George Lambert

Sermons on Various Useful and Important Subjects

Volume II.

George Lambert

Sermons on Various Useful and Important Subjects
Volume II.

ISBN/EAN: 9783337160531

Printed in Europe, USA, Canada, Australia, Japan

Cover: Foto ©Lupo / pixelio.de

More available books at **www.hansebooks.com**

SERMONS

ON

Various USEFUL and IMPORTANT

SUBJECTS,

Adapted to the

FAMILY and CLOSET.

In TWO VOLUMES.

By GEORGE LAMBERT.

VOLUME II.

I have not shunned to declare unto you all the counsel of God. PAUL.

Look to yourselves, that we lose not the things which we have wrought, but that we receive a full reward. JOHN.

YORK:

Printed by A. WARD; and sold by C. DILLY, London; J. SMITH, Sheffield; also by T. BROWNE and the other Booksellers in Hull.

MDCCLXXXVIII.

TO THE

CHURCH and CONGREGATION,

Fish-Street, *HULL*.

My dear Brethren and Friends,

THIS volume is not intruded upon you by your Minister; but is made public in answer to your repeated and earnest request. I am by no means insensible of the respect and affection you have thereby discovered to myself, but am far from being convinced that a degree of partiality, on your part, has not led to the request; you have thought more favourably of the sermons delivered to you, than I have myself. Such publications are now become very frequent and numerous; many of them, in my humble opinion, far superior to any of the sermons now put into your hands, not one of which was composed with a view to the press, or with the most distant intention of surviving the season in which they were delivered, except in their influence upon the hearts and lives of those who heard them. They are now delivered to you from the press, as near as possible, in the same garb

garb in which they appeared in the pulpit: You now have them, such as they are, and may God condescend to own and to accompany them with his blessing, then will they be further useful to you and to others likewise.

I think it my duty, and hope that none of you will consider it as servile flattery, to take this opportunity of acknowledging my gratitude to God for the long series of happiness, apparent usefulness, and growing esteem which I have been privileged to enjoy amongst you. May we still love as brethren, sympathize with each other's weaknesses, and promote each other's progress towards the heavenly country. With several of you I have long walked in Christian fellowship: Let not languor and indifference increase, the nearer we approach the end of our journey. The prize is great:—Not less important than when we first began the pursuit:—Our conduct will be attended to by our younger brethren:—Let not our example tend to abate their ardour, but rather animate and encourage them to press on, and to persevere to the end. BE FAITHFUL TO DEATH: This be the watch-word amongst us, AND HE THAT ENDURETH TO THE END SHALL BE SAVED: This be the encouragement to exhilarate us in the pursuit.—With pleasure also would I seize this opportunity to address

myself

EPISTLE DEDICATORY. v

myself to a respectable number of my *younger* brethren and friends. You have turned your backs upon the sins and follies of the age in which you live, and have set your faces towards that *Jerusalem* which is above. Persuaded I am you will never have cause to repent of what you have done: May your conduct from day to day, and from year to year, even to the end of your lives, confirm more and more your approbation of that choice you have made. Real religion is real wisdom, strength, happiness, and honour: It will fortfy your minds in danger, furnish you for every present duty, adorn your characters in the world, keep you near to God in the closet, and cause you to shine and to be useful in your families, when God shall see proper to settle you in the world. " Religion's ways are ways of pleasantness, and all her paths are peace:" And the further you pursue your journey in these paths, the fuller will be your conviction of the truth of what is here asserted. With many of you, my younger brethren, it cannot be expected that I should travel much further in this world: Though our sentiments agree, there is a disparity in our years, perhaps a greater in constitution. You, I trust, will live for the honour of *Jesus Christ* and his religion, when my lips will be closed, and I laid silent in the grave. The solemn separating day will come,

come, may come soon; but the communion we have enjoyed is not, we trust, confined to this present imperfect life. There is a day coming, a world yet remains in which we hope to *meet*—to *know*—to *rejoice* in you, as the crown of our ministry, and as our companions for eternal ages, where we shall teach you no longer in the knowledge of the Lord, but shall see, know, and rejoice in him together. Give diligence that my hopes meet not a disappointment in that day; but that you may then be found without spot and blameless. And now, brethren, I commend you to God, and to the word of his grace, which is able to build you up, and to give you an inheritance among all them which are sanctified.

There is yet another class of my hearers, whom I would by no means at this time pass by unnoticed, I mean such who have heard these sermons without any serious impression remaining on the mind after the discourse was concluded. Respecting you I have hitherto laboured in vain. After every effort on my part for the good of your souls, you remain just as you were—except it be more careless, more carnal, and more guilty in the sight of God. These discourses, which died away with the sound upon your ears, are now placed before your eyes. Read them— Reflect upon their contents—And remember that you, as well as I, have to give an account

count of them before God. Prepare to meet him:—Meet him you muſt;—but to be *prepared* to meet him ſhould be your great, your preſent, your conſtant concern. May the Printer of theſe diſcourſes, as an inſtrument in the hand of Providence, have more ſucceſs in this reſpect with you, than the Preacher had when he delivered them to you.

It is more than probable that ſome copies of theſe ſermons may fall into the hands of perſons whom I never knew, nor ſhall be acquainted with while in the body. Such will find that ſalvation by grace through faith in *Jeſus Chriſt* to the honour of God's character, and as it tends to promote the intereſt of real holineſs in the hearts of men, is the principle which runs through them all. This I apprehend to be the doctrine of the ſcripture, of our venerable Reformers from Popery, and which will be found to ſtand in that day when every doctrine, incompatible with this, ſhall be conſumed as wood, hay, and ſtubble. A doctrine which I have more than once experienced the ſupport of, apparently in the near approach of death; which, while I live, I truſt it will be my endeavour to vindicate, and when I die I hope to prove a truth. Other foundation can no man lay *(Paul* himſelf being witneſs) which can ſupport the ſoul in its laſt and ſolemn appearance before God;

EPISTLE DEDICATORY.

God; and that on this foundation all who read these discourses may build for eternity *is*, and *shall be*, the prayer of

Your sincere and affectionate Servant

in the Gospel,

HULL, March 20, 1788.   G. LAMBERT.

ERRATA.

Page.
45   Line *last* in the note, dele *this*.
78   3 for *of*, read *to*.
124 12 after *him*, add, . *This*.
150 18 for *scourge the very*, read *scourgeth every*.
202 19 for *word*, read *world*.
215 7 after *That*, add *which*.
297 Line last but three, dele *to*.
360 Line last but three, for *I*, read *ye*.

CONTENTS.

CONTENTS.

SERMON I.

Salvation in Christ alone.

ACTS iv. 12.

Neither is there salvation in any other: for there is none other name under heaven given among men whereby we must be saved. p. 1.

SERMON II.

Pride humbled and Grace exalted in the Justification of Sinners.

ROM. ix. 30——32.

What shall we say then? That the Gentiles which followed not after righteousness, have attained to righteousness, even the righteousness which is of faith: But Israel, which followed after the law of righteousness, hath not attained to the law of righteousness. Wherefore? Because they sought it not by faith, but as it were by the works of the law: for they stumbled at that stumbling stone.

p. 22.

b SERMON

SERMON III.

God honoured by an humble offering: Or, Salvation connected with a Christian Conversation.

Psalm L. 23.

Whoso offereth praise, glorifieth me: and to him that ordereth his conversation aright, will I shew the salvation of God. p. 41.

SERMON IV.

The Necessity and Advantages of Reconciliation with God.

Amos iii. 3.

Can two walk together except they be agreed?
p. 61.

SERMON V.

The Glories of Jesus Christ as the end of the Law discovered.

John i. 14. latter part of the verse.

We beheld his glory, the glory as of the only begotten of the Father, full of grace and truth. p. 79.

SERMON VI.

The Duties of Faith, Prayer, and Application to God, recommended by a great Prince, and a gracious Saviour.

Psalm lxii. 8.

Trust in him at all times; ye people, pour out your heart before him: God is a refuge for us. p. 98.

SERMON VII.

The Believer viewing a coming Saviour in his present work.

Revelations ii. 25.

That which ye have already, hold fast till I come.
p. 117.

SERMON VIII.

Divine Power magnified in the Believer's Preservation.

1 Peter i. 5.

Kept by the power of God through faith unto salvation, ready to be revealed in the last time.
p. 138.

SERMON IX.

Dying Remorse: Or, the Pangs of a wicked Man's Conscience in the Close of Life.

PROVERBS v. 12, 13.

How have I hated instruction, and my heart despised reproof? I have not obeyed the voice of my teachers, nor inclined mine ear to them that instructed me.   p. 156.

SERMON X.

Invigorating Comfort in a dying Hour: Or, the Composure of a good Man's Mind in the closing Scene of Life.

GENESIS xlix. 18.

I have waited for thy salvation, O Lord.
p. 176.

SERMON XI.

Hypocrisy exposed.

PROVERBS xxv. 14.

Whoso boasteth himself of a false gift, is like clouds and wind without rain.
p. 195.

SERMON

CONTENTS.

SERMON XII.
Gospel Visiations.

ACTS xv. 14.

Simeon hath declared how God at the first did visit the Gentiles, to take out of them a people for his name.

p. 215.

SERMON XIII.
Professing Christians warned by the dispersed Jews.

LAMENTATIONS i. 18.

The Lord is righteous, for I have rebelled against his commandment: Hear, I pray you all people, and behold my sorrow: my virgins and my young men are gone into captivity.

p. 237.

SERMON XIV.
Modern Miracles.

PSALM cxlvi. 8.

The Lord openeth the eyes of the blind: The Lord raiseth them that are bowed down: The Lord loveth the righteous.

p. 256.

SERMON

SERMON XV.

God glorified by Instruments of his own forming.

ISAIAH xliii. 21.

This people have I formed for myself, they shall shew forth my praise. p. 274.

SERMON XVI.

Happy Mediocrity: Or, an humble Plea presented to the universal Proprietor.

PROVERBS xxx. 7, 8, 9.

Two things have I required of thee, deny me them not before I die. Remove far from me vanity and lies; give me neither poverty nor riches, feed me with food convenient for me: Lest I be full, and deny thee, and say, Who is the Lord? or lest I be poor, and steal, and take the name of my God in vain. p. 294.

SERMON XVII.

God the refuge of his Saints.

PSALM lxxi. 3.

Be thou my strong habitation, whereunto I may continually resort: thou hast given commandment to save me, for thou art my rock and my fortress. p. 313.

SERMON

CONTENTS.

SERMON XVIII.

The Soul voluntarily humbled under God's sovereign and saving Hand.

1 PETER v. 6.

Humble yourselves, therefore, under the mighty hand of God, that he may exalt you in due time. P. 332.

SERMON XIX.

Dark Dispensations illumined: Or, present Twilight ushering in a glorious Day.

ZECH. xiv. 6, 7.

It shall come to pass in that day that the light shall not be clear nor dark; but it shall be one day, which shall be known to the Lord, not day nor night: but it shall come to pass that at even-time it shall be light.

P. 351.

SERMON XX.

Spiritual Gain from temporal Losses: Or, the Death of the Widow's Son.

1 KINGS xvii. 18.

Art thou come unto me to call my sin unto remembrance, and to slay my son? P. 371.

SERMON

SERMON XXI.

Chrift's Charge againſt his profeſſing People.

Psalm lxix. 8.

I am become a ſtranger unto my brethren, and an alien unto my mother's children.

p. 391.

SERMON XXII.

Acceptable Worſhip: Or, God approached through a Mediator.

Ephes. ii. 18.

Through him we both have an acceſs by one Spirit unto the Father. p. 410.

SERMON

SERMON I.

Salvation in Christ alone.

ACTS iv. 12.

Neither is there salvation in any other: for there is none other name under heaven given among men whereby we must be saved.

IN all human laws, particularly those which regard the honour of the sovereign, or the welfare of the subject, plainness and perspicuity are desirable, in opposition to all ambiguity of language or indetermination of sentiment. Thus doubts and diffidence are excluded, the mind meets the will of the legislature unmasked, the line of duty becomes plain to every honest man, and those barriers which secure our rights, or are intended to guard against fraud and transgression, are well maintained and defended. Where there is no law, there can be no transgression; and where the law is equivocal or indeterminate, there transgressions will multiply, while the transgression will be less reprehensible in its nature, and fraud will find an easier apology in order to palliate the offence: And in those cases where the life or death of the subject is made to depend upon his obedience to, or transgression of, any particular law, there the greatest care and caution become needful to guard against every misapprehension on the one hand, and every excuse on the other. Hence, in the laws of our own country, a great variety and multiplicity of words are used and crowded together to express the same thing, in order to prevent all misunderstanding, evasion, or guile. Without this, men would torture, twist, alter, yea even invert the design of the legislature.——But if such care be peculiarly requisite in human laws, where our lives and property are at stake, how much more is this precision necessary in the laws of heaven, especially those which relate to our souls and eternity? There is no sort of comparison between the life of the body and the value of the soul;—between our condition for time and our state for eternity. What would be the balance between the whole material world and an immortal soul, suppose the one gained, the other lost? In this case, the gain would be imaginary and momentary; but the loss, the enjoyment of happiness, complete and eternal in glory, and the enduring all the misery and horrors of damnation in hell for ever. " The world passeth away, and the lust thereof; but he that doth the will of God, abideth for ever." * What then

* 1 John ii. 17.

then shall a man give in exchange for his soul? In matters which relate to salvation, the revelation which God has been pleased to give us is exceeding plain and express; so plain that he that runs may read its contents. This subject is not couched in ambiguous phrases or unintelligible terms; but is adapted to the weakest capacity: And, in condescension to the ignorance of the human mind, the great God has been pleased to treat the greatest subject in language the most plain and simple. The words of the text fully evince the truth of this remark. Salvation is now to be obtained——but in no other way——through no other name than Jesus Christ: " For there is salvation in no other, nor is there any other name under heaven given among men whereby we must be saved."

The preceding chapter informs us that *Peter* and *John*, soon after the feast of *Pentecost*, going up to the temple, and observing a man at the gate, who had been lame from his birth, they looked upon him with compassion, and in the *name*, that is, by the authority and power of *Jesus Christ*, they wrought a perfect and instant cure upon him. This event happening in so public a place, soon brought a great concourse of people together. They expressed their astonishment in different ways; some gazing upon the man, whom they had long known as a deplorable object; and others on the Apostles who had effected

effected so remarkable a change upon him. *Peter* seizes this as a suitable opportunity to address himself in a very affectionate discourse to the assembled multitude: With all due humility, he first assures them that it was not through any superior power or holiness naturally resident in him, or in his fellow-disciple, that this great change was effected; but that this miracle was wrought by the power, in the name, and in confirmation of the mission and resurrection of *Jesus Christ*: Even that *Jesus*, who had been so lately crucified by them and their rulers, and exposed to shame near to that place. However, he takes it for granted that they had done this from ignorance, and had thereby been accomplishing what the Prophets had before predicted concerning the sufferings of the Messiah. He invites them, therefore, to repentance—warns them of the danger of persisting in their infidelity—and assures them, that God having raised up his Son, *Jesus*, had sent him to bless them, in turning every one of them from their iniquities.——While he was thus proceeding in his discourse, the Captain of the Temple appears, authorized to seize them, and to bring them before the Sanhedrim. The next day, the court being assembled, they are introduced, and their answer demanded to these questions: *By what power have ye done this? And in whose name?*

Instantly,

Salvation in Christ alone.

Instantly *Peter* finds his mind fortified against fear, and enlarged to speak his sentiments with the greatest freedom; addressing himself therefore to them, with all the respect due to the rulers of the people, and pointing to the poor man that had been healed, who was also present upon this occasion, he delivered himself thus: "Ye rulers of the people, and elders of *Israel*, if we this day be examined of the good deed done to the impotent man, by what means he is made whole, be it known unto you all, and to all the people of *Israel*, that by the name of *Jesus Christ* of *Nazareth*, whom ye crucified, whom God raised from the dead, even by him doth this man stand before you whole. This is the stone which was set at nought of you builders, which is become the head of the corner. Neither is there salvation in any other: for there is none other name given among men whereby we must be saved."* Some have taken much pains to debase the meaning of the word, here rendered *salvation*, insinuating that in this place it signifies only *healing:* But is there ground to conclude that all those rulers were so afflicted in their bodies as to need such a cure? Or, were the Apostles themselves in similar circumstances? No; this could not be his meaning; for it is evident that *Peter* includes himself, and all that heard him; and takes it for granted that both he and they needed to apply to *Jesus Christ*

* Acts iv. 8—12.

for spiritual healing. The miracle alluded to was only to be considered as a testimony given from heaven, to prove that *Jesus Christ* was the head of the corner; that is, the Supporter and Saviour of all who, by faith, become connected with him.—What I propose by discoursing from these words, is to shew,

I. That all mankind, since the fall, are in such a state and condition as to need salvation.
II. That though such be their condition, the generality, indeed all, while in that state, discover either the greatest ignorance how salvation is to be attained, or the strongest aversion to that way and method in which God hath revealed it. But,
III. In order to remove that ignorance, and to subdue this aversion, God is pleased in the volume of revelation, especially in the New Testament, to declare in the most clear and peremptory manner that the only way in which men can be saved, is through *Christ*, and by him.

Such is the method we propose to follow in this discourse. May God bless what shall be said to our conviction, or the bringing of our minds to correspond with the sentiment contained in the text. The first thing we propose to shew is this,

I. That

I. *That all mankind, since the fall, are in such a state and condition as to need salvation.*

What the scripture uniformly testifies upon this head, the history of all nations, and our own observations upon the conduct of mankind, confirm. In *Adam* all sinned, became obnoxious to displeasure, and died in virtue of the sentence of God's holy law. Hence they are said to be *dead in trespasses and sins*; and, *by nature* (not as originally formed of God, but as debased by sin) *children of wrath*. Under this head, we do not propose to enter upon a long and laboured disquisition of a point, which probably few or none of you doubt or deny. The whole scheme of that salvation revealed by the Gospel is founded upon this principle, that men are in a condition which needs salvation. Could that principle, therefore, once be proved false, the whole structure would crumble to nothing, as the Empress of *Russia*'s superb palace, formed of snow or congealed water, dissolved before the summer's sun. However, that we may endeavour to make our ground-work good, under this head we propose to glance at two things.

1. Every one who transgresses against God's law, thereby, at once, becomes a rebel against God, and is enthralled under the power of Satan. Sin is a transgression of the law. He that breaketh the law, dishonoureth God; he that offendeth in one point is guilty of all;
and

and curſed is the man that continueth not in all things written in the law to do them. To tranſgreſs, therefore, what the law enjoins, or to omit what it requires, is an offence againſt the law, and againſt the authority of the divine Lawgiver, ſince it is both the tranſcript of his nature, and the diſcovery of his mind and will. This law requires ſupreme love to God, as the great ſource of Being and of Bleſſedneſs——rectitude of mind, or truth in the inward parts—and perfect, univerſal, and unremitted obedience to every part of his revealed will. And who can object to the reaſonableneſs of every part of this requirement? Is it not highly reaſonable that this God ſhould be loved? That the creature ſhould preſerve thoſe powers which his Creator originally gave him; and that he ſhould anſwer the end for which he was at firſt made? In a word, is it not reaſonable that the creature ſhould heartily approve of, and cheerfully perform whatever God requires, and hate and ſtudiouſly avoid every thing that he forbids? But while our reaſon and judgment juſtify the Lord in all theſe claims, every mouth muſt be ſtopped, and each of us ſtand guilty, by our own ſentence, before God—Conſcience, in every one, muſt teſtify that we have, as individuals, ſinned and come ſhort of the glory of God. Who amongſt us all have loved this God as he ought to have been loved by us—ſerved him, agreeable to his

juſt

just and reasonable requirements—or returned unto him in proportion to those favours and benefits which he has conferred on us? Here God must be pronounced just, and ourselves guilty; and was he to enter into judgment with us, so as to mark iniquity, who of all the human race could stand before him? If then things be thus, the evidence is clear to a demonstration, that, by the deeds of the law, no flesh can be justified in the sight of this holy Lord God. On the contrary, that, as individuals, we have transgressed and stand condemned at the bar of God's holy law. We have proved ourselves to be rebels against the divine authority, and enemies in our minds by wicked works. By sin we have dishonoured God, and have been led captive by Satan. Nor is this the condition of a few individuals only, but,

2. It is the state and situation of *all, universally*, and *without exception*, considered as under the fall. "They are all gone out of the way; there is none that doth good, no not one." It is true, indeed, that the inhabitants of the several nations of the earth may, and do very much differ in their tempers, manners, customs, and dispositions; but, as one observes, "Let an impartial judge take four unconverted men, or children, from the four parts of the world; let him examine their actions, and trace them up to their spring; and, if he makes some allowance for the ac-

cidental difference of their climate, conſtitution, taſte, and education, he will ſoon find their diſpoſition as equally earthly, ſenſual, and deviliſh, as if they had been caſt in the ſame mould. Yes, as oak trees are oaks all the world over, though, by particular circumſtances, ſome grow taller and harder, and ſome more knotty and crooked than others: So all unregenerate men reſemble one another; for all are proud, ſelf-willed, impenitent, and lovers of pleaſure more than lovers of God. Sin manifeſts itſelf among black and white, ſavage and civilized nations, *Turks* and *Jews*, Heathens and Chriſtians, whether they live on the banks of the *Ganges* or the *Thames*, the *Miſſiſippi* or the *Seyne*, whether they ſtarve in the ſnows of *Lapland*, or burn in the ſands of *Guinea*." It is not the character of a particular ſect of men, of any peculiar nation, climate, or age only; but of men univerſally, and in all ages ſince the lapſe of our firſt parents, that they are dead in treſpaſſes and ſins.

The Apoſtle *Peter* was here ſpeaking to the greateſt and moſt learned men in all the *Jewiſh* nation;—that nation which God did then honour with advantages peculiar, and above all the nations of the earth, and yet he here aſſerts that even theſe men were in that condition which needed ſalvation.

Now, men being univerſally, by ſin, in a ſtate of condemnation and ſlavery, unaſſiſted

by

by divine revelation, we could have conceived of no possible way in which they could be saved, but either by repentance for their past conduct, or by a superior kind of obedience to that required by the law, in future, which should be able to make up the deficiency of the past: But repentance is not restitution; and an obedience superior to that which the law requires cannot be given by human nature; for the obedience it requires must be perfect, perpetual, and universal, and that of the best of men is defective.

Thus having glanced at the first thing proposed, viz. That all mankind, since the fall, are in such a condition as to need salvation, we proceed to remark,

II. *That though such be their condition, the generality, indeed all, while in that state, discover either the greatest ignorance how salvation is to be obtained, or the strongest aversion to that way and method in which God hath revealed it.*

1. The amazing ignorance of the generality, as to this subject, is but too evident, even at the first glance. We refer not to the inhabitants of those nations who never had or heard of the Gospel, but even of those countries who are the most privileged in this respect. It is astonishing to see how the human understanding is darkened, and what a variety of methods the God of this world has taken to blind the eyes of them who believe not,

left the light of the knowledge of the glorious Gospel of *Christ*, who is the image of God, should shine unto them. Among the Heathens, even *Socrates* is represented as intimating to his friend *Alcibiades*, the necessity of the appearance of some extraordinary messenger, in order to remove the darkness which covered the human mind, that men might know and approach God with success. Men may, indeed, have some sense of sin—some idea of the necessity of satisfaction—and conviction that something is requisite in order to their being happy; but how low, groveling, and unworthy are their conceptions of the way of acceptance with God. Let a people—a people who had the best means of knowing how God was to be approached with propriety——a people under deep conviction of the evil of sin, and in earnest to obtain acceptance before God—willing to part with any thing so that they might obtain it—let one of their number, and he the best qualified, be permitted to speak for the whole, and you will instantly discover the ignorance and folly of the human mind respecting this great subject. I have reference to the words of the Prophet *Micah*, " Wherewith shall I come before the Lord, and bow myself before the high God? Shall I come before him with burnt-offerings, with calves of a year old? Will the Lord be pleased with thousands of rams, or with ten thousands of rivers of oil? Shall I give my first-

first-born for my transgression, the fruit of my body for the sin of my soul"*? Invention could go no further, nor could conjecture rise higher. Part of the proposal was too much for any one to give; but infinitely too little to expiate the sin of the soul, or to satisfy the claims of the most high God. We will suppose the person here alluded to, to have been a man possessed of a very quick and fruitful invention; he could conceive well, and express what he had conceived with great propriety, and in the most elevated language; but in him you have a specimen (and we have supposed, not one of an inferior sort) how ignorant men are about the method of obtaining salvation.

2. There

---

* Micah vi. 6. Dr. *Butler*, Bishop of *Durham*, and Dr. *Lowth*, Bishop of *London*, with several others, understand this passage as the language of *Balak* king of *Moab*. I was once of the same opinion, but upon a more deliberate view of the subject, am now led to conclude the contrary. In the history, recorded Numbers, chapters xxii, xxiii, xxiv.——*Balak* seems to have had no such conviction of the sin of his soul, as is here intimated.—He appears, on the contrary, to have been full of rage and indignation against *Israel*.—He makes no such proposal there to *Balaam* as this in the above passage.—He seems to have been much displeased at *Balaam*, that after putting him to so much expence, he had not been able to procure a curse against *Israel*.——He dismissed the prophet with evident marks of displeasure.——And the closing advice from *Balaam* to him (*Numb.* xxv. compared with *Rev.* ii. 14.) was materially different from the language of ver. 8.—The connection of the passage seems to be this:——After the prophet *Micah* had (agreeable to the command given him) reproved the people for their ingratitude, and called upon them to reflect upon the Lord's gracious appearances for them,—they are introduced as anxiously enquiring how they might avert the displeasure and judgment of the Almighty. See *Lowth's Comment. Pool's Annotat. &c. in loc.*

2. There are others, who difcover the greateft averfion of heart to the method of falvation which God has been pleafed to open through *Jefus Chrift* Such were the perfons to whom the Apoftle firft addreffed this difcourfe: They were men of great learning—eminent in the *Jewifh* church and nation—They had read, profeffed to believe, and probably fome of them had commented upon the writings of the Prophets—They were no ftrangers to the doctrines and claims of *Jefus Chrift*—and they had now, at this very feafon, a cripple before their eyes reftored to perfect foundnefs, in confirmation of the authority of this Saviour and his doctrine; and yet, with all this evidence before them, they wilfully fhut their eyes, and would not have this *Jefus* to be their Prince and Saviour. Ignorant of God's righteoufnefs revealed in the Law, and not willing to fubmit to that brought in by the Gofpel, with confiderable ingenuity and diligence they went about to eftablifh a righteoufnefs of their own. To effect which, they were neceffitated to mutilate the divine law, and to invent fervices which God neither required, nor would accept.—But leaving thefe men, how many are there who, though they fit ftatedly under the Gofpel, never faw their need of falvation! They pay little or no attention to the doctrine of it. Perhaps defpife it in their heart, or pervert it to the vileft of purpofes. Multitudes, it is to be

be feared, in this land assume the Christian name to take away their reproach, while they are no better than *Heathens* in their creed, or *Jews* in their practice. In principle they despise him, or in practice crucify him afresh. O to see, and feel, and know our need of salvation by *Jesus Christ*, that so we may cordially submit to the righteousness of God!—As proposed we proceed to shew,

III. *That in order to remove that ignorance, and to subdue this aversion, God has been pleased in the volume of revelation, especially in the New Testament, to declare in the most clear and peremptory manner, that the only way in which men can possibly be saved, is through* Christ, *and by him.* ——" Neither is there salvation in any other: for there is none other name under heaven given among men whereby we must be saved." Here we remark three things, viz. That salvation is now revealed.—That the salvation of the whole church is here represented to be in *Christ.*——And that every one who applies for it, must apply for it in this way, to the exclusion of every other.

1. Salvation is now revealed—A salvation for sinful men—A salvation, often predicted and long expected—A salvation, the influence of which extends to soul and body, through time, and to eternity—A salvation, free, rich, great, and glorious—A salvation, which comprehends the pardon of all sin, and the communication of all the blessings of grace and glory

glory—A falvation, of which all other falvations were no more than fhadows, types, or introductions—A falvation, in which the wifdom, the grace, the holinefs, the love and power of Jehovah are more completely and more glorioufly manifefted, than they ever were, (with humility we add) than they ever could have been in any other way—Behold, Brethren, God hath brought nigh this his falvation to you. You read of it in your Bibles. You hear of it from your pulpits——May you alfo experience the introduction and earnefts of it in your fouls. To you, Men and Brethren, is this falvation fent; and all that believe are juftified from all things from which they could not be juftified by the law of *Mofes*. That name is proclaimed amongft you whereby ye may be faved.

2. The falvation of the whole church of believers is here reprefented, as being all in *Chrift*. The efficacy of his undertaking, obedience, and death, extends to millions of millions: even all who are brought to apply to, and reft on him. In him they were all reprefented; and it hath pleafed the Father that, in him, fhould all the fulnefs dwell which they require. In him they are pardoned, juftified, and accepted; and all the grace neceffary for their complete fanctification and prefervation is found in him. "In the Lord fhall all the feed of *Ifrael* be juftified, and fhall glory." In him alfo have they righteoufnefs

teoufnefs and ftrength. His grace is fufficient for every individual of them, and his ftrength fhall appear perfect in the whole body of them when collected together. "There is redemption in *Chrift's* blood, the forgivenefs of fin according to the riches of grace; and he is able to fave to the uttermoft all who come unto God by him. By the one oblation of himfelf once offered, he hath for ever perfected them that are fanctified.*" There was no occafion for a repetition of the facrifice, becaufe it was completely efficacious, nor doth it need any thing, at any feafon, to be added to it; for it is always perfect. To this Saviour believers under the Old and the New Teftament ftood equally indebted for falvation. He is the Saviour of the body, his church. The advantages and efficacy of his interpofition and death, extend backwards to the birth of fin, and forward to the clofe of time. And as the fun may be faid to introduce the day a confiderable time before it actually arife upon that fpot of the earth in which we dwell, and to protract the day for fome time after it has fet below our horizon; fo *Jefus Chrift* is found the fame under every difpenfation. No man cometh to the Father but by him; and he is the fame yefterday, to-day, and for ever. Never was there a name given under heaven, whereby men could be faved, but that of *Jefus Chrift*. In him is

Vol. II.   C   found

* Eph. i. 7.—Heb. vii. 25.—Heb. 10. 14.

found grace sufficient to justify and sanctify millions of millions of the most impure sinners, even numbers which no man can number; and power to preserve and save them to the very uttermost.

3. Every one who applies for this salvation, must apply for it in this way, to the exclusion of all hope from any other. It is not by human merit, or works of righteousness that we have done, or can do, that we must be saved; for by the deeds of the law no flesh can be justified.——It is not by any austerities inflicted upon the body, be they ever so humiliating or severe; for though we give the body to be burnt, if destitute of faith in *Christ*, and love to God, it profiteth nothing :—Nor is it through the advocacy or intercession of this or of that saint, however eminent they might be in their day; for there is salvation in none other than *Jesus Christ:* " There is none other name under heaven given to men whereby they can be saved :" Had there been any other, who could have effected what *Jesus Christ* has done, we conclude from the prayer of this Saviour in the garden, that God would have spared his Son, and would have revealed some other name.——But

Never was any other authorized and commissioned of God—or qualified to save sinners. He was set up in the counsels of Jehovah from eternity :——Was pointed to by all the Prophets, and by many of the services in the

Jewish

Jewish Sanctuary:—And an angel was sent express with this commission from heaven, that his name should be called JESUS, for *he shall save his people from their sins* *. The *Gentiles* had many gods, and many lords or mediators; " but to us," says the Apostle, " there is but one God, the Father, of whom are all things and we in him; and one Lord *Jesus Christ*, by whom are all things, and we by him." †

There is no one so fit on the part of man to be a Saviour, and at the same time so suitable and honourable on the part of God.——There is a decency and propriety necessary to be observed in this transaction, which we apprehend is signified in the verb here translated *must* ‡. It is in every respect becoming the character and conduct of the great and holy God. " It became him, for whom are all things, and by whom are all things, in bringing many sons unto glory, to make the Captain of their Salvation perfect through suffering." § He was God and Man in one Person. Not a Mediator of one, but able to lay his hands on both, to satisfy the claim of justice, and supply the lost sinner with a complete salvation

And he alone is able to save. The carnal *Jews* placed their confidence in *Abraham* as their Father, in *Moses* as their Mediator and Instructor:—And yet, neither *Abraham* nor

Moses

---

* Matt. i. 21.—† 1 Cor. v. 8.—‡ *Ib.*—§ Heb. ii. 10.

Moses could save those who trusted in them; but *Jesus* can fully answer all the dependence that we can place in him. "To him give all the Prophets witness, that through his name whosoever believeth in him, shall receive remission of sins." *

What a privilege is it to have that name announced amongst us in which there is salvation! Such a salvation we all need.—The report of it is brought to us.—It is now proposed and to be obtained. Behold, now is the day of salvation. Did men but see and feel the deplorable condition into which sin has reduced them, how would their hearts bound with gratitude, and their souls overflow with praise, to hear that there is redemption in *Christ*'s blood, the forgiveness of sin? This name of the *Lord Jesus* is a strong tower, fly to it for safety. Rely upon him, and plead this name before the throne of grace.

But how awful will be our condition, if we reject this only Deliverer: "For there remaineth no more sacrifice for sins, but a certain fearful looking for of judgment and fiery indignation, which shall devour the adversaries."† In this way salvation is to be had, and in no other. To be unconcerned or indifferent in a case of such importance is highly criminal. How will ye escape, if ye neglect
this

---

* Acts x. 43.—† Heb. x. 26, 27.

this great salvation? " In rejecting *Chrift*," says an Author, " we reject the Wisdom of God——the Authority of God——the Love of God——yea, the Salvation of God." From such an evil the Lord preserve us all, and lead us to believe to the salvation of the soul. Even so. *Amen.*

SERMON

SERMON II.

Pride humbled and Grace exalted in the Justification of Sinners.

ROM. ix. 30—32.

What shall we say then? That the Gentiles *which followed not after righteousness, have attained to righteousness, even the righteousness which is of faith: But* Israel, *which followed after the law of righteousness, hath not attained to the law of righteousness. Wherefore? Because they sought it not by faith, but as it were by the works of the law: for they stumbled at that stumbling stone.*

SCARCE is there any doctrine of revelation that we can exercise our thoughts upon, but we meet with something which bears analogy to it, either in the natural or commercial world. The more these are considered in the resemblance they bear to each other, the more is the mind enabled to understand, and the more is our faith confirmed in those interesting truths held forth by the oracles of God. Thus, for instance, when

we read over the account which the Apoſtle gives of the condition both of the *Jews* and *Gentiles* in his day; when we reflect upon the ſuperior advantages and diligence of the one, and the aſtoniſhing ignorance and inſenſibility of the other, we ſhould not only be ſurpriſed, but almoſt ſtaggered at his account of their different ſucceſs, did we not frequently meet with ſomething in other concerns of men which looks very much like it.—To exemplify what we intend: It has ſometimes been the caſe that men well acquainted with the laws and powers of Nature, after employing their thoughts to invent ſome improvement in our manufactures, and uſing every effort and every invention, have failed in the attempt; while, perhaps, a perſon of little learning, in other reſpects, of comparatively ſhallow abilities, has ſtruck out a new diſcovery which has fully anſwered what the former had long attempted in vain. The one failed with all the apparent advantages that lay on their ſide, while the other ſeemed to be indebted for all his ſucceſs to the bleſſing of the Almighty. And may we not call this the doctrine of the text, exhibited in colours furniſhed from the world which we inhabit? What then is the natural and eaſy deduction that we have to make both from the one caſe and the other, but this, that the wiſe man ſhould not glory in his wiſdom; but that he that glorieth ſhould glory in the Lord? The
intent

intent both of the plan of Providence, and of the doctrines of Revelation, is to bring men to a simple subjection of their minds to God, that he may guide them through all the business of life, and save their souls with an everlasting salvation. "The haughtiness of man must be brought down, that the Lord alone may be exalted."

In reading over this chapter, while we are constrained to bow to the divine Sovereignty, we are likewise led to admire the strength of the Apostle's reasoning, as well as the admirable skill and prudence he shews in the management of that profound and solemn subject of which he treats. In the former part of the chapter, he had been discoursing upon the election of some and the rejection of others; as also concerning the calling of the *Gentiles*, and the casting off of the *Jews*. The words we have read, as the foundation of this discourse, are the conclusion which he draws from the whole; and with what profound skill doth he manage this subject! With what amazing foresight doth he anticipate, and answer every objection that might be raised against his doctrine, as also every false inference that might be deduced from it! Did he foresee that men would, in future, charge the doctrine of the divine decrees with being the cause of the final condemnation of sinners? Or did he know that they would argue thus: That if Election be

the

the cause of Salvation, then Non-Election must be cause of final destruction? This, says *Paul*, is not the doctrine I have advanced: And should any person, in any future age of the world, presume to fix such a charge upon it, or to draw such an inference from it, let that man know that it is an unjust charge, and a false inference. True it is that I ascribe to the purposes of God's grace all the real good that men are made the partakers of, either in the present life, or a succeeding eternity; but at the same time I am careful to assert, that *sin*—and especially under the Gospel dispensation, that *the wilful rejecting of Jesus Christ* is the grand cause, and the *only* reason of the condemnation of the hearers of that Gospel. This we apprehend is the plain, unforced, and undisguised doctrine advanced by the Apostle, and comprehends the sum of his reasoning upon it in the words now before us. *What shall we say then? That the* Gentiles *which followed not after righteousness, have attained to righteousness, even the righteousness which is of faith: But* Israel, *which followed after the law of righteousness, hath not attained to the law of righteousness. Wherefore? Because they sought it not by faith, but as it were by the works of the law: for they stumbled at that stumbling stone.* That we may enter more fully into the meaning of these words, we propose to consider,

I. The

I. The mark or object here described, as aimed at by the *Jews*, not so by the *Gentiles*: This was *the law of righteousness*.

II. The condition, disposition, and success of the two sorts of persons here referred to, viz. the *Jews* and the *Gentiles*—And,

III. The reason assigned for the want of success on the one side—and for the obtaining it on the other.

We shall then close the subject with a few words by way of application.

Let us consider,

I. *That mark or object which is here described by the Apostle, as aimed at with much diligence by the* Jews, *not so by the* Gentiles. *This he calls the* Law of Righteousness. A law, we know, is properly speaking the declaration of the will of a superior, obliging his subjects to the performance of what is pleasing in his sight, and to avoid what is the contrary.—— God, as the supreme governor of the world, has been pleased to give forth the evidence of his authority and will, which we find contained in the moral law. This law requires righteousness *from* men, and is the rule *of* it to them. It prescribes, on the one hand, whatsoever he accounts just and reasonable; on the other, prohibits what is contrary to his pleasure. By this law the grand rule of righteousness is held forth; requiring supreme love to God, cheerful obedience, spiritual worship,

worship, and the constant reverence of the omnipresent Majesty; at the same time enjoining that affection, sympathy, and regard to the dignity, person, and property of our neighbour, which are comprehended in that short, but significant sentence, "Whatsoever ye would that men should do unto you, that do ye also to them." But if this law be more particularly considered with respect to the duties of the first table, it requires truth in the inward parts, and a full and perfect conformity, both of the heart and life, to God's revealed will. The obedience this law demands is spiritual, universal, and everlasting. It requires not only that man should stand possessed of the image of God, and that this image be preserved entire, but also that it be growing more strong in all its features, more glorious in all its powers, and that for ever: Not only that men should esteem all the commands of God concerning all things to be right; but that both in time and in eternity they should stand complete in the whole of his will.

But though the Law of Righteousness be here named by the Apostle, the righteousness required by that law is what he particularly intends:—for it was this which the *Jews* followed after. The law itself they had in their temple, it was read in their synagogues, and copies of it were found in their hands; so that there was no occasion for so much diligence to be used in order to obtain that:

But as transgreffors, they had all come short of the requirements of this law; and, as profeffors of the true religion, fome of them, at leaft, fpared neither pains, diligence, or expence that they might attain to the righteoufnefs which it required. By the Law of Righteoufnefs, then, muft here be meant the Moral Law, or rather that righteoufnefs which it required.——We now pafs on to confider,

II. *The condition, difpofition, and fuccefs of the perfons here referred to, viz. the* Jews *and the* Gentiles.

1. As to the *Jews*. They, as was obferved before, *had the rule of duty*. To them pertained the giving of the law, and the ordinances of God and the fanctuary. They might eafily know what it was that God required of them, for they had a full and clear difcovery of the mark they were to aim at continually before them. Their minds were left in no uncertainty as to what God required of man, his word being as a light to their feet and a lamp to their paths.—It is a great privilege to have the mind and will of God in our hands, that we may confult it in all our courfe through this wildernefs. To this we are to give heed as to a light fhining in a dark place. Where men have no rule refpecting the line of duty, every thing is left to conjecture and uncertainty.

Nor had the *Jews* the law of the Lord only, but many of them aimed at conformity to the requirements

requirements of it. They laboured with desire, with diligence, and perseverance, to attain that standard which this law set before them. Zealous for this law, they went about, sparing no pains, to establish their own righteousness by it; but, continually disappointed in their pursuit, they endeavoured to lower the requirements of this law to their imperfect attainments, till at last its very spirit was so disguised and obscured, that little more than the letter was regarded. While things were viewed in this light by the Apostle *Paul* previous to his conversion, he tells us that touching the righteousness of the law he apprehended himself blameless. He fasted, he prayed, he laboured abundantly, as did also many of the *Pharisees;* but when he saw that a covetous desire was forbidden; when the commandment came not only in the letter, but in its spirit and power, then sin revived, and he died to every hope of obtaining eternal happiness by his own obedience. This, however, was far from being the case with all of that sect; some we find had the effrontery even to go into God's presence, and there to boast of their good dispositions, and the superiority of their character, when compared with others. Witness the *Pharisee* in the temple as represented in the parable.—— They thought by their zeal, their diligence, and their long round of duties, that they were doing God service. Mistaking the letter for the spirit of the law; substituting shadows for

for the substance, and the oblations of the hand for the love and obedience of the heart, they followed after righteousness. They had a zeal of God, as our Apostle himself bears them witness, but it was not according to knowledge. Ceremonies were rigidly observed, sacrifices voluntarily offered, the form of godliness diligently maintained, while they remained destitute of its power.——This subject is wisely calculated to shew us the danger of mistakes in matters of religion. Some have zealously espoused the sentiment of the innocency of error, and have warmly contended, that if a man means well, though there may be many errors in his creed, and many imperfections in his conduct, yet no doubt he stands approved in the sight of God. How far this may apply to the case of those who were never favoured with a divine revelation, we pretend not to say; but as to those who are favoured with that advantage, the opinion of the Apostle is here determinate. Not to enter into any long reasoning upon the subject, the only question that lies before us is this—Did our Apostle give a true description of these *Jews*, or did he not? If not, the reflection must fall upon himself; but if he did, then the description that he gives us of them is this—They *did follow* after the law of righteousness, and yet they *did not obtain* that which they followed after. The reason that he assigns is this—That they sought it not in the right way, *not by faith, but*

but as it were by the works of the law. They had false ideas of what this law required, and of what alone could satisfy its demands. In this lay the ground-work of their error. For though they followed after the law of righteousness, yet they *did not attain* They came infinitely short of the mark; and the event, sooner or later, proved to each one of them, that " by the deeds of the law no flesh could be justified in the sight of God, for by the law is the knowledge of sin." The whole power of that law with respect to an unconverted sinner, is either to convince him of sin, or to condemn him for it.

2. Respecting the *Gentiles*, their case was very different. Their condition, their disposition and success, are drawn out in very different colours.

They were grossly *ignorant:* For although some traces of the law of nature remained upon their minds, yet these were faint and very imperfect, compared with what divine revelation held forth to the *Jews.* True, indeed, their consciences, in many things, accused or excused them; but ignorance of God was deeply impressed upon all that they professed or practised.

Nor were they only ignorant, but *unconcerned* likewise. Their ignorance did not put them upon the enquiry after truth, or stir them up to seek the Lord: But they are represented as *sitting* in darkness, and in the
valley

valley of the shadow of death; *insensible* of danger—*unaffected* with their condition, and *at ease*, as to the state of their souls. Instead of following on to know the Lord, or enquiring, where is God my Maker? They do not seem so much as to have desired the knowledge of his ways, or inclined to retain him in their thoughts.

Nor was this all: Ignorance and want of concern is far from constituting the whole of their character; they were *unholy* likewise. Instead of following after the law of righteousness, they were notoriously wicked—wicked even to a proverb; and this their wickedness appeared even in their more solemn and public acts of devotion. They gloried in their very shame, were reprobate to every good work, and wrought all manner of uncleanness with greediness. The *Jews* were very careful, diligent, and laborious; they did a great deal to recommend themselves to the divine favour; but these *Gentiles* had done nothing to merit favour at the hands of God—all that they deserved was wrath and misery; and yet we are told that *they attained* to that righteousness which they had not been following after. How evident is it from this representation of the Apostle, that human merit has nothing to do in the salvation of a sinner. Evident it is, that the salvation of these poor *Gentiles* (as indeed of every sinner) is of pure free mercy. In their case, as in many

many others, the Lord is " found of them that fought him not, and manifefts himfelf to them that enquired not after him." Their falvation was not by works of righteoufnefs that they had done, but freely of Grace. In their cafe, God fhewed the way, the only way in which he would in every age accept finners. Human merit and human diligence are in this cafe entirely excluded in the acceptance of a finner before God, and it is proved to be " neither of him that willeth, nor of him that runneth," for in that cafe the *Jews* had fucceeded in their purfuit; but thefe *Gentiles* found it to be entirely of Him who fheweth mercy. To them was made known the unfearchable riches of *Chrift* by the preaching of the Gofpel; with joy they received the word, mixing it with faith, and embracing it as a report worthy of all their acceptance, that " *Jefus Chrift* came into the world to fave the very chief of finners."—— Though once *ignorant, unconcerned, unholy,* tranfgreffors of, inftead of followers after, the Law of Righteoufnefs, now they obtained mercy, and *attained to righteoufnefs,* even the righteoufnefs which is of faith. This naturally introduces the third thing we propofed to confider, viz.

III. *The reafon affigned for the want of fuccefs on the one fide, and for the obtaining it on the other;* and fo far is this from being refolved into any decree or purpofe of God, that, on the contrary, we find it traced to and resolved into the different principles by which these opposite characters were influenced.

1. *The Jews sought it not by faith, but as it were by the works of the law.* The very same method of acceptance with God was proposed to them that was also proposed to the *Gentiles:* yea, the first publication of it was to the *Jews;* and what was still more in their favour, this method of salvation came recommended to them by the writings of *Moses* and the Prophets. However, they rejected this way of obtaining righteousness, though it was the only one that God had appointed, or would ever suffer to be crowned with success. They would not be indebted to another for a righteousness which was both to answer the demands of the law and give them a title to the heavenly inheritance. No, such a proposal was too debasing to their pride. They turned away from it with contempt, and rejected *Christ* and salvation by him.

They sought it not by faith, but, *as it were, by the works of the law.* This was the case with the *Pharisees* in general; while they rejected *Jesus Christ*, they sought acceptance with God by their own obedience to the law: And even the judaizing Christians we find were for uniting the systems of *Moses* and *Christ* together in that, in which they could never unite—seeking justification, *as it were,* by the works of the law; that is, partly through the obedience of *Jesus Christ*, and partly by their own. Even *Peter* himself seems upon a particular occasion to have given but too much countenance to this opinion by his own conduct: But the Apostle to the *Gentiles* nobly opposed him in his conduct, and as ably defended the cause of Christian liberty. The case was this: Before that certain brethren came from *James* to *Antioch*, *Peter* eat with the *Gentiles*; upon their coming, he withdrew himself, fearing those who were of the circumcision. The effect was, that the other *Jews* dissembled with him, so that even *Barnabas*, who had been *Paul*'s companion when he laid the case of the *Gentiles* before the church at *Jerusalem*, was carried away with their dissimulation. " But," says *Paul*, " when I saw that they walked not uprightly, according to the truth of the Gospel, I said unto *Peter* before them all, If thou, being a *Jew*, livest after the manner of the *Gentiles*, and not as do the *Jews*, why compellest thou the *Gentiles* to live as do the *Jews?* We who are *Jews* by nature, and not sinners of the *Gentiles*, knowing that a man is not justified by the works of the law, but by the faith of *Jesus Christ*, even we have believed in *Jesus Christ*, that we might be justified by the faith of *Christ*, and not by the works of the law; for by the works of the law shall no flesh be justified: But, if while we seek to be justified

fied by *Chrift*, we ourselves also are found sinners; is *Chrift* therefore the minister of sin? By no means;"* That is, if we now profess that something more than what *Jesus Chrift* formerly taught, be necessary to our acceptance with God, we own that we have been doing wrong, and in effect charge our divine Master with being the minister of sin; for he taught, that whosoever believed in him had passed from death unto life, and should not come into condemnation. It is in vain, therefore, to hope to mix, or to compound the matter: Justification is "freely by grace through the redemption that is by *Chrift Jesus*." Neither an external nor partial obedience can satisfy the demands of the law; it requires that which is perfect. We pity those, therefore, who are going about to establish their own righteousness, and would charitably hope that many of them are sincere in their views as *Paul* was before his conversion; but they are mistaken; and unless grace correct this their mistake, it will prove as fatal to them as it did to the *Jews*. Rejecting *Jesus Chrift*, and relying upon themselves, was the reason why the *Jews* attained not to the Law of Righteousness: Ignorance, Pride, and Unbelief were the causes of their disappointment. But,

2. The *Gentiles* which *followed not after righteousness attained to righteousness, even the righteousness which is of faith*. The free remission

* Gal. ii. 14—17.

mission of sin, and complete salvation by grace, through faith in *Jesus Christ*, were by the Gospel published to them. To this report they attended, as to tidings of great joy. They believed the report—they embraced the Saviour and his righteousness, as proposed to them in the word. Informed, that through *Jesus Christ* was preached unto them the forgiveness of sin; that he had made peace by the blood of his cross; had brought in an everlasting righteousness; and that he was the end of the law for righteousness to every one that believeth—they cordially embraced the tidings. Contented to be saved without money and without price—willing to be wholly and eternally indebted to free mercy—having nothing to bring, to plead, to boast of, in themselves, these sinners received the Gospel, believed on *Jesus Christ*, and were reconciled to God. In a moment—by a single act of faith in *Jesus Christ*, they attained what the *Jews* had been so long, and with so much labour, searching for in vain. "They were accepted in the Beloved to the praise of the glory of grace." But observe *how* they attained it, not by the works of the law, but by faith in *Jesus Christ*: And observe farther *what* they obtained, viz. Righteousness; that is, embracing the Saviour which *Paul* preached to them, they found him to be full of grace and truth, to justify them through the righteousness imputed or placed to their account—to

justify

justify them from all things from which the law of *Moses* could not justify its most strenuous votaries: And in *Jesus Christ* they saw a fulness likewise to subdue every evil, to sanctify them in body, soul, and spirit, and finally to present them holy and unblameable before the throne, just such as the law required. How complete then are those that are found in *Christ Jesus!* Acceptance in him gives glory to God and peace to the conscience. Faith in him purgeth the conscience from dead works, and purifieth the heart: And every believer in this *Jesus* is complete in him; there is no condemnation against such, for they are made the righteousness of God in him.

But, to draw to a close, we would consider these words as descriptive of three characters.

1. How descriptive are they of those persons who shew no concern about a righteousness in which they may appear with acceptance before God? Such was the condition of the *Gentiles* before the Gospel was sent amongst them: But how inexcusable are you who hear of a judgment to come, of an holy law, and of an all-seeing Judge, and yet discover no concern how you may appear with acceptance? How inexcusable are you who hear of *Christ*, and salvation by him, and yet treat that report with a cold indifference? Sure ye do not discover the same rationality when spiritual subjects claim your regard, as ye do
when

when your temporal interest lies before you. You are concerned to procure those things that are calculated for the support of your health, or for the removal of your infirmities; and are your souls left to perish when the grand remedy is brought nigh to you? O infatuated, inexcusable conduct. Sure it will be more tolerable in the day of judgment for poor benighted heathens than for you.

2. Another class of persons here described are those who are much concerned to obtain righteousness, but, though their object be right, they pursue it in a wrong way. They engage in their own, not in the strength of the Lord God. They are ignorant, awfully ignorant, of what God *is*, of what his law requires, and of their own depravity and helpless condition. Hence they go about to establish their own righteousness, and submit not to the righteousness of God revealed in the Gospel. They labour in vain, and spend their strength for nought; for as soon might they touch the sun, or turn the tide, as reach the standard of perfect righteousness, or answer the extent of the law's demands without an interest in *Jesus Christ*.

3. A third class of hearers are those who, by humble faith, take God at his word, and receive *Jesus Christ* as their wisdom, righteousness, sanctification, and redemption. They are content to be nothing, that He may be the great ALL in their salvation. They
place

place no confidence in the flesh; they flee for mercy to the hope set before them in the Gospel; and they desire to be found in *Christ*, not having their own righteousness which is of the law, but that which is by the faith of him. In a word, they look to *Jesus* as the Author and Finisher of their faith; hope one day to receive the end of that faith in the salvation of their souls, and to have an abundant entrance ministred unto them, into his everlasting kingdom. Of this character may we all be found at last, even in *Christ Jesus*. *Amen.*

SERMON

SERMON III.

God honoured by an humble Offering; or Salvation connected with a Christian Conversation.

PSALM L. 23.

Whoso offereth praise, glorifieth me: and to him that ordereth his conversation aright, will I shew the salvation of God.

HOW very singular, my brethren, would it have appeared to the children of *Israel*, if, during their long and hard bondage in *Egypt*, they had sometimes heard their cruel task-masters address them in some such language as this: "We sincerely pity you, O ye *Israelites*, under this your hard servitude; but know, that while we exact this toilsome labour at your hands, your God has something further in view. The end—the only end that he intends in all this, is to raise your hearts in faith and prayer towards himself—to lead you wholly to despair of all help from yourselves, or from any other human aid, and to bring you to an entire dependence upon him alone

alone to accomplish your deliverance." Such language, I say, would have sounded very different in their ears from the crackling of whips—the angry demand of brick without straw—or the constant clamour of, Ye are idle, ye are idle; to your work, to your work. Nor would it appear much less strange to the posterity of this people afterwards, while yet the yoke of ceremonial institutions lay heavy upon their necks, as a burden which neither they nor their fathers were able to bear, to hear such language as that contained in the text proceed from the heavenly oracle.—— While, perhaps, some were dragging their sacrifices along to the altar, and others bringing their thank-offerings in baskets upon their shoulders, to hear *Jehovah* himself give forth this proclamation, *Whoso offereth praise, glorifieth me: and to him that ordereth his conversation aright will I shew my salvation.*——Such a declaration one would have thought was sufficient even then to indicate that he required something more than these sacrifices——. that it was the worship of the heart which alone was acceptable to him; and that he had farther discoveries to make to those who looked through the means of his appointment to the intention he had in the appointment.— This was one way by which he preached the Gospel to them then, as well as unto us; and those who were enabled to mix faith with the

word

word both saw and waited for God's salvation.

The Psalm, which is concluded with the words of the text, opens with a very magnificent description of the promulgation of the ever-blessed Gospel. "That God who, at sundry times and in divers manners, spake in times past by the Prophets to the Fathers, in these last times by his Son hath spoken to us." The difference of the two dispensations is marked out with great precision in ver. 1, 2. The Law of *Moses* was delivered from mount *Sinai*, the Gospel from *Sion*—that in terror, this in beauty—the one from a *cloud*, the other in *brightness*—the former to a *peculiar people*, but the latter is directed to *all the inhabitants of the earth*, from the rising of the sun to the going down thereof.

This pleasing description of the publication of the Gospel is followed with an intimation of the awful and terrible manner in which God would judge his apostate people the *Jews*. In this solemn work he appeals to heaven and earth, to angels and men, to vindicate the rectitude and propriety of his conduct, ver. 3, 4. *Our God shall come and shall not keep silence: a fire shall devour before him, and it shall be very tempestuous round about him. He shall call to the heavens from above, and to the earth, that he may judge his people.*

The summons is sent forth; the criminal nation appears at the bar, and *Jehovah* himself

self brings forward the charge against them. It is granted that they had not with-held the sacrifice from his altar; but they had placed an undue confidence in their offerings, and had vainly supposed that their God was pleased, and satisfied, and rendered propitious to them by such things, ver. 5—13.

These ceremonial institutions are therefore set aside, and a service more spiritual is required. Prayer, Praise, and Obedience are the sacrifices which he now demands: *Offer unto God thanksgiving, and pay thy vows to the Most High. And call upon me in the day of trouble; I will deliver thee, and thou shalt glorify me.* Ver. 14, 15.

The impenitent *Jews*, while they boasted of the law, had greatly dishonoured it by their traditions. While they taught that men should not steal, they had robbed God of his honour; and, to crown their vile conduct, they at last reviled *Jesus Christ* his own Son, and slandered those who placed their dependence on him. Such is the charge preferred against them, ver. 16 —— 20. Upon these accounts they are threatened,——exhorted to repentance,——and encouraged to embrace that Gospel which represents *Jehovah* as a God who freely pardoneth iniquity, and saveth to the uttermost all that approach him by *Jesus Christ.*——*Whoso offereth praise, glorifieth me: and to him that ordereth his conversation*

verſation aright will I ſhew the ſalvation of God.† Such are the outlines of the Pſalm.*

As to the words of the text, we propoſe to conſider them in the order in which they lie, and as holding forth the moſt intereſting inſtruction under the two following branches:

I. They ſhew us how God is to be glorified by ſinful men in the preſent ſtate. And,

II. They encourage us to purſue that courſe of conduct, with which he has been pleaſed to connect the greateſt of all bleſſings, the ſalvation of God.

Theſe things conſidered, we ſhall cloſe with a few inferences from the whole.

I. *Theſe words afford us inſtruction how God is to be glorified by ſinful men in the preſent ſtate:* "He that offereth praiſe, glorifieth me:" Under this branch of the diſcourſe we ſhall attempt three things; 1ſt, To explain the word here rendered *praiſe*; 2dly, Shew how this is to be *offered*; and, 3dly, Prove that ſuch an offering is acceptable to God, as it tends to *glorify him*.

1. We ſhall lay before you what we conceive to be the meaning of the word here tranſlated

---

† Ver. 21. 22, 23.

* See an excellent *Commentary on the Book of Pſalms,* by *George Horne,* D. D. A work eminent for learning and piety, deſerving to be read by every ſerious Chriſtian; and which can ſcarcely be read without the much pleaſure and profit.

lated *praise*. An expositor has greatly the advantage of a translator, as he moves in a larger circle, and is not limited or confined in the work he undertakes. He can multiply words, and mould them into a variety of sentences to convey his meaning to his audience. In almost every language certain words are found, to which various senses have been affixed, and which convey a variety of ideas to the mind. Those who are well informed in any of these languages, have this variety ever before them, so that they can fix upon this, or that, or pass in their reflections from one to another: but a translator, whose business it is to pass one language into another, is under a necessity to fix upon one word alone, and, therefore, can convey no more of the original idea than that word contains. Thus, for instance, the primary and proper meaning of the original word here made use of, signifies *Confession*; and this idea perfectly agrees and corresponds with the context. Their crimes had been specified in the 21st, and some preceding verses. These things they had done; and because the Lord kept silence, they supposed that he was altogether like themselves; but he resolves to reprove them, and to set their sins in order before their eyes. This they are called to consider, and to reflect upon the awful consequences of such sentiments and conduct, lest he tear them in pieces when

there

there would be none to deliver, ver. 22. Upon which they are invited to acknowledge their offences with humility before God. *Whoso offereth confession glorifieth me*, ver. 23. To excuse, or to extenuate our offences before God, is to act as though we supposed that he were such an one as ourselves, and, like ourselves, could be imposed on by ignorance, or by the artifice of others: But ingenuously to *confess* our sin, is to *glorify God*; seeing therein we acknowledge that he searcheth the heart, and that it would be just in him to take vengeance upon us for our iniquity. The same word here rendered *praise*, is, in *Joshua*'s address to *Achan*, translated *Confession*, and in the very same connection in which it is found in the text. *Joshua* vii. 19. And *Joshua said unto Achan, my Son, give, I pray thee, glory to the Lord God of* Israel, *and make* Confession *unto him: and tell me now what thou hast done, hide it not from me.* He was there called to own that God was righteous—that he had been justly displeased—and that he had manifested his great wisdom in bringing his transgression to light; and, in *Joshua*'s esteem, this was to give glory to God, even that glory which was due unto his name. In like manner in the text, the Lord himself declares, that to offer confession was to do him honour. But upon this we shall have opportunity to speak more fully presently.

The

The word likewise signifies *Thanksgiving* or *Praise*, as it is rendered in the 14th verse, and many other places. Nor are these words so very different from each other in meaning as they appear in sound; for, when it is rendered praise or thanksgiving, the primary idea of the word is not given up, but virtually retained. For what is praise but a confession of some benefit received, and of the obligation that we are thereby laid under to him that conferred that benefit upon us? Under the law, you will recollect, there were two kinds of sacrifices or offerings appointed; under the one, sin was acknowledged and confessed; as were gratitude and devotedness to God, under the other. So the ingenuous confession of our sin, and thanksgiving for mercies innumerable, are the two grand sacrifices which are both required of us, and accepted from us, under the gospel dispensation. And with such sacrifices God is well pleased, for thereby he is glorified.

2. In all our offerings we are to have particular respect to the Lord *Jesus Christ*, as the great High Priest of our profession. Under the *Mosaic* dispensation, no sacrifice for sin could be admitted at God's altar but through the interposition of *Aaron*, or his successor in office; nor could the thank-offering be accepted but as coming through his hands. And is there not something similar to all this still? Our very confessions would

would vindicate our condemnation, rather than procure favour, was there not a reference to *Jesus Christ* in all of them. Was it not for the merit of his blood, and the prevalence of his intercession before the throne, we should confess, and be confounded. And where must all our praises centre but in this? *Blessed be God for Jesus Christ.* He is the root of all our mercies, whether spiritual or temporal. He is the ground-work of all our hopes of heaven, and an eternity of happiness. If we bless the Father, it is as he hath manifested himself in and by the Son. Thus the Apostle *Peter:* " Blessed be the God and Father of our Lord *Jesus Christ*, who hath blessed us with all spiritual blessings in heavenly places in *Christ*." *Jesus Christ* is the priest who presents all our sacrifices, and the altar which renders them acceptable to God. " By him, therefore, let us offer the sacrifice of praise to God continually, that is the fruit of our lips, giving thanks unto his name." Out of him, there is no access, no acceptance; in him, both are enjoyed, and enjoyed with confidence.——— We remark,

3. That such sacrifices glorify God more than thousands of rams, or ten thousand rivers of oil. He that offereth *praise*, or *confession*, in the full sense of the word, glorifieth God. Confession of sin glorifies both the justice and the mercy of God at the same in-

stant. The soul is favoured with this happy discovery, that God can be just and yet display his mercy; and that the sovereign is satisfied, while the sinner is freely pardoned. Thus the poor publican in the temple honoured God, while he smote upon his breast, and cried out, God be merciful, or *propitious*, to me a sinner. And thus every sinner gives glory to God, who flees for refuge to the hope set before him in the gospel, and depends upon *Jesus Christ* for pardon, peace, and salvation. Such are led to exult in this view of the divine character, and to say, " Who is a God like unto thee, that pardoneth iniquity and passeth by transgression? Thou retainest not thine anger for ever, because thou delightest in mercy."

Such likewise are grateful for their mercies. They see how the mercy of God is displayed in the pardon of sin—in the provision of a Saviour, and in the fulness deposited in him. Even temporal and relative blessings they consider as flowing to them through the channel of an everlasting covenant, and the language of their hearts is, What shall we render to the Lord for all his benefits conferred upon us!—These are the sacrifices that tend to glorify God—and to glorify him more than all those which were offered under the law. *Those* were only offerings from the flock, or from the field;— *these*, from the heart. *Those*, were from without

out the man,—*these*, from within. *Those* the labour of the hands—*these*, the act of the mind. *Those* were but the shadows, of which *these* are the substance. The declaration of God then was, *I will have mercy and not sacrifice*; and these are the offerings which mercy requireth, and which likewise are produced by discoveries of mercy. Thus confessions of our guilt and misery, and of our obligations for favours innumerable, are those offerings which glorify God. We then glorify his mercy, and glorify his goodness, when we venture our eternal all upon the bottom of the one, and pour out our praises into the bosom of the other. " God hath set forth his Son to be a propitiation, through faith in his blood, to declare his righteousness in the forgiveness of sin:" and the soul gives honour to this report, when it builds all its hopes, and derives all its confidence from that consideration. Then it appears, with indubitable evidence, that " there is redemption in *Christ*'s blood, the forgiveness of sin, according to the riches of grace."

We have now seen how these words tend to instruct us as to the manner in which God is to be glorified by sinful men in the present state. *Confession*, or *praise*, are the offerings which he requires—these are to be *presented through Jesus Christ*—and, as accepted in him, *they glorify God*.—We pass on, II. To

II. To consider these words as tending to encourage us to pursue and persevere in that course of conduct, with which the greatest encouragement respecting the future life stands connected. "To him that ordereth his conversation aright, will I shew the salvation of God."

Under this head we shall take a view of what is meant by *ordering the conversation aright,* and of the *privilege connected with it.*

1. As to the meaning of this phrase, *ordering the conversation aright.* By *conversation* we understand the habitual course of a person's conduct, both towards God and man. By faith and prayer the correspondence is kept up with God in the manner already described. Not a day passes but we have to confess that, in many instances, we have sinned, or come short of the glory of God: But his mercy appears new every morning, as doth his faithfulness every evening. Daily shall we find the inestimable advantage of holding converse with God, while we read his word, or meditate upon his covenant, grace, or promises. The conversation must be kept up in heaven, if we wish to live above the world, to mortify sin, or to overcome temptation. By daily coming to Jesus, and holding fellowship with him, the soul is both encouraged and edified; it obtains renewed strength and additional support. What is the life of a real christian but a walking with God,

God, listening to his word, and acquainting him with our various wants and weaknesses? Brethren, converse with him as your friend, your father, your God reconciled towards you in *Christ Jesus*. By prayer, with supplication and thanksgiving, let all your requests be made known to him. The way is now open for the interesting correspondence to be carried on, and it is your province to guard against every thing that would, in the least, impede or interrupt it.—And amongst men also, " let your conversation be as it becometh the gospel of *Christ*." See that ye shine as lights in the world. " As much as lieth in you, live peaceably with all men." Owe no man any thing, except it be that debt of love which is always due, and which ye should be continually paying. Study to conquer the prejudices of men, to silence their objections against religion, and to win their souls to *Christ*. In every situation in which you may be placed by an all-wise Providence, be it your constant concern how you may do the least injury, and all possible good. Be pitiful, be courteous; and should ye be reviled, revile not again. Study the character, and, as much as lies in your power, imitate the conduct of *Jesus Christ*. Frequently look up to God by prayer, to teach you how to glorify him best in your day and generation; that while sinners behold your

conduct,

conduct, they may be condemned, saints encouraged and edified, and all around you benefited.

But when the Psalmist speaks of the *ordering* of our conversation, it supposes that *there is some rule* laid down, *whereby our conversation is to be ordered.* This rule is no other than the whole of that revelation which God has given us in the scriptures. In every difficulty, duty, and concern, this will point out to you the way, and direct you how to pursue it. This will inform you what God *is*, how he is to be approached, and what he requires from you. This will inform you respecting the person, the offices, the character and grace of *Jesus Christ*, and direct you to the Holy Spirit, as the great instructor and applier of all the grace and truth that is in *Christ.* This word will unfold the purposes, the promises, and the providences of God to your view, shewing how all of them are so united, as to make all things work together for good to those who love him.—And as to men, this rule will teach you how to order your conversation towards the sinner and the saint; towards friends and enemies; towards relations and strangers. By this rule you are required to walk orderly towards them that are without, giving no offence to *Jew* or *Gentile,* or to the Church of God. In short, this word will be found as a light to your feet and a lamp to your paths, profitable for all things;

things;—and, walking according to it, you will have peace.

In order to the accomplishment of this, let it be seen that *your converſation is in Chriſt* *. It is by the grace, wiſdom, and ſtrength that you receive from him, that all this is to be effected. Without him ye can do nothing. His grace alone will be ſufficient for you, and his ſtrength is made perfect in weakneſs. Your work then is to receive him, and to walk in him day by day. Lean not to your own underſtanding, but go in the ſtrength of the Lord God, relying upon him, even him alone. You will never be able to make any progreſs in the divine life, but by a conſtant application to this Saviour, and the uſe you make of him by faith. Without him, the correſpondence between God and you muſt fail for ever:—And without *Jeſus Chriſt* you will do no good amongſt men. He that lives a life of faith on the Son of God, will be active, tender-hearted, ready to ſupply the wants of his fellow-creatures according to his ability, diſpoſed to forgive injuries, and will be concerned above all for their ſoul's profit. He will do all this through Chriſt ſtrengthening him, and will own that all his ſufficiency is of God.

2. As to the privilege connected with this ordering the converſation aright, it is added, that *to ſuch ſhall be ſhewn the ſalvation of God*.

The

* 1 Pet. iii. 16.

The difcovery of this every true believer has, in a greater or lefs degree, at prefent; but the more full manifeftation, as well as the complete enjoyment of it, is referved for the future world.

The fubject to be manifefted is the *Salvation of God*; fo called, we apprehend, for its great magnitude. Hence we find large trees, ftiled trees of God, and great mountains, mountains of God. It may alfo be called God's falvation, on account of its excellency and importance. He is the great author and end of it. And this falvation is a *great falvation*, as it incircles the whole church of believers, extends from eternity to eternity, and includes all the glory of God: It proceeds from him, centres in him, and the complete manifeftation of himfelf is feen in the whole of it. O how great muft that falvation be, which has grace enough in it to pardon all our fins, to fanctify all the powers of the mind, to fupply every want, to fubdue all oppofition, and to fatisfy every defire and demand of the foul. To every believer it appears a great falvation—but every believer fees but a part of it—yea, all the deliverances which all of them put together have enjoyed, are no more than the furface of it: Still the greatnefs of it remains, which will be found fufficient to extend itfelf, fo as completely to fill all the ages of eternity. How great then muft that falvation

tion be, of which God himself is the centre, and eternity the circle that surrounds it.

This salvation is now almost ready to be revealed. That day, which shall disclose the important secret, approaches nearer and nearer every sabbath, and every hour. At present, time, like a vail, separates you from the prospect. The work is now in hand—every day brings it nearer to its consummation—and, when completed, it will appear to be worthy of God in every part of it. Hence an Apostle represents the people of God, as kept by his mighty power through faith unto salvation, ready to be revealed in the last time. *——And

The revelation of this salvation will fully satisfy the souls of God's people with everlasting pleasure and delight. " I will shew, or, I will make him to see, the salvation of God;" that is, he will both give the discovery, and the faculty also properly to conceive of it, and take it in: And if harmony can delight, what must it be to see a company composed of millions of millions, even all the ransomed of the Lord, each present to bear his part in this glorious song of salvation! If the enjoyment of the greatest delicacies can delight, here the whole treasure of divine goodness, grace, and mercy will be displayed! Or, if grandeur can strike the mind, here all the glory of God will be revealed, and every perfection manifested in

* 1 Pet. i. 5.

its full proportion! It will be a filling subject to all the people of God; and the vision will be growing more bright and more extensive, as the ages of eternity roll along. There *Jehovah* will make all his goodness pass in review before his adoring people, and will be glorified in his saints for ever and ever. Upon the whole we infer,

1. That if sincere confession be the way to glorify God, there are multitudes who withhold this honour from him.—It is not barely saying I have sinned, or, that I am verily guilty in this or that instance; but it is to be humbled, to be abased, to be annihilated as it were before God, upon the account of sin. It is to feel displeasure, resolution, and vengeance against sin. To see how it dishonours God, defiles the soul, and brings darkness and condemnation upon the mind. Renouncing then all confidence in, or dependance upon, yourselves; nay, loathing yourselves because of your iniquities, have ye joined issue with the law in condemning sin, while ye have fled for refuge to the hope set before you in the Gospel? Has sin been confessed, pardon implored, and justice honoured, while ye have taken sanctuary in the arms of the God of mercy? This is to abase self and to honour God.

2. From this subject it appears to be vain and presumptuous to hope to see and enjoy

enjoy the falvation of God, where there is not a ftudious defire to order the converfation aright. Sanctification is no lefs a part of falvation than juftification; but both of them are from *Chrift,* and both of them through faith in him. By union with *Jefus Chrift,* the foul is not only abfolved from guilt, but in him has a title, and from him a meetnefs for glory. And the intent of the Gofpel being preached to the race of fallen *Adam* is, that they may receive forgivenefs of fins, and an inheritance among them that are fanctified by faith that is *Chrift Jefus.* * Such are faid to be wafhed, yea they are fanctified: And fhould it be afked, how are they fanctified? the anfwer is, *relatively,* being juftified in the name of the *Lord Jefus,* and *really* by the Spirit of our God.

3. How much caufe have the followers of *Chrift* to be humbled on account of their deficiencies in this refpect! In many things they all offend; but perhaps in nothing more than in this, a want of realizing views of, and dependance upon, *Jefus Chrift.* To this fource may be attributed all the defects of their converfation and conduct. Did they live more on him, they would exprefs more of his image in their conduct, and thereby adorn the doctrine of God their Saviour in all things. That we may be more convinced of this defect, more humbled on the account of it, and

---

* Acts xxviii. 18.

and led into more lively and conſtant acts of dependance on him, God grant of his abounding mercy, for the Redeemer's ſake. *Amen.*

SERMON

SERMON IV.

The Neceffity and Advantages of Reconciliation with God.

AMOS iii. 3.

Can two walk together except they be agreed?

NO; it is impoffible that they fhould; for fuppofe that they fet out at the fame time, yet if it be not from the fame place; or fhould they fet out from the fame place, yet if it be not at the fame time, they cannot walk together; or fhould it be the cafe that they ftart at the fame time and place, yet if there be any previous difagreement between them, if they really diflike one another, they will foon feparate. "Friendfhip is the very life of fellowfhip, and concord of communion." The evidence of this we fee continually in the world at large; but more from the want of friendfhip than from its genuine effects. From whence arife all thofe envyings, bickerings, perfonal contefts, open ruptures, or numerous law-fuits—whence all thefe, but from the difagreement there is found in men's interefts, principles, or tempers?

pers? They infringe upon each other's rights, or they impede the execution of one another's schemes; or there is that want of affection, of public spirit, and concern for the good of others equally with their own, which is essential to happiness and order in society.—— Even in the natural world, we see that things which are different in their nature, are so far from uniting, that they oppose each other with all their force: Thus darkness and light seem to struggle for a separation, or to gain the superiority. Thus water and fire mutually oppose each other; and oil, while it adds rage to the one, entirely divests the other of its fury. If poured upon fire it increases the blaze; but if upon the tempestuated ocean it reduces its rage, and begets a perfect calm. But to come to the subject before us.

Notice had been taken in the preceding chapter of the sins of *Israel*, of the peculiar aggravations which accompanied their conduct, and of the desolating judgments with which, on that account, they were about to be visited. To this they are required to pay the most serious regard as to a message from God, ver. 1. *Hear this word that the Lord hath spoken against you, O children of* Israel, *against the whole family which I brought up from the land of* Egypt. Though *Amos* was the messenger, it was the word of the Lord which he delivered.—This word is directed to *Israel,* as *a family.*——To the *whole* family.
That

That family which the Lord had formed, preserved, built up, multiplied, and wonderfully appeared for. From this we remark, that God sees and is much displeased with the sins of his own family. If his children transgress, he will visit their iniquities with a rod, and their transgressions with stripes. Though he be the Father of the family, he will assert and maintain his authority therein. He loves his children, but it is not with a blind partiality, for he sees that folly is bound up in their hearts, and he will employ the rod of correction to drive it away: " Whom he loves he chastens, and scourgeth every son whom he receiveth."

The Lord's conduct, we find, had been very gracious towards his family, but they had not rendered according to the goodness done to them: They had returned evil for good, and unkindness for his generosity.— Ver. 2. *You only have I known of all the families of the earth; therefore I will punish you for all your iniquities.* As *God*, he knew all the families, that is, all the nations of the earth; but, as a *Covenant God*, he had not discovered such affection and regard for any other nation as he had for *Israel*. To them he had given a good inheritance; had favoured them with the knowledge of himself and of his will; established his worship amongst them, and, by a special providence, watched over and defended them. But though, as a family,

family, they had been thus highly favoured, having God so nigh unto them, yet they had grievously departed from him; though, as children, he had brought them up with such tenderness, and delivered them from such misery, yet they had rebelled against him; loaded with benefits, they had proved ungrateful, rejected the revelation that had been given them, and distrusted or denied his providence. Their sins were more aggravated and heinous than those of other nations. The time was now come that judgment should begin at the house of God. Slighted mercies and abused privileges lay a once-protected people open and exposed to the most awful and desolating judgments.—The Lord had been long amongst them, and had received many affronts from them; but now their situation was become desperate. Things had got to such a pass, that a separation was absolutely necessary. How could they expect that he would any longer walk with them, when every day he saw himself affronted to his face? His promises were not believed, his commands were disobeyed, his worship was polluted with their own inventions, his providence disregarded, and his Prophets either despised, insulted, or murdered: He refers therefore the decision to themselves, whether it were possible, things being so circumstanced, that they could walk any longer together. Evident it was, that the parties were entirely disagreed,

disagreed, and therefore it was time to separate: For, *Can two walk together except they be agreed?*

What is here said of *Israel* in particular, may, in a more general view, be applied to mankind at large. Once they and their Creator walked together in the strictest agreement; many were the favours with which they were then loaded; great their advantages:—But man being in honour continued not; he walked contrary to the Lord, and thus the communion was broken. In this discourse we propose to shew,

> I. That there is a very great disagreement between the Lord and mankind in general.
> II. What it is for God and Men to be reconciled, or agreed. And,
> III. That one end of this agreement, or reconciliation, is, that men may walk with God.——These things being considered, we shall close with an inference or two from the subject.

The first thing we have to shew is,

I. *That there is a very great disagreement between the Lord and mankind in general.* The evidence of this mournful fact is so plain, that little need be said in confirmation of it, if God be what the word of revelation expresly declares that he is, and what right reason also teaches us that he must be, or he cannot be God:—And on the other hand, if men in general are what our eyes, our ears, and our experience prove them to be, it is not only impossible that they should be agreed, but it is further manifest that the disagreement between them must be very great. This will appear if we consider the general *conduct* of mankind, or their *temper* and *disposition*.

1. The *conduct* of the generality of mankind shews that there is a very great disagreement between God and them;—such a disagreement, that it is impossible, things continuing as they are, they should walk together: For instance, God is an holy God—He requireth truth in the inward parts.—This is his command, " Be ye holy, for I the Lord your God am holy."—And this God cannot be deceived with any false appearances, for he " searcheth the hearts and trieth the reins of the children of men." The wicked conduct of men is an indubitable evidence what enemies they are to this God in their minds. What a scene of abomination is every day passing in review before him! Thousands of thousands of transgressors, all at work at once; each of them exerting all his wiles and all his powers in the practice of iniquity. The Lord is represented as looking down from heaven upon the habitations of the sons of men; and what was the result of the enquiry? He saw that they were all gone out of the

way; that they had all done abominably; that there was none of all the sons of *Adam* that did good; no, not one, strictly considered as his descendant. Astonishing forbearance, that he does not at once sink such a wicked world under the weight of the most awful and complicated judgments! It is not from any want of power, nor is it because he is not displeased, for God is angry with the wicked every day; but it is because he waits to be gracious to those who will accept of his grace, and that all the rest may be rendered eternally inexcusable: But, though he thus delays the stroke; though he even continues to load his very enemies with his bounty, we are not thence to conclude that he is agreed with them: quite the reverse. Scripture informs us that he endures with much long-suffering the vessels of wrath fitted for destruction.— Earthly sovereigns are acquainted only with a few of the discontents and murmurings that may be amongst their people; they do not apprehend in how many instances their laws are broken, and their revenue injured; but the Lord sees all the wicked works, he hears all the wicked speeches that there are in the world, wherever transacted, or by whomsoever spoken. Now, if God's way be a way of truth and holiness, and if this be the course of the inhabitants of the world at large, how evident is it that they do not walk together, and the reason is plainly this, they are not agreed.——But,

2. The *tempers*, as well as the conduct of men, is another proof that there is a great disagreement between God and them. This is the will of God even their sanctification. He demands of them the love, the subjection, and the obedience of their hearts: He requires that they should bow to his sovereign will, realize his presence in all places, and at all times feel their hearts attached to his glory: But is this the case? So far from it, that many are said to hate him in their hearts.— They are at enmity with his law, and could we hear that language which he both hears and understands, one is saying, Depart from me, for I desire not the knowledge of thy ways—another, I will not obey his voice— and a third, Tush, God seeth not. Could we see as God seeth, that the hearts of the sons of men are set in them to do evil, what an awful and distressing prospect would it be to behold every heart unvailed at once, and all the windings and workings of sin laid bare to our view in a moment; but God seeth all this without the least interruption or intermission. Men are proud, passionate, unclean, and unholy; actuated by the lusts both of the flesh and of the mind. And how, suppose ye, is it possible that God should agree with such? They have affronted his holiness, and injured his justice, and spurned at his authority, and

rebelled

rebelled against his government; have defpifed his Son, and refifted his grace, and how can he be reconciled unto them?—Thus the outward *conduct* and the inward *tempers* of natural men fufficiently evince that there is a great difagreement between God and them.—But we haften to fhew,

II. *What it is for God and Men to be reconciled, or agreed.* Something feems neceffary on each part. In the Lord *Jefus Chrift* the grand fcheme of reconciliation hath been opened on the part of God. He himfelf provided a Deliverer—one who had the intereft of each party at heart—one who was fully able to remove all the obftacles on either fide that lay in the way of a reconciliation—one altogether qualified to effect a reconciliation upon the moft equitable and honourable terms, and to render the fuccefs of his interpofition of permanent advantage to every fucceeding age. "God was in *Chrift* reconciling the world unto himfelf, not imputing their trefpaffes." Juftice is now fatisfied, wrath removed, holinefs honoured, truth vindicated, the law magnified, the throne of mercy erected, and the reign of grace eftablifhed. The minifters of religion are likewife fent forth in the name, and by the authority of *Jefus Chrift* to pray you to be reconciled to God. All things are now ready, and behold the Lord waiteth to be gracious.—But upon the part of man likewife

likewife two things are found neceffary, in order to this agreement.

1. It is neceffary that man fhould be made willing *to accept of God's free favour; to receive his* Chrift, *and to bow to the fceptre of his fovereign grace.* God has refolved to glorify himfelf in his Son *Jefus Chrift*, and in the falvation of finners through him. The mind of the finner muft be brought fully to acquiefce therewith. He muft cordially receive the reconciliation, and fay from the heart, Let God have all the glory; yea, and let him be eternally glorified in faving me and my fellow-finners in this way. When this is the cafe, men begin to be reconciled to the holinefs, and to the juftice, and to the authority and law of God. They then begin to fee that fin is that evil and bitter thing which God's word defcribes it to be; that it deferves that punifhment which he has denounced againft it; and that it is reafonable and abfolutely neceffary, that fatisfaction fhould be made on account of it. The fcheme of Redemption and Salvation, by *Jefus Chrift*, now begins to appear a very glorious fcheme, every way worthy of the counfel of God to devife, and of his character to accomplifh. It now appears a report truly " worthy of all acceptance that *Jefus Chrift* came into the world to fave finners—that he fuffered for fin, the juft for the unjuft—and that he is able to fave to the very uttermoft all that come unto

to God by him."—But reasonable, wonderful, worthy of God, and glorious as this scheme appears in itself to the enlightened mind, nothing can be more opposite to the proud and self-sufficient heart of the natural man than freely and fully to acquiesce in a salvation which is entirely of God; and, as such, to embrace it. In this salvation there is not the least room left for the creature to glory: God possesses the whole honour. The exceeding greatness of the divine power is found necessary to make a people willing to accept of grace as God's gift, and of salvation as his work: Thus it is in *Christ* alone, that this agreement between God and men can take place. Men never agree with him till they are brought to approve of his plan, of his *Christ*, and that he himself should be the great ALL in ALL of their salvation. *Christ* is our peace, opening the way for this reconciliation by his obedience and death; and, by his Spirit and Grace, reconciling the minds of men, and bringing them cordially to receive his favours.—In order to this reconciliation, or agreement, being complete,

2. It is requisite that men be *reconciled to the whole will of God*, so as to approve what he approves, and to hate what he hates. The mind must be disposed to esteem all his commandments concerning all things to be right, and to hate every false way. Their minds are so reconciled to the will of God, that they

they follow him as his dear children; they enter into his mind so as to approve of it from their hearts, and delight in his law after the inward man. Imperfections are indeed evident in the whole conduct of the most eminent believers; for they see but in part, and are sensible that they come amazingly short of that which they see and approve to be right: But though there be great evidences of imperfection in their obedience, yet they are not partial in their regard to the will of God: They do not follow one precept while they wilfully reject or transgress another; but they approve of them all, and desire to stand complete in the whole will of God: They see a beauty in holiness; they long to be transformed into the image of a holy God, and this alone will fully satisfy them. Their desire is *to believe all that God hath revealed.* Such read the scriptures, and pray to have their understanding and hearts led into every revealed truth, and bow their souls to the mind and will of God revealed in the scriptures. Such persons would not wish to have one chapter, or even a single verse left out of the Bible; but, with a mind open to conviction, their prayer is, " that which we see not, Lord teach thou us."—Such persons approve of all God's precepts, they neither charge *that* as too hard, nor *this* as too restrained; but their language is, Lord, thou shalt guide us with thy counsel.—They have

likewise

likewise a desire to bow to the sovereignty of God in the dispensations of his providence, and would bless his name whether he gives to, or takes away from them.—It is also their desire to honour the Lord, as the great institutor of ordinances, doing what he has required, because he has required it, and endeavouring to keep up communion with him in all his appointments. Knowingly they would not turn their backs upon any divine institution, but would be found walking in all the commands and ordinances of the Lord blameless. But where any of the doctrines of divine revelation are obstinately rejected, any of God's commands disregarded, any of his providences rebelled against, or any of his ordinances habitually slighted, it proves that such persons are not fully reconciled to God, or they would be found walking with him. Thus we have seen, that to accept of God's grace, and to be obedient to his will are the evidences of the soul's reconciliation to God. This being proved, we pass on,

III. To shew *that one end of this reconciliation, or agreement, is that men may be brought to walk with God;* and how glorious doth the work of man's Redemption, the whole plan of his Salvation, and the operations of God's Spirit upon the heart appear, when viewed in this light! Can that doctrine tend to licentiousness, which is expressly designed to bring men to walk with God? And we assert that the doctrines of Justification by faith, of Salvation entirely of grace, and of the Spirit's operations and influences upon the heart, have this direct tendency: Their proper and necessary influence, where truly received, is to encourage and to enable men to walk with God; and nothing but a licentious abuse of those grand articles of the Christian Faith can possibly prevent this. *That man* doth not really believe those doctrines with his heart, who does not both feel and give evidence to others, that they have this influence upon him.

To walk with God, how great the idea! What an *honour* conferred! What *advantages* must result from it! And what circumspection and *studious concern* are necessary to preserve and promote it!

1. What an *honour* is it conferred upon a sinful and imperfect creature to walk with God! Angels bow before him, but believing sinners are permitted to walk with him. The honour, though ineffably great, is invisible to an eye of sense, otherwise sure the courts of princes would be left thin, and princes themselves would step from their thrones to seek this more exalted honour of walking with God. This was the honour conferred upon *Enoch*, upon *Abraham*, upon *Hezekiah*, and upon all good men in every age. This is the honour of all the saints; for truly " their fellowship is with the Father, and with his Son *Jesus Christ*."

Christ."—And as the honour conferred upon them is great, so,

2. The *advantages* resulting from it must likewise be *great*. They who walk with God *are under his peculiar care*, and he has wisdom sufficient to guide, and power to keep and to defend them. His eye is always upon them, and his ear open to their cry. He has promised never to leave nor forsake them; to watch over them by night and by day; to keep them as the apple of his eye; and to preserve them by his mighty power through faith unto salvation.—Being in his company, they shall also have his friendly *counsel in all their difficulties*. He has promised that the secret of the Lord shall be with them that fear him, and he will shew them his covenant.—Walking with him, they *shall* likewise *have his support*, and come up from the wilderness leaning upon their beloved. He will strengthen them for all their journey with him, and for all the service that he requires at their hands; and his grace shall be sufficient for them; his strength shall be perfected in their weakness: God being in their company, they shall want nothing that is really good for them.

3. In walking with God great *circumspection* is also necessary. Remember ye are under the eye of him who can detect the least deviation from the rule of the precept and from the line of duty. Your God seeth you. "All things are naked and open to the eye

of him with whom ye have to do;" and you will have need frequently to addrefs him as one of old did, " Search me, O God, and know my thoughts; prove me, and know my ways; and fee if there be any way of wickednefs in me, and lead me in the way everlafting. Who can underftand his errors, cleanfe thou me from fecret faults; keep back thy fervant alfo from prefumptuous fins, left they have dominion over me."——But though he be infinitely wife to detect a failure, he is alfo full of compaffion. He knows your frame, and remembers that ye are but duft. The believer may often ftumble in his way, perhaps fometimes fall; but his face is ftill towards *Zion,* and he rifes again to purfue his courfe.

4. In walking with God, *a ftudious concern is neceffary to keep up the agreement.* See that God and you fall not out in the way. He is not unreafonable in his demands: All that he requires of you is, that ye fhould look to him for fupport and direction in every ftep, and not lean to yourfelves. The conftant exercife of faith upon his wifdom, promife, and power is neceffary to your walking with him. Lofing fight of him, ye will loiter or wander. It is by faith the intercourfe muft be kept up. By faith ye walk, ye run, and fhall finally prevail.—Having now concluded what we propofed, we fhall draw to a clofe in an inference or two from the fubject. And,

1. How

1. How awful, pitiable, and diftreffing is the condition of thofe who are not in a ftate of agreement with God! Their own confciences fometimes proves to them how awful their condition is: Where fhall we borrow language or images whereby to reprefent it? They are at hand: What do you fuppofe muft a poor animal feel which beholds a lion approaching in all the majefty of power— furrounding it with a leer of anger and difdain, and ready to fpring upon it and feize it for his prey? Or how will the poor bird flutter and pant, when caught in the fnare of the fowler, and taken by his hand? Thefe are the images employed in the fubfequent verfes: *Will a lion roar in the foreft, when he hath no prey? Will a young lion cry out of his den, if he have taken nothing? Can a bird fall upon the earth, where no gin is for him? Shall one take up a fnare from the earth, and have taken nothing at all?* Such is the condition of finners, and this the warning which an holy and powerful God gives them, "Confider this, ye that forget God, left I tear you in pieces and there be none to deliver"*. It will be found a fearful thing to fall into his hands, if he then be our enemy.

2. They who are reconciled to God, and walk with him upon earth, fhall be admitted to walk with him alfo in glory: They fhall fee his face; fhall enjoy his company; be owned as his friends; led to his treafures of glory,

* Pfalm L. 22.

glory, and be delightfully satisfied in his presence. The Lamb which is in the midst of the throne shall feed them, and lead them of fountains of living waters, and God shall wipe away all tears from their eyes. In his light they shall see light, shall drink of the rivers of his pleasure, and be led by him from happiness to happiness, from glory to glory, throughout all the successive ages of eternity. That it may be our present privilege, and our future honour thus to walk, God grant for *Jesus*'s sake. *Amen.*

SERMON

SERMON V.

The Glories of Jesus Christ as the end of the Law discovered.

John i. 14. latter part of the verse.

We beheld his glory, the glory as of the only begotten of the Father, full of grace and truth.

IT was God's purpose from eternity to create this world, the inhabitants of which you and I are a part. Had angelic minds been left to conjecture what sort of a world it would be when completed, notwithstanding all the superior advantages they had of knowing God, as well as their superior capacities to conceive properly of him, yet it is highly probable that their idea would have come amazingly short of what it afterwards appeared to those heavenly intelligences, when this work was actually finished. Then they *saw*, and were *satisfied* with the complete order of the great design:—The power, the wisdom, and the goodness displayed in this great production of Omnipotence,

potence, caused all these morning stars to sing together, and all those sons of God to shout for joy. A scene was then opened, sufficiently extensive and various, to employ their contemplative powers. The opening glories of creation exhibited themselves more and more to their view, and in all, they saw and adored the great Creator.—But soon, probably very soon, this harmony was broken—disorder was introduced. Sin threw its thick vail over all the beauties of the lower creation. Man rebelled, and God withdrew his smile of approbation from that very creature which once bore his image. Scarce was that divine image impressed, but it was obliterated, or greatly obscured.—We presume not to say what effect this awful change would have upon the minds of angels. Probably they expected what man himself seems to have expected, viz. that judgment would immediately erect its throne; and, having consigned the criminals to hell, would reduce this world back to its primitive chaos.—God's thoughts, however, are not like our thoughts. His designs exceed even the capacity of angels. He had other discoveries to bring forward, and other scenes still more grand and glorious to open. Scenes in which more of the marvellous of the Godhead would be displayed, and more of his complete character would be exhibited to the minds, both of sinful men and of admiring angels. REDEMPTION

TION was now to be proclaimed, and gradually to be introduced. Sin having entered, God has opportunity, in the ages to come, to shew forth the exceeding riches of his grace, in his kindness towards us, by *Christ Jesus*. Nor must the knowledge of an event, at once so interesting and important, be limited to that age in which the great work was to be accomplished, or to the few ages that might succeed it. The benefits resulting from this glorious work were to extend themselves backwards and forwards, even to all the ages of time. It became, therefore, necessary that the discoveries of it, though, perhaps, at first more dark and distant, should be afforded to the human race; accordingly we find, that it was intimated to our first parents. The discovery of it kept enlarging gradually under the ministry of *Moses* and the prophets; at length, " God sent forth his Son, made of a woman, made under the law, to redeem them that were under the law, that we might receive the adoption of sons." The character, the complete character of this glorious personage is clearly and fully described in that chapter from which the text is taken. His divine—his human—and his complex character, as mediator, is here abundantly set forth. As the *eternal* WORD, subsisting in the one *Jehovah*, he *is*, and *ever was*, God over all, blessed for ever. He was *with* God—*was* God—and by him *all things were*

were made.—Confidered in his low eftate, he *was made flefh*. He affumed the human nature into union with his divine; and, as God manifeft in the flefh, he dwelt, or *tabernacled*, amongft us. Viewed in this his complex character as mediator, there appeared fuch a glory in him, as then drew forth, and ftill continues to draw, forth, the admiration of all that converfe with him. In him dwelleth all the fulnefs of the Godhead bodily. All the counfels, the purpofes, and the promifes of *Jehovah*, meet in him. He is their centre;—their fubftance—their glory: And low, mean, and defpicable as was the appearance he made while here upon earth, through all that fhade which furrounded him, his own difciples *beheld his glory, the glory as of the only begotten of the Father, full of grace and truth.*——What I propofe to your confideration from thefe words, is,

I. The glory of the auguft perfonage, defcribed in the text.
II. The peculiarly gracious way in which this his glory is made manifeft, viz. in the *fulnefs of his grace and truth*.
III. The way and manner in which this was feen formerly, and is to be difcovered ftill; we *faw*, or *beheld* it.

You need no information what are our ideas of this phrafe, *the only begotten of the Father*.

Father. Many eminent in the church, both for their learning and piety, have understood and explained the phrase of the eternal generation of the divine nature of the Son in the Godhead. We have supposed, and still suppose, that this description has reference to the eternal constitution of *Christ*, in the covenant of grace, to be the mediator. As such, he was set up from everlasting ages, and his delights are said to have been with the sons of men. As such, he engaged for the whole church of believers in every age, and graciously undertook to act that part for them which should capacitate him finally to bring them to God. Eternal generation, if the idea be restricted to the divine nature of our Lord, must, we apprehend, indicate some inferiority or subordinate existence; at least, some infer this from it; but this, we assert, is not the doctrine of the scripture, nor is it the intention of those who maintain that sentiment: But upon this head, we presume, our sentiments are sufficiently known already—we see no reason for alteration—nor need we repeat. We proceed, therefore,

I. To consider *the glory of the august personage, described in these words*. The apostle saith, *we beheld his glory*.—Under this head we remark,

1. That, as subsisting in the Godhead from all eternity, this everlasting WORD possessed all divine, and every possible perfection and glory.

glory. He *was*, and continueth to be, *one* with the Father, in such manner as no words can explain, no image illustrate, nor any imagination conceive. To him, in equal conjunction with the Father and the Holy Spirit, every glorious perfection and attribute of Deity pertains. He is before all, and above all, and in all his works. Considered strictly as God, no man hath seen him at any time, nor can any flesh behold him and live. True it is, at seasons, the rays of his Deity broke out, and shone through his words and actions: But these were not direct, but transient, partial, and secondary discoveries of his proper divinity. In his divine nature he is God over all blessed for ever; that blessed and only potentate, who is King of kings, and Lord of lords; that King eternal, immortal, and invisible, who is the only wise God. How far we may be indulged with brighter and fuller discoveries of the divine nature in heaven, we presume not to say; but we apprehend that all our discoveries, even there, will be accommodated to us, and enjoyed by us, through the human nature of the Lord *Jesus Christ*.—It is probable, that in every period, throughout eternity, the fulness of the Godhead will be found to dwell in *Jesus* bodily.—But, though the apostle *John* and his brethren were all of them well satisfied respecting the proper Deity of their blessed Lord, though this may not only be inferred from the beginning of the chapter, but is expressly

expressly asserted there; yet this, we apprehend, is not that glory to which he here particularly refers. We remark, therefore,

2. That this divine personage has a glory, considered as mediator; and to this the words of our text particularly apply. The apostle speaks here of his glory, as the glory of the only begotten of the Father; that is, as he was appointed, raised up, and sent forth, to be the grand medium of all communications, and of all access, between the great *Jehovah* and his sinful creatures, men. He is God and man, in one person. Had he been God alone, he could not have suffered; and had he been man alone, his sufferings could not have been satisfactory for others; but, being both in one person, while, as man, he bled upon his cross, and now pleads before the throne; as God, he throws an infinite merit into all that he did and suffered in our nature, and on our account. His blood hath efficacy to cleanse from all sin; and, through his intercession, he is able to save to the very uttermost all that come unto God by him. A treasure is deposited in him, which neither all the ages of time, nor those of eternity itself, will be able to exhaust. Through him it is that God shineth into the hearts of men, to give them the light of the knowledge of his glory; and, beholding that glory, the whole church are transformed into the same image, by the accompanying influence

ence of the Holy Ghost. We apprehend, therefore, that the apostle, in the passage before us, refers to our blessed Lord, in the character of mediator, both by his describing him as *the only begotten of the Father*, and immediately adding, *full of grace and truth*; representing this, as the glory that they *beheld in him*. Proceed we, therefore, in the *second* place,

II. To consider *the peculiarly gracious way in which this glory of Christ was then, and is still, made manifest.* " Full of grace and truth." GRACE and TRUTH constitute the glory that is here said to have been manifested. And this grace and truth are placed by our apostle in opposition to that law which was given by the ministry of *Moses*, ver. 17. *The law was given by* Moses, but *grace and truth come by* Jesus Christ. To form a proper conception of the contrast, we are to remember that the law delivered by *Moses* was partly *moral*, partly *ceremonial*. The *moral* law evidenced what God *was*, and what man, his creature, *ought to be*.—It provided no security against the entrance of sin; it revealed no remedy for that awful havock which it has since made of human nature, still it required that man should love God with his whole soul; should serve him with his whole strength; and should worship him with his whole heart. This law admitted of no imperfection in the obedience of the creature;

ture; and it required truth in the inward parts.—The *Ceremonial Law* had respect to man as a sinner. It allowed him to acknowledge his guilt, and to present his sacrifice before God: But even those sacrifices, tho' of divine appointment, were not intended to satisfy the demands of justice, or to remove guilt from the conscience, they only marked out, as with a shadow, the sacrifice of that glorious Saviour, who, by the oblation of himself once offered, was completely to take away sin, and for ever perfect all the sanctified. All the appointments of that law were but the shadows—the body is *Christ*.— As perfectly answering, therefore, the end of this law of *Moses*, in both its parts, *Christ* is here said to be full of *grace* and *truth*.

1. He is *full of grace*, and this is his glory. There is grace with him, commensurate to all the parts of that glorious plan of grace which was laid in the everlasting counsels. Was it, for instance, God's resolve to bring many sons unto glory by *Jesus Christ?* All the grace requisite to accomplish this great design, though millions of millions of subjects were to be included in its vast embrace; and though it was to extend its influence throughout all the generations of time, and the more durable ages of eternity, yet all the grace, requisite to this great undertaking, is found deposited in, and with, *Jesus Christ*. He is full of grace, and it is a fulness which

he

he has to communicate to all his family, juſt as the ſun communicates light, life, and beauty to the ſeveral parts of the vaſt creation. In order to ſee the beauty of this contraſt, you have only to place one object over againſt the other. The law was given by *Moſes*; and this law, conſidered as *moral*, required perfect holineſs, or full conformity of heart and life to the will and image of that God who is therein revealed.—This law we have each of us broken—by this law we all ſtand condemned—From this law we can derive no hope and no help; but *Jeſus Chriſt is full of grace*. There is grace ſufficient in him to juſtify millions of millions of ſinners—to juſtify *every one* that applies to him by faith. "Through this man is preached unto you the forgiveneſs of ſins; and by him all that believe are juſtified from all things, from which ye could not be juſtified by the law of *Moſes*."

Further, this law of *Moſes* not only condemned ſin, but it alſo *requires holineſs*, perfect and complete holineſs.——But be it ſo; *Jeſus Chriſt* has a fulneſs of grace to ſanctify the *unholy*; to cleanſe them from all filthineſs of fleſh and ſpirit; and to ſanctify them in body, ſoul, and ſpirit. It is through faith in him that the impure are made holy, and the ſoul enabled to go forward from ſtrength to ſtrength, till it appears perfect before God in *Zion*. In him, believers are

created

created unto good works; and by him they bring forth the fruits of righteousness to the praise and honour of God. What is sanctification but a growing up into Christ in all things, and thereby proving, in an experimental manner, the truth of that saying, "My grace is sufficient for thee, for my strength is made perfect in weakness?" To him coming as to a living stone, disallowed indeed of men, but chosen of God and precious, the church is built up an holy temple in the Lord. This *coming to him* is, we apprehend, descriptive of the whole course of a believer's life. It is in this way that the life of grace is supported, maintained, and carried on to its perfection in eternal life. We must depend upon *Jesus Christ*, and apply to him daily, yea constantly, just as the children of *Israel* did to the waters of that rock which followed them in the wilderness. That rock, taken in a natural view, might be said to be a *living stone* to them; as, by the waters which they constantly received from it, their natural lives were preserved and supported. What that rock was to the children of Israel literally, that, all that, *Jesus Christ* is to his church in a spiritual view. Was there a fulness of water in that rock to supply the whole family of *Israel* for forty years successively? There is also a fulness of grace in *Jesus Christ* to justify, to sanctify, and eternally to save the whole church of believers in every age.

Thus then you see, that as the *moral* law came by *Moses*, so the grace that fully answers all its requirements, comes by *Jesus Christ*.—Remember, sinner, he is full of grace, and therefore apply to him for the pardon of all your sin, be it ever so great, heinous, or aggravated.—And, believer, apply *thou* to him to make thee all that which the law of God requires that thou shouldest be. And let both remember, that the riches of his grace are unsearchable. We notice,.

2. That *Jesus Christ is full of truth*. Grace has been already exhibited, as it stands opposed to the requirements of the *moral law*, let us now consider *truth*, as equally opposed, by way of counter-part, to all the shadows of the *ceremonial law*. This law, you will remember, came by *Moses* no less than the other. All those shadows and services which were enjoined by that law, pointed out some better thing that was to come. Under the idea of the ceremonial law, we include not only the ordinances instituted by it, but the whole ministry, as carried on by the different priests and prophets who appeared under that dispensation.——But all that is found in *Jesus Christ*, which substantiates, all those shadows;—— fills up all those prophecies, and answers all those promises. He is the *truth*; that is, the *end*, the *fulness*, the *substance* of them all. His *sacrifice* not only fully answers to, but supersedes all their sacrifices.

His

His *priesthood* sets aside their priesthood, and abolishes the law that first established it. To him give all the prophets witness, and in him is found all *that* which stamps eternal truth upon *all* they predicted. *He is the way, and the truth, and the life* *: The *way*, seeing he is full of grace, and, as such, the end of the moral law for righteousness to every one that believeth:——He is also the *truth*, as before him all the shadows of the ceremonial law vanish, having fully answered their end in giving intimation of his coming:——And now, under the gospel-dispensation, he is the *life* of the church; and, as such, will be owned and adored, both in time and in eternity.

Jesus Christ is *full of truth*, as all saving discoveries of God, whenever made, or to whomsoever granted, have been, and are, in and through him. His followers have been, in every age, supported and sanctified by the *truth as it is in him:* And the promises of God, whether they relate to present support, or to future and full salvation, are all in him yea, and in him amen, to the glory of God by us. In him also, truth stands engaged to fulfil all the promises that he has given. He will support——will supply——will never leave or forsake the humble dependant believer. But, as a great dignitary in the church remarks, " when *grace* has brought us to him, *truth* will keep us with him; and, thro'
grace,

* John xiv. 6.

grace, we shall accomplish what *truth* requires at our hands."——Did God, therefore, formerly reveal himself in the services of the *Jewish* tabernacle, and in the ministry thereof? That was but a shadowy revelation; but, to realize those shadows, "the WORD was made flesh, and tabernacled amongst us." The great mystery of that dispensation was this, that God should be manifest in flesh. And now, in the person of the Redeemer, you have the prophetic, the sacerdotal, and the regal offices all united. He is our *temple*, our *altar*, our *sacrifice*, our *all*. The shadows are all fled, and the true light now shineth; and by this light we are enabled to contemplate the glory of *Jesus Christ* the Mediator, as full of *grace* and *truth*. Proceed we,

III. To attend to *the way and manner in which this was seen formerly*, and is still to be discovered by us. "We beheld his glory, the glory as of the only begotten of the Father, full of grace and truth." This, perhaps, does not allude to any visible glory, as to the outward manifestation. His visage was marred more than any man's, and his form more than the sons of men. He had no form nor comeliness in him, nor any *outward* glory that men should desire him; yet, saith the apostle, we *beheld* his glory——full *of grace and truth*. But in what did they behold this?

1. It

1. It appeared *in what he said.* His word was with power. They saw and they felt its evidence.——Never man spake as he spake. Grace was poured into his lips, and it flowed continually out of them. The glory of this grace and truth was discoverable in all the *doctrines* that he taught——in all the *invitations* that he gave——in all his *conversation,* whether in private or in public. His whole ministry was one grand and continued display of the fulness of that grace and truth which dwelt in him. Never did either of them appear so glorious before; and all the subsequent discoveries that have been made of this glory, in every age, have been made in him, and through him. Only reflect for a moment upon those gracious words which proceeded from his lips, and the evidence of what has been said must appear manifest to every one. These are his words, " Come unto me, all ye that labour and are heavy laden, and I will give you rest.—He that cometh to me, I will in no wise cast out. He that cometh to me, shall never hunger; and he that believeth on me, shall never thirst. I give unto my sheep eternal life, and they shall never perish, neither shall any pluck them out of my hand*." Such are his declarations; and there is a fulness of grace and truth with him to answer all the encouragement held out to you in these and many such expressions.

2. The

---

* Matt. xi. 28.—John vi. 35, 37.—John x. 28.

2. The fulness of that grace and truth which was in him, appeared also *in all that he did.* When upon earth he went about doing good was never weary in that delightful employ: By night and by day, in secret and in public, this was his constant course. He always discovered the greatest readiness to teach the ignorant, to succour the distressed, to comfort the mourner, and to heal the sick. Who ever met with a repulse from this gracious Saviour? Or if repulsed, it was only the repulse of a moment, and intended either to quicken the ardour of their application, or to prepare the way for larger and fuller discoveries of his grace and glory in their relief. His words and actions, while he dwelt among us, were a full demonstration to all who conversed with him, that he was full of grace and truth.

Such was the glory that was then manifested. It was seen by faith; and such were the means, whereby his disciples had the discoveries of it formerly; and it is only in the very same way that we can have the privilege of beholding it at this day. That *Jesus Christ* is full of grace and truth, the word declares; and when God is pleased to open the eyes of the mind to behold the wonderful things which are therein contained, then have we, in some measure, similar ideas of the glory of *Jesus Christ.* In all that he he hath done formerly for others, or is now doing, the fulness of his grace and truth is exhibited. May we both see its glory, and have proper conceptions of the great encouragement that it holds forth to us, then shall we also unite with the apostle in saying, "we beheld his glory, the glory as of the only begotten of the Father, full of grace and truth."

But to draw towards a close: From what has been advanced upon this subject, it becomes us seriously to inquire what discoveries we have had of the glory of this great Redeemer? It is the privilege *now*, as well as formerly, for his disciples to see this glory. This glory is to be seen in the same instances, and in the same way. Faith still beholds *Jesus Christ* as full of grace and truth; and this appears in his word, which, though it no longer sounds in our ears, is put into our hands, and is continually under our eye. It is no less manifest in all that he hath wrought for the support of his cause in the world, and in all that he hath wrought in the hearts of his people in every age. The wonderful acts of his grace have been many, and the efficacy of divine truth has been manifest in each of them. But have the eyes of the mind been opened, so as to see the encouragement these discoveries open to you, and the glory which they reflect upon him? Having contemplated the suitableness, the ability of this Saviour,

have

have ye fled to him for refuge, for help, for salvation? They who know his name will put their truft in him. But how many read the fcriptures, fit under the clear and faithful difpenfation of the gofpel, have tranfient convictions, and fome flafhes of comfort, and yet never have their eyes fo opened as to behold the glory of *Jefus Chrift?* Others remain infenfible of their danger, unaffected with their ftate, unacquainted with this Deliverer. They fee no more form or comelinefs in him, than the very men who crucified him. But remember, my brethren, that they who never fee the glory of Chrift's grace and truth on earth, and fee it fo as to feel its influence upon the heart, fhall never be permitted to fee it in heaven.

This view of the glory of Chrift will have its effects in all who are bleffed with it. Such will neither be barren nor unfruitful in the knowledge of the Lord. The love and the power of fin will not prevail in fuch. Quite the reverfe; beholding this glory of the Lord, they will be changed into the fame image, from glory to glory, even as by the fpirit of the Lord. This image reflected upon the mind, will affect the heart: Chrift will be loved—will be depended upon—will be imitated. And thus will he be formed in the heart, and his temper, conduct, and grace be exemplified in our deportment. His falvation

tion will operate within; and grace and truth will, in its measure, shine forth in his disciples. May the same mind that was in *Christ Jesus* appear in us also; and while we behold his glory, may we severally be enabled to advance and spread it. Even so. *Amen.*

SERMON VI.

The Duties of Faith, Prayer, and Application to God, recommended by a great Prince, and a gracious Saviour.

PSALM lxii. 8.

Trust in him at all times; ye people, pour out your heart before him: God is a refuge for us.

IT has been a common practice, in different ages and countries, for Princes to issue out proclamations for the advice, the caution, or the instruction of their people. In our own land, and within the compass of a few years, we may recollect proclamations calling the people to fast and humble themselves before God, during the late war, as likewise for a day of general thanksgiving at the conclusion of it. By the Psalm before us we are introduced as it were into the presence of a great Prince, who had been led through a variety of difficulties, and compassed about by innumerable dangers: Influenced by a principle

principle of pure and undefiled religion, he stood undismayed, contended in the strength of his God, till he had surmounted every opposition, and finally attained both honour and peace. Long had he been detained in the school of adversity; hard were some of the lessons which he learnt in it, and painful the methods by which he was instructed. At length he is brought out of this school of experience, and placed upon the throne of *Israel*. He finds himself fixed at the head of a great people; a people highly distinguished by their God, and remarkably honoured with the revelation of his mind and will. But how does he begin to act in that exalted station? Resolved to unite all his authority and influence, for the spiritual and permanent good of his subjects, as a true father to his people, he steps forward from his throne, teaching them how to love and rely upon the Lord; to trust in him, to pray and make application to him in all their difficulties: This was the proclamation of the *Israelitish* Monarch to his people, *Trust in him at all times; ye people, pour out your heart before him: God is a refuge for us.*

The Psalm from which the text is taken opens with a solemn resolution to trust in God alone, without having recourse to any sinful expedient, or dependance upon an arm of flesh, ver. 1, 2.——The Psalmist then expostulates with his enemies, and predicts their ruin,

ruin, ver. 3. *How long will ye imagine mischief against a man? Ye shall be slain all of you; as a bowing wall shall ye be,* which is out of plumb, *and as a tottering fence,* which has no cement to bind the stones thereof to each other.—He saw that the efforts of his adversaries were to withhold from him the honours which God had promised to confer upon him, or to deprive him of them, ver. 4. This consideration led him to recline, if possible, more firmly upon the Lord, and there alone to ground all his confidence, ver. 5—7. And the advantages which he derived from such conduct, led him to recommend this same method to his people in all their trials; *Trust in him at all times; ye people, pour out your heart before him: God is a refuge for us.* Such is the literal explication of the words in the connection in which they stand: And a glorious prospect it must have been, to behold one of the potentates of the earth, stepping forward to recommend real religion to his subjects; and, what was more, to recommend it from his own example and experience.

But what if, under all this, a greater than *David* be understood as addressing himself to us in the words of the text? *Jesus Christ,* when he appeared as man's Redeemer, trusted only in God that he would deliver him. He would not accept of deliverance from his sufferings, even when he was invited to it; and when no more was required to effect it than
the

the exertion of that power which he possessed. If he be the King of *Israel*, said the *Jews*, let him come down from the cross and we will believe him, ver. 1, 2.—*Jesus Christ* also expressly foretold the dangerous and tottering state of the *Jewish* church and nation, agreeable to ver. 3. He saw through all the consultations and proposals of his enemies, how they were calculated to prevent him from executing that work he had engaged to perform—to withhold from him that honour which was the reward of his work, even the joy which was set before him, ver. 4. This led him with the greatest confidence to commit himself wholly into the hands of his Father, ver. 5—7.——And now, as victorious over all opposition, as the great head of the Christian Church; yea, and as one who sympathises with all his members in their various trials and difficulties, he invites, exhorts, and by his own example recommends this important duty to us; *Trust in him at all times; ye people, pour out your heart before him: God is a refuge for us.* These words we propose to consider as a call or invitation,

I. To Faith.
II. To Prayer; and,
III. To a personal and particular application to the Lord, at all times, and under all our troubles.—We shall then conclude with two or three inferences from the subject.

I. These

I. These words are to be considered as a call or invitation *to faith* in God at all times. By faith in God we mean that affiance in him and dependance upon him, which is proportioned to the manner in which he discovers himself to the soul, and also to the degree in which that discovery is enjoyed: Now there is no other discovery which God hath given of himself, which can produce or nourish such a trust, but that revelation which he has made in *Christ Jesus*. The light of nature exhibits no such discovery.—The covenant of works affords no such encouragement; for while the one shews that we have all transgressed, the other proves that, as transgressors, we have forfeited all claim to every privilege: But, in and through *Jesus Christ*, all the attributes and perfections of *Jehovah* are viewed in harmony, are viewed, as engaged by compact to save to the very uttermost all that come to him by this Saviour. We are all in a state of dependance. We cannot subsist as of ourselves, either with respect to the soul or the body. In ourselves we have no *strength*, no *stock*. We have many enemies and many wants. It is as vain to lean upon any arm of flesh, as to rely upon ourselves: But it is *reasonable*——it is *highly reasonable*——it is highly reasonable, *at all times*, that we should lean upon the Lord; or, as the text expresses it, that we should *trust in him*. We apprehend this phrase, *at all times*,

times, is to be considered as applicable to the several branches of the text. It is reasonable that we should trust in God at all times; that we should pour out our hearts before him at all times; and that we should make him our refuge at all times; that is, in every season, and upon every occasion. The reasonableness of this *trust* is what we propose to enlarge upon under this head of discourse.—— And,

1. It is reasonable that we should trust in the Lord, because *he is possessed of every possible perfection*. Were men required to trust, that is, to place their confidence in the princes of this world, one would make choice of *this* prince, because he is *powerful*; a second of *that*, because he is a *wise* and *prudent* governor; a third of another, because he is renowned for justice and equity in all his dealings with his subjects. Probably it would be difficult, if not impossible, to fix upon one, in whom all these qualifications would be found equally united. Was that the case, and were men left to their choice, that sovereign would probably have the greatest number of subjects, if he were not owned universal monarch: But every perfection is found in God; for he is powerful, wise, compassionate, holy, just, good, and true. All these excellencies meet in that blessed and glorious Being, on whom we are called to place our confidence. He is able to defend us in every danger,

danger, to inſtruct us in every difficulty, and to load us with every benefit. He is equal in his diſtributions, faithful to his promiſes, and holy in all his works. We could not wiſh for a quality which is not to be found in him; for he can guide us by his counſel, keep us by his power, ſanctify us by his truth, and ſave us to the eternal honour of his grace. Poſſeſſed of every poſſible perfection, he is able to make us both holy here, and happy for ever. His ability is equal to every thing that we can wiſh or want. Such a Being, therefore, certainly deſerves our truſt, and of us he has a right to claim it.— But,

2. As he is poſſeſſed of every poſſible perfection, ſo *in him every perfection is infinite*; that is, it is carried out to the greateſt poſſible extent and degree. The wiſeſt of men have not unlimited wiſdom; the greateſt of potentates have not unlimited power; the beſt of princes have not unlimited goodneſs: But God is infinite in power, in wiſdom, in holineſs, in goodneſs, in juſtice, and in truth. He neither is exceeded in any of theſe his perfections, nor can he be equalled. With him inclination and ability, the promiſe and the performance, the purpoſe and the production, are equal.—Nothing is too great for him to promiſe, nor is any thing too hard for him to do. He cannot come too late in any of your diſtreſſes, for he is infinitely wiſe, and
knows

knows the crisis of the difficulty:—He cannot come unprepared to assist you, for he is infinitely powerful:—He cannot be exceeded by the creature's wants or guilt, for he is infinitely good, and infinitely gracious.—— There is no searching of his understanding— no exhausting of his treasures—no contending with his power—no eluding of his justice— no frustrating of his purposes or promises. He can do all his pleasure, and there is ground to conclude that he will, for he is infinite. He can pardon the greatest guilt; can sanctify the most notorious sinner; can subdue the strongest corruption; in short, can do exceeding abundantly above all that we can ask or think: And as he *can* do all this, so he certainly *will* do it for that soul which comes through *Jesus Christ* to place all its confidence and dependance upon him.——But, as an additional reason why we should trust in him, we add,

3. That as he is possessed of every possible perfection, and as every perfection he is possessed of is infinite, so, to render him the most proper and suitable object for our trust, we remark further, that *in all these perfections of his nature he is immutable.* Solomon was a wise prince, but his widom failed him; *Alexander* was a great conqueror, but he fell a sacrifice to his own lusts; *Nebuchadnezzar* was a great prince, but his pride degraded him to rank with brutes; *Josiah* was a good prince,

but

but his imprudence coſt him his life. *Immutability*, however, is the glory of all the divine perfections; with our God there is no variableneſs or ſhadow of turning. This is propoſed as the foundation of the confidence and ſafety of his people. This is the language in which he addreſſes thoſe who truſt in him; " I am the Lord, I change not, therefore, ye ſons of *Jacob*, are not conſumed." Men are not found the ſame upon all occaſions, or in every place; but God is always the ſame: His arm, which was extended formerly, is not ſhortened now; his ear is not heavy now which was attentive then; his mind is not now altered from what it was a thouſand years ago; he ſees the ſame; he ſpeaks the ſame; and he is the ſame as ever. He is not agitated as we are by different paſſions, or affected by different frames; now awake to attention, and anon dull and ſtupid; or now active, and preſently indiſpoſed for action. He is immutably the ſame to the children that fear him that he was to their fathers; as able, as ready, as gracious, to equal and to exceed your expectations as he was to exceed all the prayers and hopes of the Fathers in former generations. What he was formerly he is at preſent; and what he is now, he will be in every age. The ſun and moon may, through intervening objects, afford to the earth a leſs quantity of light at one ſeaſon than they do at another; but with that God, who

is

is expressly stiled, " the Father of lights, there is no variableness or shadow of turning."

Having thus pointed out the three arguments which, we apprehend, proves the reasonableness of our trust in God, let us collect them all into a single point, and see their force when united. If God be possessed of every possible perfection, then *there is ground to trust in him:* If each of these perfections be *infinite*, then there must be ground for *the most unshaken trust*; and if *immutability* be the crown, the glory, the very life of all those perfections, then what can be more reasonable than this requirement of the text, that *we should trust in him at all times,* and trust him with all our concerns. Trust in him at all times, ye people—in affliction, for he can support you in it, and sanctify you by it—in temptation, for he can succour you under it, and save you from it—in darkness, for he can guide you through it or enlighten you in it—in persecution, for he can make the wrath of man to redound to his praise, and enable you to honour him in the fires—in poverty, for then there is a more favourable opportunity for him to supply you, and for you to see his appearance in your behalf—in life, for it is he that must support—and in death, for he has promised even then to keep that which you have committed to him. O trust, Brethren, in that blessed Being, who has

has power to make you happy, who poſſeſſes every perfection in an infinite degree, and who is able to conduct the work that he begins in you, and to complete the deſign which he has formed concerning you.—*Jeſus Chriſt* found all thoſe excellencies in his Father, when he was engaged in the work of man's redemption. He truſted in his God, and was not confounded; and through him you are now invited to come and place your truſt and confidence in the ſame God. *Truſt in him at all times.*—We propoſed to conſider the words,

II. As a call or invitation to *prayer. Ye people, pour out your heart before him.* And this is a duty which is incumbent on you *at all times. Jeſus Chriſt,* as a man, was much given to prayer, and ſpent whole nights in it, and, from the advantages he himſelf found in that duty, he invites all his friends and followers to be found in the ſame practice.

To pour out the heart before God is expreſſive of unfeigned humility, undiſſembled ſincerity, and unreſerved freedom: It is ingenuouſly to expoſe all before God, holding back nothing however it may criminate our conduct, or evidence the folly or the preſumption of our hearts. There are two ways in which the heart may be ſaid to be poured out:

1. In *Confeſſion.* When the humble ſinner approaches his God, he acknowledges *what he has done,* and what he deſerves in conſequence of ſuch conduct. All hope in himſelf

self is relinquished; there remains no more of this spirit in him: His soul is poured out as water before the Lord, and he prostrates himself in the very dust of humility. Such was the disposition of the Publican in the temple—*he smote upon his breast*, and cried out, *God be merciful to me a sinner!* This was all that he could express—indeed it contained the very soul of grief, of humility, of self-abasement, and of faith—if more was poured out upon that occasion, it was comprehended in sighs, and groans, and tears.—*David* also was an example of the same frame of mind, when, pricked to the very heart with a sense of his sin, he poured out his soul in this language——" Against *thee*—thee *only*—have *I sinned*——and have done *this evil*——in *thy sight*."

It is in vain to attempt to conceal sin before God——To see its evil nature, though distressing, is necessary—To confess it before the Lord in all its infinite aggravations, is our duty; and let the heart be poured out in real contrition and self-abasement while ye are thus engaged.

2. In *Supplication* also the heart may be poured forth when we go to God with the ardent desires of faith and expectation. The soul approaches the throne of grace with boldness to request counsel, or ask help from the Lord. Distress and desires unite their influence to carry out the heart in this important

portant duty of prayer. Thus the royal suppliant was engaged, as he describes the frame of his own soul: *I cried unto the Lord with my voice: with my voice unto the Lord did I make my supplication. I poured out my complaint before him: I shewed before him my trouble.* * Thus *Hannah* also refuted the unjust censure of *Eli*, by assuring him that she had been *pouring out her soul before the Lord.* † To pour out the heart before God then is, to make free with him—to be importunate—to wrestle for the blessing—and to tell him all our wants. And this is our duty and privilege *at all times,* intimating that it should be our concern.

To keep up a regular correspondence with our God. To pray without ceasing; to pray always, and not to faint. Every day brings with it fresh wants, presents fresh arguments, and lays you under fresh obligations to be found in the practice of this duty. On the entrance of every day, therefore, pour out the heart in supplication, and in the close of it you will see cause both for confession and for thanksgiving: Yea, and frequently in the course of the day, let the heart be poured forth in ejaculatory petitions.

At all times pour out your heart before him; that is, *acquaint him with all your affairs, and consult him in the manner of conducting them.* Lean not to your own understanding; for that

* Pf. cxliii. 1, 2.—† 1 Sam. i. 15.   is

is to be wife in your own eyes; but in all your ways acknowledge the Lord, and he has promised that he will direct your steps. You need his friendly counsel in temporal no lefs than in your fpiritual concerns; and was God more confulted by us, perhaps in general, fuccefs would be more common. It is the moſt weak and foolifh thing imaginable for fuch of you who are men of extenfive bufinefs, to truſt your property, and that which is to be the fupport of your families, in fo many hands, without looking up by prayer to that God who has all their hearts in his hand, who allows you the privilege to confult him, and who is able to keep every thing that you commit to his care: Keep not the Lord, therefore, out of your fecrets; but in all things, by prayer, with fupplication and thankfgiving, let your requefts be made known to him.—— The title which he hath affumed is no lefs glorious to himfelf than it is encouraging to you, *The God that heareth prayer.* Be it your concern to honour him under it.

Once more; when we are exhorted at all times to pour out the heart before God, it intimates *that it fhould be our ftudious concern to preferve an holy fervour in our prayers.* It is not fufficient to draw near to God with our lips, if the heart be far from him. Words are foon loſt in air, but prayer is the labour of the heart: When engaged, therefore, in that duty, remember with whom ye have to do;

do; remember the importance of the business ye have to transact with him; and that as God is a Spirit, so he seeketh such to worship him, who worship him in spirit and in truth. Guard against a customary formality in your devotion. Stir up your hearts to lay hold upon the Lord, and give him no rest till he stablish, strengthen, settle you, and finally perfect that which concerneth you. He will be found of them that seek him; but he will be sought with the whole heart. Plead, O plead therefore with him to pardon your sin, to strengthen his own work in your souls, to guide you in every step, to prosper the work of your hands, and to perform all that which he hath spoken to you of.——Thus the heart is poured out in *Confession* and *Supplication*. And when it is said that we should do this at all times, it intimates that it should be our concern to keep up *a regular correspondence with God—to acquaint him with all our affairs—consulting him in the manner of conducting them—and to preserve an holy fervour in the whole of our devotion.*——We have yet to consider the words,

III. As a call or invitation to make *a personal and particular application to God at all times.* " God is a refuge for us." Considered as the words of *David*, they represent this to be the common privilege both of the king and his subjects. There was equal access and encouragement for the poorest subject as for the

the greatest prince. They all stood in need of God for their refuge; and all who applied to him in truth found him such.——But viewed as the language of *Jesus Christ* addressed to the whole church, the words intimate that he considers them all as his brethren, and is not ashamed to own them as such; that though he be the head, he acknowledges them as his members; and that through him they have access to the same privileges that he himself enjoyed while engaged in the arduous service which he performed, and sufferings which he endured on earth. In all their afflictions he is afflicted, and of all their joys he is a partaker; and for the encouragement of the whole body, and of each individual, he says, *God is a refuge for us.* This intimates,

1. That now *there is access to God* through *Jesus Christ*: He who might justly have destroyed, is become our Deliverer. The way is now open——the wrath removed——God is reconciled——He waits to be gracious——He stands engaged by word, by covenant, and by oath, to save to the very uttermost all that come unto him by *Jesus Christ*. This God is a refuge and strength to his people, and a very present help in every time of trouble. There is now access to him, and acceptance with him through *Jesus Christ*.

2. When it is said that God is a refuge for us, it proves that *there is room with him.*——

Millions have fought refuge here, and what they fought they have happily attained; yet there is room for millions of millions more. He whose perfections are infinite cannot want room to embrace numbers which no man can number. There is room for the whole church; room for the greatest of sinners who repent and turn to the Lord—room for the weakest that believe—room for those who have the least ground to expect it on account of their complicated offences.

3. When it is said God is a refuge for us, it shews likewise *that there is security and support in him for all his people; security at all times*, against all their fears, and from all their enemies; enough to supply all their wants, to satisfy all their desires, and to save their souls with an everlasting salvation; they shall never be ashamed nor confounded world without end.

The inferences from this subject are such as these:

1. That faith, prayer, and application to God are not only the privileges, but the duty of all the hearers of the Gospel. That faith is their duty, is evident from such considerations as these: Whatever is pleasing to, or acceptable in, the sight of God, must be right in itself; but when the *Jews* inquired of *Jesus Christ*, what they must do to work the works of God, the answer he returned to them was: " This is the work of God" which he

he both requires and will approve, "that ye believe in him whom he hath sent." Further, to omit that which is not our duty can be no sin, and what is no sin, can deserve no punishment; but where punishment is inflicted, guilt is always supposed; but he that believeth not shall be damned. Now, as damnation comprehends in it the greatest punishment that the human mind can conceive; and as this punishment is said to be annexed to unbelief, it must prove that this want of faith is a sin, and a great sin, and in the sight of him who is the most competent judge, a sin deserving of eternal damnation.——That prayer also is a duty, may be inferred from many passages of scripture, particularly from *Peter's* address to a man whom he had pronounced to be in the gall of bitterness and in the bond of iniquity; yet he requires even that man to pray to God that the thoughts of his heart might be forgiven him.—It is therefore our duty to " seek the Lord while he may be found, and call upon him while he is nigh;" yea, " that the wicked should forsake his way, and the unrighteous man his thoughts, and turn to the Lord!" What can be more reasonable—more proper.

2. From this subject, how blameable are even God's own people? How much do they distress themselves, and dishonour him, by not making more use of him as their refuge. They fly to creature-refuges; they complain

to their fellow-mortals, they confult them in difficulties, inftead of flying by faith and prayer to God as their refuge. This is blameable.

3. Hence it appears to be a very reafonable duty, as well as a delightful employ, to comfort others with the comforts wherewith we have been comforted of God. O blefs the Lord, all ye faints of his; fpeak of his goodnefs all the day long, point others to him as a refuge; declare what he hath done for your own fouls, and when heart and flefh fhall fail, may this God be found the ftrength of our hearts, and our portion for ever, for *Jefus's* fake. *Amen.*

SERMON

SERMON VII.

The Believer viewing a coming Saviour in his present Work.

REVELATIONS ii. 25.

That which ye have already, hold fast till I come.

THE want of connecting the present with the future, both in our ideas and conduct, is the foundation of many errors, and the reason why many of our privileges become vain and unprofitable to us. In the concerns of the present life, men are generally wise and provident; but, in what relates to the future, they are thoughtless, inattentive, or unconcerned. With a view to a future harvest, the husbandman exhausts his strength, and relinquishes a part of his property. He breaks up his fallow ground with labour, and he scatters his seed with liberality; and in both he plows and he sows in hope of being repaid with a plentiful crop. With the hope of enjoying restored health, the infirm gives up his present pursuits or pleasures, and resigns himself to the prescriptions and regimen appointed by his physician; and every man

man exerts and employs his little skill, influence, or property, in order either to support or to aggrandize his family. They snatch the present moment, and wish to improve every apparent advantage, in order to attain that which they account more valuable or desirable than the present enjoyment. In natural concerns, a sense of honour makes men faithful to their trust; but does the same principle influence them in matters of infinitely greater importance? Thus, for instance, you are intrusted by the great Lord of all with the care of an immortal soul; with the volume of divine revelation, and the privileges of gospel-institutions; but where is that anxious care—that ardent solicitude for your souls—that serious attention to their worth and wants—that solicitous desire for their safety, which becomes you as reasonable creatures?—You have the bible; but is it read with that attention—examined with that care—esteemed and valued in that proportion that it ought? Or, are the ordinances of God attended upon with that serious reverence, diligence, or constancy,—with that sense of God's presence in them, or of that last solemn and strict account that you have to give of them? Alas, How many neglect their souls and their bibles, while others attend upon the means of grace only occasionally, and when it suits their convenience, or, if constantly, with a trifling indifference,

difference, instead of hearing for eternity, mixing faith with the report of the gospel, or pressing into the kingdom of heaven with resolution. Instead of all this, they trifle with the first concern, they tempt God to anger, and do every thing in their power to fill up the measure of their iniquities.

In order to stimulate your mind seriously to attend to the things which concern your everlasting peace at this season, we claim your regard to these words of the faithful and true witness, addressed to the church of Thyatira. The author of the epistle to this church, is *Jesus* the son of God, represented as having his eyes like a flame of fire, significant of his infinite wisdom and his penetrating knowledge, both into men and things. His feet are also described as brass, denoting the steadiness of the proceedings of his providence, his strength to support his friends, and his power to crush his foes. In this epistle he approves their general conduct, pronouncing it to have proceeded from a right principle, viz. *love:* He accepts their services, is pleased with their faith, commends their patience, and confirms his approbation of their conduct, by this honourable testimony, that *their last works were more than their first*, ver. 19. But after all that is said in a way of commendation, an exception follows, to shew that perfect churches and perfect characters are not to be found upon earth.

erath. The fault charged upon some in this church is, that they had too much connived at those who assumed the character of inspired teachers, and who, in order to avoid persecution, had endeavoured to seduce some of that community to commit fornication, and to eat things offered unto idols. *Jezebel* is particularly mentioned; but whether we are to understand some individual person, or those false teachers, who too closely copied the example of that woman, we pretend not to say; but great is the wrath which is denounced against them, ver. 20—23. *Thou sufferest that woman* Jezebel, *which calleth herself a prophetess, to teach and to seduce my servants to commit fornication, and to eat things sacrificed unto idols. And I gave her space to repent of her fornication, and she repented not. Behold, I will cast her into a bed, and them that commit adultery with her into great tribulation, except they repent of their deeds. And I will kill her children with death; and all the churches shall know that I am he which searcheth the reins and hearts; and I will give to every one of you according to his works.* From all which it appears, that some of that church had been snared and taken by these diabolical delusions; such they are represented to be: However, the great Head of the church declares, that it was not his intention to lay any unnecessary burden upon his followers.

His

His yoke they had cheerfully taken upon them; his name they had professed; and the power of his grace they had experienced. The direction and command that he requires them to regard is comprehended in these words: *But unto you I say, and unto the rest in* Thyatira, *as many as have not this doctrine, and which have not known the depths of Satan, as they speak, I will put upon you none other burden. But that which ye have already, hold fast till I come.* In this discourse we propose,

I. To mention some things which true believers *have* already in distinction from others.
II. Their duty respecting these things, which is to hold them fast.
III. The encouragement which is proposed to excite them to this duty, and is taken from *the coming of Jesus Christ*.

That there is a very great, and, indeed, an essential difference between believers and unbelievers, is evident from the different principles by which they are actuated, and their opposite practice; from the testimony of scripture, and the whole history of the world and church: But this difference will be peculiarly manifested in that last and great day, when the precious shall be separated from the vile, and the Lord himself, as the judge, shall distinguish between those that served him, and such as served him not. Then the grand line of separation will be drawn, and all the inhabitants of this earth shall stand in their proper company, to mix no more, or change their character for eternity. But, as proposed, we shall,

I. *Mention some things which true believers have in distinction from others.* The persons mentioned in the text are represented as having something, which it was required they should hold fast. To particularize in two or three instances,

1. True believers have received the knowledge of the method of salvation by *Jesus Christ* alone. This doctrine has been published in their ears, and has been embraced by them. They have been led to view themselves in the very same light in which the scripture represents men to be under the fall: Not only as dead, by a legal and just sentence, but also as dead in trespasses and sins. They see sin to be what God's word represents it to be, infinitely odious to his nature, diametrically opposite to his holy will, and eternally ruinous to that soul who, in the hour of death, is found under its power. To them it appears, a clear scriptural truth, that, by the deeds of the law, no flesh can be justified in the sight of God; that without shedding of blood there is no remission; and that the death of *Jesus Christ* was absolutely necessary to bring sinners to God. To them no other way

way appears so suitable to the state and condition of man, or so honourable to the character of God. They see further, that by the one oblation of this Saviour once offered, he hath for ever perfected them that are sanctified; that his blood has an infinite efficacy to cleanse from all sin; and that as the righteousness which he wrought out and brought in, is held forth to all the hearers of the gospel in the dispensation of the word, so it is upon all them that believe. They can conceive no other way in which the great *Jehovah* could be just to himself, and yet justify the ungodly. This is a fixed and settled principle with them, that it is not by "works of righteousness that they have done, but through the washing of regeneration, and the renewing of the Holy Ghost," that they must be saved. Nor are these matters of mere speculation with them. They are not trifling, uninfluential notions, but doctrines, in their esteem, of infinite importance. They have received, and still do receive it as a faithful saying, and worthy of their acceptance, that " *Jesus Christ* came into the world to save sinners," such as themselves, even the very chief of sinners. These are doctrines in which they see the glory of the divine character maintained—in which the dignity of the Saviour's person and work are exhibited—in which the holiness and spirituality

tuality of the divine law is demonſtrated—doctrines, in which the miſerable and helpleſs condition of man, by the fall, is ſet forth—in which the types and promiſes of the Old Teſtament appear fully anſwered—and in which the glory and grace of the goſpel are admirably advanced and exalted. Theſe are doctrines which affect the heart, influence and adorn the conduct, and keep up the moſt lively views of the perſonal excellency of *Jeſus Chriſt*, and of the ſoul's conſtant need of him, is ſurely an inquiry of infinite importance. How ſhall a ſinner appear with acceptance before God? And that doctrine, which gives a full and ſatisfactory anſwer to this queſtion, muſt enter into the very eſſence of chriſtian faith and of chriſtian practice. This lays the foundation for true faith, genuine humility, and ſincere obedience.

While, therefore, ſome deny the doctrines of juſtification by faith alone, and of ſalvation entirely by grace; and, while others receive them in notion only, the true chriſtian believes, and obeys them from the heart, as truths delivered down to him by prophets and apoſtles; yea, by *Jeſus Chriſt* himſelf. The teſtimony of *Chriſt* is confirmed in ſuch, and they receive and rely on him daily, as "made of God to them wiſdom, and righteouſneſs, and ſanctification, and redemption." Such, like the great apoſtle of

the

the Gentiles, desire to be "found in *Christ*, not having their own righteousness, which is of the law, but that which is by the faith of *Christ*, the righteousness which is of God by faith."—This then is that heavenly doctrine, that divine, influential sentiment, which the true believer hath, and which it is his duty, and should be his constant desire, to hold fast.

2. Such, likewise, have convictions of the evil of sin, of the vanity of the world, and of the inestimable value of the soul. Transgression against an holy, gracious, and glorious God appears to them to be no trifle. They have seen it to be an evil and bitter thing, that they have sinned against the Lord their God. They see that sin has not only exposed them to the just displeasure of the Almighty, but has likewise deranged all the powers of the soul, and made that awful breach between God and them, which no known method, except the obedience and death of *Jesus Christ*, could heal. They consider sin as the most dangerous, the most unreasonable, and the most destructive principle that there is in the whole world: A contrariety, not only to the will of God, but to the happiness of men: A bar both to present peace and to future glory. Nor is this a transient view, which only possesses the mind while under their first convictions, but it abides with them. At seasons it revives with

with greater strength in the soul, and is carried out to a greater extent as they grow in experience. They loath themselves because of their iniquities, and both desire and pray to be delivered from that body of sin and death which they carry about with them.

They have convictions also of the vanity of this present evil world. Its riches appear to them unsatisfying; its honours fading; and its pleasures deceitful. The unsearchable riches of *Jesus Christ* are what they seek; the honour of fellowship with him, what they are ambitious to obtain; and the pleasing, profitable, constraining experience of the joys of his salvation, what they thirst for. They are convinced that an object, which is always changing, and perpetually fleeing from the embrace of its deluded votaries, cannot possibly satisfy. God says, this world is not your rest; and while their judgment corresponds with his in the same sentiment, their experience corroborates the truth of both. It is a better country that they seek, not from any petulance of temper, or morofeness of disposition; but from the most clear and rational conviction, that it is in vain to seek permanent happiness or substantial good from that object which cannot, in the nature of things, afford it.

The inestimable value of the soul likewise is a conviction with which believers are impressed. In their view, this sentiment of the
Redeemer's

Redeemer's appears in all its divine reasonableness, "What shall it profit a man if he gain the whole world, and lose his own soul, or what shall a man give in exchange for his soul?" This is a subject which has occasioned them many serious reflections. Others may indulge every trifle and impertinence, so as to avoid such questions as these. Have I a soul or not? If I have, what does it need to make it happy? Am I attentive to its real interests? But the persons of whom we speak, see the care of the soul not only to be highly reasonable, but absolutely necessary. They see, and are deeply sensible, that the loss of the soul must be an infinite and irreparable loss; as, on the contrary, its salvation must be everlasting gain.—Once more,

3. These persons have received *Jesus Christ*—a principle of grace, and found real pleasure in the ways of God and religion.

Christ has been received by them in all his fulness, as their life, their treasure, and their all. They have seen him to be suitable to all their wants, and altogether precious. This conviction has led them to live in him, to walk in him, and to depend upon him for all they want. Others may see no need of him, and no form or comeliness in him; but this is not the case with believers: To them, this divine Saviour appears the chief of ten thousand, and altogether lovely. In him they have all, and abound.

Partakers

Partakers likewise of a divine nature, they are influenced by this, as a living principle, in their conduct. The seed of real holiness is sown in their hearts; and, being sown, it shall be preserved there, notwithstanding the corruptions they feel within; it shall be defended, notwithstanding all the opposition they may meet with from without, till, at length, it breaks forth in the full-ripe fruit of everlasting obedience. *Jesus Christ* has given to them this principle of eternal life, and they shall never perish, neither shall any pluck them out of his hand.

Nor are believers strangers to that solid pleasure which is found in the ways of God and religion. They have tasted that the Lord is gracious; their hearts have been happily enlarged to run the way of his commandments; and to them wisdom's ways are ways of pleasantness, and all her paths are peace. In their esteem there is no peace, no pleasure, no honour, compared to that which is to be found in close converse with God. His word is as bread to their souls; his presence, as life; and his ordinances, as breasts of consolation. In fine, in keeping of his commandments, they have a present and a great reward.

Having glanced at some things which true believers *have* already in distinction from others, we proceed,

II. To

II. *To point out their duty with respect to these things*, viz. to hold them fast. This you will remember is the command of *Jesus Christ*, and it implies in it, not only a duty on our part, but a danger to which we are liable. Our work, under this head, will be to review and apply what was said under the preceding. And

1. Have ye received the true knowledge of salvation by *Jesus Christ* alone? Then hold it fast. Ye may be called to contend for the faith once delivered to the saints, if not against persecutors, yet against those errors which may be propagated in the age and place in which ye live. Beware then that none move you from the stedfastness of your faith which is in *Christ*. Though the gospel have been long and faithfully preached amongst you, errors may be introduced. See that ye be not carried about with divers and strange doctrines; let your hearts be established with grace, that so ye be not imposed upon by that cunning craftiness whereby men may lay in wait to deceive. An itch for novelty, mistaking zeal for truth, and substituting the hearing of many sermons in the place of serious reflection, meditation, and self-examination after, prepare the way for, and finally introduce that evil of which we speak: But be it your concern to acquire a sound judgment, to converse much with your bibles, and often to review the principles

ciples of your creed. This is the way to grow in grace, and in the knowledge of the Lord and Saviour *Jesus Christ*, so as not to be moved from the hope of the gospel. Especially beware that the doctrines of justification by faith, and of salvation by grace, do not become trite and trifling subjects in your esteem. Often renew the reflection upon their importance, and examine what influence they have upon your temper and conduct. Probably the *Galatians* had no doubt but they had firm hold of these sentiments; but the apostle proved that they had let them slip. Hold fast then the true knowledge of salvation in a sound judgment, and in a pure conscience.

2. Have ye been convinced of the evil of sin, the vanity of the world, and the inestimable value of your precious and immortal souls? Hold such convictions fast. " Salvation is not to be obtained but by striving against the stream; nor is it sufficient to make a few efforts in order to obtain it. They must be repeated. If ye yield to the tide of opposition but for a moment, there is danger of your being carried away by it." Sin indulged, will, in the event, gain the ascendency. Maintain, therefore, a constant watch against it, and be afraid of its consequences. Stand in awe. It is both deceitful in its attacks, and destructive in its tendency.—Beware that ye be not diverted by the cares of this

this world, or drawn away by undue conformity to it. Miſtake it not for your home, ſeeing it is intended only for an inn in the way to the heavenly inheritance.—Above all, hold faſt the views that you have been favoured with of the value of your ſouls. Trifle not with convictions, either of your danger or of your duty; but improve upon the one, and comply immediately with the other. Attend to preſent duty in the proper ſeaſon; and remember that every day ye ſpend upon earth, ye are living and acting for eternity; that your ſouls are of infinite worth; and that an intereſt in Chriſt is a concern above every other concern.—But do all, who have experienced ſuch convictions, hold them faſt? Many perſons, perhaps at different times, have felt ſtrong and lively convictions of the worth of their precious ſouls; but thoſe convictions, and the temporary concern produced by them, have ſoon wore off. They once had ſome view of their ſtate and danger, but now they have almoſt forgotten what manner of men they then appeared to themſelves to be, as alſo the reſolutions which were then made. Inſtead of holding theſe faſt, they have let them ſlip, and are returned like the dog to his vomit, and like the ſow that was waſhed to wallow in the mire.

3. Have ye received *Jeſus Chriſt*—a principle of grace, and found real pleaſure in the ways of God and religion? Hold theſe things faſt,

fast, so as to preserve the lively sense of them upon your minds. There is danger of settling upon the lees, or sliding into formality: In order to prevent which, look much to *Jesus Christ*, and converse much with him. You need him still—need him daily—need him as much as ever; though ye have been ten, twenty, many years in his service, it is as much a truth *now* as it was the first day ye came to him, that *without him ye can do nothing*. To them who believe he is always precious, always needed, always sufficient. Hold fast the head, brethren, and see that ye grow not weary, either in waiting, or in the warfare. The righteous have the promise that they shall hold on their way, and wax stronger and stronger; and the trees of righteousness shall bring forth fruit even in old age, to shew that the Lord is faithful.— Endeavour, therefore, to preserve upon your minds a lively sense of the preciousness of *Jesus Christ*. Maintain the power of internal religion in the soul, and desire to experience more of that divine, invigorating support which is to be found in an habitual converse with God. Though ye have not yet attained, press forward towards the mark for the prize of the high calling of God in *Christ*. There is more to be known——more to be experienced——more to be enjoyed in God and his ways, than any of us have hitherto attained.——The duty then required is, to *hold fast*; and,

III. The

III. *The encouragement proposed to excite you to this duty is taken from the coming of Jesus Christ.* His second coming is, no doubt, intended here. The proper consideration of which solemn event is a grand encouragement to hold fast what we have; and did our minds enter more fully into this solemn consideration, it would animate us to look for, and hasten the coming of this day of God. We should be found more in the frame of the primitive christians, who looked for this blessed hope, and the glorious appearance of their Lord and Saviour *Jesus Christ.* But to be more particular; Behold he cometh,

1. To put an end to all those trials and temptations which his followers ever experienced, in their maintaining their hold of him, of his truth, and of his ways. The long and tiresome conflict will then have a final and an honourable close: Satan shall tempt them no more—sin deceive them no longer—nor shall error, with its blandishments, allure or impose upon them again. Then the whole store of Satan's temptations will be exhausted, his hour concluded, and the power of deceit destroyed. Every principle and relick of sin will then be completely eradicated from the hearts of God's children, and every power of their souls be perfectly and eternally sanctified.

2. Behold

2. Behold he cometh to confirm all the grand articles of the Chriftian's faith. Juftification will then appear to be entirely free, and falvation full and complete. Iniquity, if fought for, fhall not be found, for all the *Ifrael* of God fhall be faved in the Lord with an everlafting falvation, they fhall not be afhamed or confounded world without end.

3. Behold he cometh to confirm all thofe convictions ye have had of the evil of fin, of the vanity of the world, and the ineftimable value of your fouls. How evil will fin appear when all its ruinous confequences to the fouls of men fhall be made evident! When thoufands fhall come forth loaded with its guilt, and finking under its condemnation into the blacknefs of darknefs for ever.— In what colours will the vanity of the world be difplayed, when the heavens fhall rend, the earth be diffolved, palaces be confumed, mountains totter, and oceans be drained? Where then will be found the painted pleafures, the tranfient joys, the falfe honours which it once held forth? Sceptres and crowns, and mines of gold, where then will they be found. Fled, vanifhed, confumed.— And however men may affect to treat the fubject at prefent, in what a light will the value of the foul appear, when they, who faw the care of it to be neceffary, fhall be called up to the kingdom of glory; while fuch

such as trifled with that great concern shall be banished from the presence of the Lord, and from the glory of his power. This sentence, then pronounced, "Depart ye cursed into everlasting fire, prepared for the devil and his angels," will eternally demonstrate on the one hand the evil of sin, and on the other the wisdom of seeking the welfare of the soul.

4. Behold he cometh to realize; yea, and more than realize, if I may so speak, to *eternize* all the experience such have had of his preciousness, of the power of internal religion, and the pleasure they have found in his service. He comes fully to be enjoyed by his saints; to take them, with all those principles which he has implanted in their hearts, along with him to heaven, and to capacitate them there to serve him day and night in his heavenly temple, without weariness or end. They shall see him as he is; shall serve him as they wish; and shall completely enjoy him for eternity. Only hold fast, brethren, and all this shall be your own.

From this subject, let every one of us examine what is our hope. The soul must have hold of something, either real or imaginary. It sinks without a support; and nothing can support when heart and flesh fail; nothing can support when heaven and earth shall flee away, but *Jesus Christ*. How pitiable, how deplorable will be the condition
of

of those who will have no hold of him then. The door of mercy shut—the day of salvation over—and the fixing season for eternity come. None will find him to be their support then who do not now flee to him for refuge. Sinner, what wilt thou do in that solemn day? If not found in Christ, all thy hopes, thy resolutions, thy promises, will suffer shipwreck, and thy soul be launched naked into an everlasting storm of divine wrath; a sea of liquid fire. Thou art not in Christ. Solemn thought! Escape then for thy life; seek the Lord while he may be found; call upon him while he is near, and remember that this is the day of salvation.

From this subject we are all called to guard against formality and declensions in religion. To be formal here is criminal; it is slighting *Christ*, and doing injury to your own souls. Every thing claims your diligence, and demands dispatch. Behold, the judge standeth at the door; beware, lest he take you by surprize.

And let one and all of us remember, that *Jesus Christ* is coming—he comes to own his friends—to crush his foes—to confound the world—to confirm the report of the gospel—to honour the faith and patience of the saints—to conclude the present dispensation of things—and to open eternity. Each of us is concerned in that appearance; each of us must bear our part in the solemnities of that

that day; and when he appears, (for every eye shall see him) may we be found of him in peace, accepted in the beloved, to the praise of the glory of grace; and shouting, "even so, come, Lord *Jesus*." *Amen*.

SERMON

SERMON VIII.

Divine Power magnified in the Believer's Preservation.

---

1 PETER i. 5.

Kept by the power of God through faith unto salvation, ready to be revealed in the last time.

THE wisdom and the power of God are represented by the sacred scripture as manifold; that is, they are exceeding various, and gradually open their excellencies to us in different periods, unfold their evidence under different dispensations, and exhibit their workmanship by a great variety of parts.— Thus while, with pleasing admiration, we examine any particular species of his work, every opening fold fills the mind with increasing wonder, and furnishes matter for advancing praise. As by these means we gradually approach the Deity, every step raiseth us to more elevated discoveries of his great designs, and exhibits more extensive prospects of his amazing productions to our view. Those perfections

perfections of the great Creator are but faintly shadowed forth in the exterior parts of his workmanship. It is by penetrating the surface that the glory of the discovery opens more fully upon the mind: Thus, for instance, a Peach is put into our hand; we admire the form, the exquisite bloom, the delicate down with which it is covered, and the firm skin with which it is surrounded; we taste the delicious flavour with which it is endowed, and in all are led to admire and adore the wisdom and power of that God, who hath fabricated this little delicacy of nature with such amazing skill: But while our senses are thus regaled, our thoughts thus employed, we find that we have penetrated to an hard stone, indented with a variety of cells, each of them containing certain nerves, or fibres; with difficulty we break this shell, and therein find a small kernel inclosed in a double covering of skin. Here the power of God appears contained in a very narrow compass. This kernel, some tell us, contains the stamina of a future tree, perhaps of all the fruit to be produced by it for many a succeeding year. We cry out, O the depth both of the wisdom and power of God! The mind is overwhelmed with astonishment, and labours to speak forth the praises of him who appears thus wonderful in working! Think not, brethren, that I am going to entertain you with a discourse upon the nature, the laws,

laws, or the progress of vegetation. No: The Peach we have described is but a representation of the world we inhabit. Philosophers have said much respecting its admirable structure; they have examined its surface, and, in their contemplations, penetrated almost to its very centre. They have in general united in pronouncing it the workmanship of an infinitely wise and powerful Being; one who deserves the praise, and ought to be honoured by all intelligent creatures. With pleasure have I read several volumes upon this delightful subject, but have always found that pleasure greatly heightened by that short, but expressive, description which *Job* gives us of God's power, where he says, *He hangeth the earth upon nothing.* *——Now, as every Peach contains the stamina of an entire tree, which, under the direction of Almighty Power, may one day flourish and bring forth fruit—so there is, if I may so speak, a spiritual world included in that which is material. And though the power of God be so remarkably displayed in the latter, yet it will be far more gloriously and more durably displayed in the former. *Believers are kept by the power of God.* The world knows them not—takes no notice of them—never penetrates the shell in which they are secured—often casts them away without respect or regard; but the all-revealing day will come, the season will arrive in which this world which now contains them

* Job xxvi. 7.

them shall be removed and done away; then shall they be manifested to be the prodigies of the God of power and salvation: " He will then be glorified in his saints, and admired in all them that believe." * *Now* he is glorifying himself in their daily support and preservation; *then* will he be exalted in their everlasting vigour and perfection.

All further introduction may seem unnecessary, except it be to inform you that the Apostle *Peter* is here speaking of the privileges and honours that pertain to the true believer; concerning such he asserts, that they *are kept by the power of God through faith unto salvation, ready to be revealed in the last time.* The method we propose to follow in this discourse is,

    I. To speak of that Salvation which is here referred to.
    II. Shew you the medium whereby every believer is now connected with it, and shall eventually be preserved to it.——— And,
    III. Point out the infallible support and security of that frail medium of connection.———Let us glance,

    I. At *the Salvation here referred to.* Indeed it is but a glance that we are able to take of it at present. Like the sun, we behold it, and are sensible that it is very glorious; but the prospect

* 2 Thess. i. 10.

prospect we have of it is both distant and imperfect. The glory of it is too splendid, its dimensions too great, its duration too extensive for the mind to conceive in the present state. However, it is here described as a *salvation ready* or prepared, in order *to be revealed in the last time*; and in the preceding verse it is spoken of under the idea of *an inheritance incorruptible, undefiled, and that fadeth not away, reserved in heaven for us*. It cannot decay—is incapable of being defiled—and will flourish for ever, without abatement either in its beauty or its glory. In describing this Salvation we beg leave to remark, that it is the contrivance and work of the great God himself—that, when finished, it will prove the most bright and complete manifestation of his glory that was ever exhibited—and that there is a period fixed in the divine purpose for its full discovery.

1. This Salvation is the contrivance and work of the great God himself; and where unlimited wisdom draws the plan, eternal benevolence furnishes the materials, and almighty power executes the design, what may we not expect? If we may be allowed to form the estimate from this material world, which, as was already observed, is no more than the shell, and which most probably was formed only to endure a few thousands of years, what may we conceive of that spiritual world which is the substance, and which is to endure for
millions

millions of millions of ages. Certain it is that the builder difcovers a part of his fkill, even in the ftructure of the fcaffold which furrounds the building; but nothing of it when compared with what he intends in the edifice, to which that is only fubfervient. For that removed will only make way for the more clear difplay of his inventive fkill and effective powers. This is a falvation fo complete, as to comprehend every poffible good in it, and exclude every poffible evil for ever from it. A falvation, wide as the ftretch of eternity, deep as the purpofes of *Jehovah*, high as his throne, and durable as his nature. Salvation in this paffage refpects not only the falvation of an individual believer, but comprehends that whole complicated work which will be continued throughout all ages, extending to every member of *Chrift*'s myftical body, and including both faints on earth and faints in heaven. It is the grand device and glorious production of the Lord God Omnipotent. Unlimited as is the defign, he comprehends the whole and every part of it in his mind; great as is the undertaking, he will neither faint or grow weary till the whole be accomplifhed; large as is the ftructure, and long the feafon that is required to complete it, yet " he will bring forth the top-ftone with fhoutings, crying, Grace, grace, unto it."— All the fpiritual " *Ifrael* fhall be faved in the Lord with an everlafting falvation; they fhall

not

not be ashamed or confounded world without end."

2. When finished, this salvation will appear the most bright and complete manifestation of the glory of God that has ever been exhibited to men or angels: All his other works will give place to this. This glorious work will outshine the sun in splendour, surpass the treasures of the ocean in fulness, and outlive the old rolling world in duration. His other works are but so many appendages to this: Creation, with all its wonders; Providence, with all its deep-laid and well-executed schemes; Revelation, with all its enlivening discoveries and soul-supporting promises, are no more than his instruments in this great undertaking, and necessary only for the completion of this God-like design. Let yon sun sink into the darkness of an eternal night; let the globe which we inhabit be whirled from its ancient basis, and plunged ten thousand fathoms deep into the gulph of forgetfulness; yea, let every remaining trace of creation be blotted out for ever; were all this done the glory of God would suffer no eclipse. The grandeur of the Deity would sustain no diminution: So far from that, in this work of salvation, his glory will acquire additional brilliancy, and his grandeur be displayed to greater advantage. Other objects will be removed that this may become more conspicuous, and illumined to a greater degree;

degree; and the glory of this salvation will at once comprehend and exceed all the glory that he now derives from his works of creation and providence. To something of this nature probably the Prophet alludes, when he says, that "the light of the moon shall be as the light of the sun, and the light of the sun shall be seven-fold, as the light of seven days, in the day that the Lord bindeth up the breach of his people, and healeth the stroke of their wound."* And again, addressing the church, " the sun shall be no more thy light by day, neither for brightness shall the moon give light unto thee: but the Lord shall be unto thee an everlasting light, and thy God thy glory." † Now, to have light and glory thrown upon an object, and that light and glory immediately from God himself, is what we can have no proper conception of in the present state; but that it must be peculiarly great, and infinitely superior to any thing we can conceive at present, may be safely concluded from that *secondary* light and glory with which many of the parts of the creation are illumined. This salvation will be the most bright, the most complete, and the most durable manifestation of his glory that has ever been made to his creatures.

3. There is a period fixed in the divine purpose for the full manifestation of this salvation. Hence it is called a *Salvation ready to be*

---

* Isaiah xxx. 26.—† Ib. lx. 19.

be revealed in the last time. The great God will "come to be glorified in his saints, and to be admired in all them that believe." * At prefent we have but very limited and inadequate conceptions of it. Did men in general only know those treasures of riches, honour, and pleasure that are comprehended in this word *Salvation*, the miser would relinquish his hoarded store, the potentate his elevated throne, and the voluptuary his sordid pursuits, each to seek the only satisfying good in the God of Salvation: Nay, to rise higher still, even those who themselves are the happy subjects of salvation——those who are marked out for it in the purposes of *Jehovah*, and are now training up for it by his Spirit, even those have but very imperfect conceptions of it. Now, says one of them, "are we the Sons of God, and it doth not yet appear what we shall be: but when he shall appear we shall be like him, for we shall see him as he is." † Nay, further, even those who are so far honoured as to be employed in publishing and advancing this great work by their ministry, see but in part, and therefore can speak of it only in part. ‡ Should we imagine an angel to have existed a thousand years before the creation of this world; and suppose some idea of God's intention to create this globe had sprung up in the mind of this angel: Imagine farther, that

he

---

* 2 Theff. i. 10.—† 1 John iii. 2.—‡ 1 Cor. xiii. 9.

he had stretched the power of thought, in order to guess what sort of a work it would be——would his conceptions, think ye, have exceeded? or rather would they not have fallen far, very far short of what God has since produced? No doubt the latter would have been the case. Yet, as was hinted before, salvation is the kernel of the creation; *this* forms the foot-stool, but *that* the throne of the Deity. What a glorious exhibition then will that be when the work is completed! Salvation shall be brought forth to be admired, and to be enjoyed, by all the saints; to be enjoyed as the marvellous work of the Deity, and as the glory of the great God. Then shall it be seen what infinite wisdom could plan, grace could accomplish, and power effect. The vail that now covers the glorious work will then be taken off, that every eye may see, and all the ransomed of the Lord may be eternally filled with the glory and honours of his salvation. It is *ready to be revealed in the last time.*——Proceed we,

II. To consider *the medium whereby every believer is now connected with this salvation, and shall eventually be preserved to the full enjoyment of it* through faith. "Kept through faith unto salvation;" that is, he is preserved by a dependance upon the Lord *Jesus Christ*; and by humble expectation of a full, though future, salvation. "The life he now lives in the flesh, is by the faith of the Son of God."

From him he derives strength, support, encouragement, comfort, and confidence.—In a word, all his help, and the whole foundation of his hope, is out of himself. He looks to *Jesus* to slay his sins, to perfect his graces, and to complete and crown the work of salvation in him. Faith bears him up while on a tempestuous ocean, and brings him support in the storm. Looking to *Jesus* is his work, his strength, and his victory.—This simple method is the appointment of the all-wise God. He approves no other, has instituted no other, and will admit of no other. Looking to *Jesus*, the Author and Finisher of our faith, is the only successful way to lay aside every incumbering weight, disengage ourselves from besetting sins, and run with patience the race that is set before us.* But simple as this method may appear, there is hardly any thing more difficult than to keep the soul in this humble, this self-degrading, this Christ-exalting frame.—In this concern the true believer labours under many disadvantages.

1. From the different views he has of the same object at different times. There are seasons when he is favoured with such enlarged views of the merit of the Redeemer's death, and the completeness of the salvation procured by him, that had he ten thousand souls he could venture them all with confidence upon that bottom. He sees that where

* Heb. xii. 1, 2.

sin

sin hath abounded, grace doth much more abound; that the riches of mercy are unsearchable; and the promises of God appear to him so many breasts of consolation streaming with comfort.—At other seasons the Redeemer is almost out of sight—guilt intervenes, and hides the only refuge and remedy from his view; promises seem to have lost their savour, and to be exhausted of their treasure. He views them, as with different eyes, hears their language with different ears, and feels different emotions within respecting them. His faith is very languid—it staggers, it sinks under accumulated burdens, and were it not for the power of God it must expire. O affecting season! in which the soul seems to have lost all prospect of a precious *Christ*, and of a promised salvation.

2. Faith labours under great disadvantages also at seasons from the suggestions of Satan. His devices are deep laid, and the season of his attacks well chosen. He has his thousands of games to play, and thousands of objections to raise against the believer and his faith: nor will he leave one mean untried in order to break the bruised reed or quench the smoaking flax. He will accuse, examine, and cross-examine your faith, and employ every artifice to invalidate its claim. *Peter*, while in this conflict, was sore tossed and broken. His Lord alone could discern that living principle which, had it not been under the

the protection of his own power, had been entirely loft. Is the foul exercifed with a variety of trials? The adverfary will infinuate that were you a believer this would not be the cafe; and though your mountain have ftood ftrong for a feafon he will affault it, and endeavour to fhake your confidence, to fap your hopes, or to rob you of your comforts. If, on the other hand, all things have worn a fmooth and placid afpect for a confiderable feafon; if there have been no perfonal affliction, no domeftic trial, no cloud upon your fecular concerns, he will infinuate that were you an accepted child, you would certainly be an afflicted one; and, perhaps, back the infinuation with this fcripture, that " whom the Lord loveth he chafteneth, and fcourge the very fon whom he receiveth; if therefore ye be without chaftifement, whereof all are partakers, then are ye baftards and not fons."

3. Faith labours under great difadvantages alfo from the variety of trials it meets with both from without and from within. Your connections in life, your employments in the world, as well as inward fears, doubts, and difcouragements have a tendency to keep your faith very weak and languid. You do not fee that progrefs and fuccefs in the divine life as you formerly expected. Little advantage feems to have been gained againft your common enemies—little progrefs made in the Chriftian

Christian course; nay, at seasons, perhaps, you are ready to conclude that you are more defiled, and more exercised with doubts and distresses than ever. You are brought almost to give up the very hope of salvation, to yield to the torrent of temptation, and to conclude that it is in vain to wait for the Lord any longer. Once more,

4. The length of time likewise that the soul hath to wait for this salvation is a great trial to faith. At first ye were willing to wait: It then appeared a duty, and a resolution was formed that you would wait for the God of your salvation; but after some time is elapsed, and little evidence of the progress of the saving work in the heart is seen, strong corruptions, unsanctified tempers, and unruly passions are felt, ye would entirely faint did not the promise assure you that now is your salvation nearer than when ye first believed—You must inevitably fail, unless faith had hold of that power which is able to make the promise good. A soul thus born up for years, in the midst of all the adverse winds of temptation, though tossed with the billows of corruption, is surely no less than a prodigy of the divine power, and to that our text ascribes it—which leads us to notice,

III. *The infallible support and security of that frail medium of connection which subsists between the soul and salvation:* It is kept by the power of God. This shews,

1. That

1. That faith, and all the other graces of the Christian, are under the guardianship of the divine power, and that sin, and all his other enemies, have to contend with Omnipotence itself. What an animating and exhilerating thought! Kept by the power of God, faith lives, hope out-rides the storm, and grace prevails. The bruised reed is still supported, and the smoaking flax is yet supplied. With this in view, the weakest believer may exult with the greatest of the Apostles, and say, having obtained help of God,' I continue to this day! It is because his care is unremitted, and his compassions fail not, that we are not consumed.

2. Though this support be sometimes imperceptible to the believer himself, it is always real. The Lord keeps him by night, when he cannot see his protector, as well as by day, when he can more clearly discern him. Unseen, he guides him still, and unfelt, he supports. Probably at seasons the true believer is no more able to describe the manner of his support than he can tell how soul and body are held together from year to year. He perceives it no more than a babe, hanging at his mother's breast in a besieged fortress, is sensible of the means of his protection. And such is the idea that seems to be conveyed by our Apostle in the original. *Kept* as within an impregnable garrison un-

der the observation of an all-seeing eye, and under the protection of an Almighty hand.

3. As this support is constant, so is it likewise sufficient. Is any thing too hard for the Lord? No, he is able to do exceeding abundantly above all that we can ask or think.—He fainteth not, neither is he weary. Look back to ancient generations—collect into one view all the wonders he hath wrought, and then remember for your encouragement, that "his arm is not shortened that it cannot save, nor his ear heavy that it cannot hear." His power is infinite, and all the church shall know what is the exceeding greatness of this his power towards them that believe, according to the working of his mighty power.* The Father is greater than all, and none shall be found able to pluck them out of the Father's hand. †

The inferences we deduce from the subject are these:

1. How great is the privilege of the true Christian. He is secured to an inheritance, and secured so as no heir to an earthly inheritance can be. Nothing shall intervene between him and his patrimony; nothing prevent his future and full enjoyment of it. No, not all the trials of life, the conflicts of a dying hour, or the assaults or accusations of his grand adversary. His God stands engaged to him by promise and covenant, and he knows

* Eph. i. 19.—† John x. 29.

knows in whom he has believed, and is perfuaded that he is able to keep that which he has committed to him againſt this day of ſalvation. Though oppoſed, grievouſly oppoſed, he ſhall ſtand, for his God is able to make him ſtand. *

2. That ſame power, which will finally reveal and bring forth ſalvation for the enjoyment of ſaints, has alſo treaſured up, and will at laſt inflict wrath upon ſinners. The day is coming when all their hard thoughts of God, and their rebellious conduct againſt him, will be expoſed to view. Judgment will be protracted no further, nor patience longer ſuffer abuſe. Vengeance ſhall be taken upon them that know not God, and obey not the Goſpel of *Jeſus Chriſt*——They ſhall be baniſhed from the preſence of the Lord, and from the glory of his power, and will find it an awful thing to fall into the hand of the living God. Conſider this, ye that trifle with *Chriſt*, with your ſouls, and with the Goſpel. Fly for refuge to the hope that is now ſet before you; take ſanctuary under the ſhield of Omnipotence: Kiſs (that is, ſubmit to, and embrace) the Son and be happy. Our God waits to be gracious—is ſlow to anger—ready to pardon——and declares that he that cometh to him he will in no wiſe caſt out.

3. From this ſubject learn to look to, rely on, and take comfort from the Majeſty of God, as engaged to ſave to the uttermoſt all that

* Rom. xiv. 4.

that come unto him by *Jesus Christ:* Look to him and be ye saved: Be strong in the Lord, and in the power of his might: Go forth in his strength, relying upon him who promiseth to give power to the faint, and to increase the strength of those who have no might. Thus out of weakness will ye be made strong, and as having nothing, will enjoy all things. And thus, as in the case of the Apostle *Paul,* " his grace shall be sufficient for you, for his strength shall be perfected in weakness." * " Now unto him that is able to keep you from falling, and to present you faultless before the presence of his glory with exceeding joy; to the only wise God our Saviour, be glory and majesty, dominion and power, both now and ever. *Amen.*" †

---

* 2 Cor. xii. 9.——† Jude ver. 24, 25.

SERMON IX.

Dying Remorse: Or the Pangs of a wicked Man's Conscience in the Close of Life.

PROVERBS v. 12, 13.

How have I hated instruction, and my heart despised reproof? I have not obeyed the voice of my teachers, nor inclined mine ear to them that instructed me.

IT may be said of human laws that they are the very life and support of society in every civilized state: without them all would be disorder, rapine, and distress—in them the magistrate, as with the finger of authority, draws the line of defence around both our persons and property. The laws of this land take every individual under their protection, and place the executive power, armed with the authority and support of the whole nation, as a terror to them that do evil, but a praise to them that do well. Considered in this light, human laws are to be viewed as strong and necessary pales, fixed upon the precipice of destruction, to guard the

the thoughtless and the rash from falling. But laws, however pure in their principles, reasonable in their requirements, just in their prohibitions, kind and salutary in their tendency, or good in their end; I say laws, with all these qualifications, hold forth but the shadow of protection to the industrious, or the phantom of destruction to the rapacious, unless penalties and punishments be annexed to them. The order and advantage of society requires that, in some cases, these penalties be enforced; yet these punishments are not only for the satisfaction of justice, and for the reformation of the transgressors, but also for a warning to others against similar crimes.

Few principles appear more reasonable in themselves than this, that every man should securely enjoy that life which his God gave him, and quietly possess that property which the great disposer of all things has allotted to him. Upon this simple foundation the laws of our country are built; and that man who would infringe upon another's right in either of these cases, deserves to be deprived of his liberty, or excluded society. But how many, tempted by the prospect of what another possesses, leap over this inclosure, hoping to bear it away with secrecy, and enjoy it undetected. Under this delusion, many have ventured upon sin, and, perhaps, when too late, have bewailed their folly and their crime. Locked up in a gloomy prison,

loaded

loaded with galling fetters, and pierced to the very foul by the sting of remorse, they have given vent to the bitterness of its anguish in such language as this: "What have I done! Into what shame and disgrace have my covetous desires, or unbridled lusts plunged me! My folly has deceived me. By presumption I am undone; and what now remains but a publication of my guilt——the sentence of judgment——and the approach of death in a public execution."

But human laws, however useful and necessary, cannot inforce every duty, or prevent every crime. They can only take cognizance of the outward action. In this God's laws have greatly the pre-eminence, they reach the principles of action, and extend their authority to our very thoughts. A perfect copy of this sacred code is to be found in the volume of *Revelation*. Ministers, like magistrates, are to publish these laws, use their vigilance, and exert all their ability in inforcing and carrying them into execution. It is true they are not invested with the power of the sword, or required to punish the offender: Their duty is to warn the unruly, invite the inattentive, and steadily to persevere in commending the truth to every man's conscience, as in the sight of God, assuring every man that God hath appointed a day in which he will judge the world in righteousness by *Jesus Christ*.

The

The minister's office is to point out the reasonableness of the divine command; the advantages that stand inseparably connected with obedience; and the promises of divine aid in the way of duty. Men are to be informed that the claims which God makes upon them are founded in love; that their present good and future advantage are all he aims at; and that it is no unreasonable service which he requires at their hands. Not only so, but while we proclaim the reasonableness of what he requires of you, we are commanded to open the treasures of his grace, and display them before you. By the gospel, even those who have rebelled are invited to return to their allegiance, and " the wicked forsaking his way, and the unrighteous man his thoughts, and returning to the Lord, shall find mercy and abundance of pardon." Such is the gracious remedy; but if this be rejected, "there remains no more sacrifice for sin, but a fearful looking for of judgment which shall devour the adversary." Thus sinners are graciously invited and solemnly warned; but how many spurn at the authority, resist the grace, trifle away the day of salvation, defy the judgments of Omnipotence, and finally make room for painful and hopeless reflections, crying out for eternity, *How have I hated instruction, and my heart despised reproof? I have not obeyed the voice of my teachers,*

teachers, nor inclined mine ear to them that instructed me.

Waving all attention to the preceding context, suffice it to remark, that these words are represented as the dying reflection of a wicked man on the borders of the grave, with his bones filled with the sins of his youth. In the words we propose to consider,

 I. The view, the comprehensive view of a minister or a parent's duty, respecting sinners in general, or young people in particular.
 II. The duty required of those who are possessed of these advantages.
 III. The manner in which too many treat these privileges.—And
 IV. The future and awful effect of such conduct.—After which we shall close with a few general reflections upon the subject.

 I. *The comprehensive view this passage affords us of the minister's or parent's duty, respecting sinners in general, or young people in particular,* comes first for our consideration. This is represented as consisting of two parts, viz. *Instruction* and *Reproof*.

 1. It is the minister's duty and province to instruct men in the way that leads to holiness and happiness; how they may honour God while upon earth, and finally attain the full

full enjoyment of him in heaven. The only way to be happy, my fellow-sinners, is *now* to seek acquaintance with God—to consign yourselves over to his care and service—to bow to the sceptre of his grace—and to derive all your help and comfort from that blessed and inexhaustible treasure which he has laid up in *Jesus Christ*. It is our office to invite you to be reconciled to God—to shew you the way in which this invaluable privilege is to be obtained—and to set before you the advantages, *the inestimable advantages*, that are to be derived from it, both in time and eternity. With pleasure we meet you, from time to time, to instruct you in that divine scheme, wherein our God can be just, yet justify the ungodly sinner who believeth in *Jesus:* In which there is a discovery made how sin can be freely forgiven, peace possessed, and real pleasure enjoyed. Our desire, as well as our duty, is to inform you how the ignorant may be made wise; the weak valiant; the fearful courageous; the guilty accepted; and the impure made holy. The amiable, yet honourable character of God; the humility, grace, offices, and glory of *Jesus Christ*; the works of the Holy Spirit; the necessity of conversion; the privileges and duties of the real Christian; and the grand scheme of salvation in its several parts: These are the subjects to which we devote our thoughts, and in which we anxiously desire

sire to be the happy instruments of instructing our fellow-mortals. To point you to the path of life, the treasures of *Christ*, and the mansions of glory. This is the delightful task we have undertaken, and which is committed unto us by our great and divine master. At other seasons we endeavour to lay before you the various devices of Satan, the deceitfulness of sin, and the depravity of the human heart; while, at the same time, we direct you to the armour of God, the treasures of divine wisdom, and the promises of strength, support, sanctification, and salvation. We inform you how temptation may be resisted with success; how sin is to be vanquished by a steady looking to *Jesus*; and how a depraved heart is purified by faith. In a word, we assure you, that yet there is room in the arms of divine mercy for the very chief of sinners, and admittance into the kingdom of heaven. We have God's authority, I say, to assure you that all things are now ready for the acceptance, sanctification, and salvation of every sinner that cometh to him by *Jesus Christ*; and that he who thus cometh to him shall in no wise be rejected.

And while the faithful minister holds out the necessary instruction to his people, godly parents are no less careful to inculcate instruction upon their tender charge. They furnish you, my young friends, with God's word, intreating you to examine its contents,

and

and to take heed that ye order your way according to the direction it holds forth. They caution you against youthful lusts, and with pleasure inform you that their God loves them who love him, and that they who seek him early shall find him. They endeavour to guard your minds against those temptations with which the world abounds, and assure you that wisdom's ways are ways of pleasantness; that early piety ensures a crop of real pleasure; and that converse and communion with God are an honour which is attainable. They intreat you to cultivate an acquaintance with the God of your fathers, and to serve him with a perfect heart and a willing mind; assuring you, that if ye seek him he will be found of you; but if ye forsake him he will cast you off for ever. Thus they warn, instruct, and intreat; mix their prayers and their tears; testify what advantages they themselves have found, and beseech you to acknowledge God in all your ways; declaring that they who make God their friend, will find him faithful to guide them through life, support them in death, and bless them for ever.——But

2. *Reproof,* as well as *instruction,* is a necessary branch, both of the minister's and parent's duty. We warn every man, and reprove every man, that we may present every man perfect in *Christ Jesus.* Dear as your favour may seem to us, we dare not purchase

it at the expence of being unfaithful to your souls. We scorn to flatter you in your faults, or to lead you blindfold to damnation. Knowingly we will not suffer sin to rest upon you undetected or unreproved; we dare not; but, disagreeable as it may be to have your frown, we will account that a weight much easier to bear than the blood of your souls.—And how many have we to reprove this day, who, though they have long enjoyed the means of grace, still neglect the only remedy, who have often felt convictions, which have been as often stifled in the very birth. Ye have seen the only way to safety, but have ye followed it? Or have ye discovered that sincere, that persevering concern for your souls, which ye once saw so necessary? Rather, like the sow that hath been washed, have not many of you again returned to the mire of your former abominations? Sirs, it is awful thus to trifle with convictions, for he that, being often reproved, hardeneth his neck, shall suddenly perish, and that without remedy*.—And even amongst many of you who make greater professions of religion, is there not too great conformity to the world? Ye are carnal in your pursuits, covetous in your desires, and conform too much to the temper, the language, the course of the world Brethren, these things ought not so to be. Others, perhaps, are negligent respecting the means of grace, and slight these institutions, without due attention to which, your souls cannot

* Prov. xxix. 1.

not prosper. Our God, who is jealous of his honour, will remember them who remember him, and has promised that such as wait upon him shall renew their strength; but they who despise him shall be lightly esteemed. Professors, see that ye love not the world; beware that ye be not intoxicated with its cares, allured by its smiles, or entangled with its comforts. Abstain from every appearance of evil. Keep yourselves pure: Remember the Judge standeth at the door: Be looking for that blessed hope, and the glorious appearance of the great God and Saviour *Jesus Christ*. Let your loins be girded about, your lamps burning, and ye yourselves as those who look for the coming of their Lord.

And, ye parents, be faithful in reproving sin in your children. Shew your displeasure against lying, prophaneness, pilfering of little things, and every advance towards indelicacy or immorality. Walk within your houses with uprightness of heart, and let your families see that it is not only your desire to be instructors, but let your conduct be an example of what ye wish to recommend, as well as reprovers of the contrary. Had the first approaches of those sins, which afterwards became habitual, been noticed early, and had their evil consequences been faithfully and affectionately pointed out by parents to their posterity, how much sin, which now prevails, might have been happily prevented. But these tares were sown, they
sprung

sprung up, acquired strength, and spread before they were noticed; or, perhaps, the reproof and remonstrance came when the authority of the parent had lost its weight and influence. Sensible I am, that parents cannot renew the hearts of their children; but let them remember, that the breaking forth of sin, is like the letting out of water; the restraint will generally prove most successful in the beginning. *Eli's* false tenderness was the means of precipitating the ruin of his sons; and let his error, and their fall, be a warning to all those who are intrusted with the care and instruction of the rising generation.

From this general view of the duty, both of the christian minister and parent towards their respective charges, we proceed to shew,

II. *The duty required of those who are possessed of these advantages.* Privileges they really are, however some may estimate them, or whatever their conduct may be respecting them. Now the duties required, you will observe, are *Attention* and *Obedience*.

1. We remark, that the great, the interesting things contained in the gospel demand *Attention*. They relate to the happiness of your souls and eternity. And shall God himself speak from heaven? Shall his own Son descend to our world, to publish his mind and will? Shall ministers be raised up, one after another, from age to age, to invite sinners to be reconciled unto God? Shall the value, the capacities,

pacities, the great concerns of your fouls be laid before you? Shall the joys of heaven, the miferies of the damned, the profpects of eternity, be exhibited to your view? Shall the commands of the great fovereign be publifhed, and his invitations and promifes, his cautions and threatnings announced? Shall the thunder of *Sinai* roar, and the trump of the gofpel be blown, and, like the deaf adder, will men ftop their ears? In the name of the great God and his Son *Jefus Chrift*, we demand your audience: As ye value the happinefs of your fouls and their everlafting falvation, we intreat you to attend to the things that make for your peace: As ye would wifh, at laft, to avoid the pain of this ftinging reflection, *I have not inclined mine ear to them that inftructed me,* let me now befœch you to attend to the one thing needful; for this unfecured, ye are miferable for eternity.

And ye, my young friends, liften to the inftruction of your godly parents. Believe that they love you—that they confider themfelves really interefted in your prefent fafety and future felicity; at leaft admit the thought, that long experience may have made them wifer than yourfelves. They long to efpoufe you to *Chrift*, and to introduce you to that friend on whom all their hopes and confidence are founded. Their inftructions proceed from a fenfe of that duty which they owe both to God and to you:

Incline

Incline then your ears to them that would instruct you—But,

2. This *Attention* must be accompanied with *Obedience*. The demand that the ministers of the gospel have upon you is, the obedience of faith; the obedience of the heart to that form of doctrine which is delivered unto you; and the voice of your teachers is to be obeyed, so far as what they advance and require is supported by the sanction of God's word. They pretend to no dominion over your faith, nor authority over your conduct, further than the rule they hold out to you. May ye know the truth, obey it from the heart, transcribe it in your practice, and adorn it by your lives.

And ye, children, obey your parents in the Lord. View them as the guardians which divine providence hath placed over you; honour them as the guides of your youth; receive the law from their mouth; subject yourselves to their reasonable authority, and believe that the very restraints they lay upon you are intended for your good. Studiously guard against the future intrusion of this painful reflection—*I obeyed not the voice of my teachers;* but as the subject would swell too much, were we to carry it on in this double point of view, in what remains, we shall confine our thoughts to the former branch alone.—Proceed we, therefore, to consider in the next place.

III. The

III. The light and indifferent *manner in which too many treat these privileges.*

Some pay little or no attention either to the instructions or reproofs of ministers. They seldom come under the sound of their voice, and therefore cannot possibly derive any advantage from them—or, if they do attend, of the great numbers who crowd under the means of grace, how few comparatively give evidence, that they reap any saving advantage. Their minds enter not into the important truths that are delivered; and, by a fatal presumption, they ward off all the arrows of conviction which are employed against them. The secret language of their heart is, I shall have peace, though I walk in my own imaginations. Thus the danger of sin, the necessity of conversion, and the judgment of the Almighty appear to them but as idle tales. *They do not incline their ears to instruction.*

Others, again, are so far from inclining their ear to it, that they really *despise* it. In their hearts they have an opposition and distaste to the gospel; for " the natural man receiveth not the things of the Spirit of God, they are foolishness to him, neither can he know them because they are spiritually discerned." If, therefore, the particular vices they are most addicted to, be exposed and struck at, they immediately despise the reproof

proof—resolve to run the dreadful venture—to procrastinate the necessary reform—or to thrust from them the word of life and salvation.

Others, necessitated to attend by the authority of parents or superiors, even *hate* the gospel. They are detained before the Lord; but this is the language of the heart, When will the sabbath be over? How long will it be ere yon babbler hath finished his tedious harangue? The doctrine advanced galls their consciences; under it they find no rest; yet from it can obtain no release. Thus are they dragged to it with reluctance, sit under it with dislike, and retire from it with disgust.

Others again act a contrary part to the spirit and precepts of the gospel. They are proud, passionate, earthly-minded, intemperate. In words they own God, but in works deny him. These are strong marks that such persons have not *obeyed* the voice of their teachers. Either, Sirs, adorn the gospel, or do not injure and disgrace it by your profession. It is in vain to say, Lord, Lord, if we do not the things that he hath commanded. If this gospel do not transform the hearts and lives of men, their profession of it is a trespass made upon the grace of the dispensation.——Brethren, the compliance of the heart with the gospel, and the conformity of the life to it, are indubitable evidences that ye really love it: But if the temper and

walk

walk be contradictory to this gospel, profess what regard for it ye may, these are the evidences that ye *hate it* in your hearts.

Such is the conduct with many; but as a guard against it, we have proposed to consider,

IV. *The awful effects of such a conduct, if persisted in to the close of life.* Such will mourn at the last. They will cry out in the bitterness of their souls, when the storm of death commences*. *They shall mourn at the last, when their flesh and their body are consumed, saying, how have we hated instruction, and our hearts despised reproof. We have not obeyed the voice of our teachers, nor inclined our ears to them that instructed us.* But in particular,

1. With what painful reflections may we suppose such persons must review the course of their lives, if reason and recollection be then in exercise.—O painful review, privileges slighted—warnings disregarded—a soul neglected—a Saviour crucified afresh—heaven contemned—and hell deserved. An ancient naturalist remarks, that the mole never begins to see, till it is about to die. The truth or falsehood of this we pretend not to say, but O what an awful view have some persons had of murdered time and slighted mercies,

---

* The word here translated to *mourn*, signifies also to *roar*, as a *lion* when pressed with hunger, Prov. xxxviii. 15: or like the *ocean* in the time of a storm, Isai. v. 30.

mercies, when they come to the borders of eternity. Confider then in time, Sirs; what can ye do in that folemn day, when death refufes to quit his prey, and God to comfort? A reflecting feafon *will come*. May that feafon not come too late.

2. Bitter remorfe is, no doubt, included in the reflection. In that honeft hour, finners will both fee and condemn their folly. Every vain excufe will then be difmiffed; fhadows retire, and realities affume their proper form and place. In that feafon God will be juftified, minifters juftified, parents and faithful friends juftified, and men will condemn themfelves, and charge the guilt to their own account. O what a confeffion will be extorted, when the finner comes to lie upon the rack of his own confcience.

3. They will then fee that they have committed an irretrievable miftake. Haftening to the grave, and no repentance there. The fummons into eternity muft be obeyed—the fentence—the final irreverfible fentence muft be pronounced——the everlafting ftate be fixed; and what horrors of defpair! What agonies of diftrefs! What anticipations of damnation will then torture the departing fpirit! Dreadful fcene! The moment of diffolution approaches—the door of mercy finally clofes——life and time expire——eternity—and, what is ftill more awful, damnation commences.

commences. In that moment hope perishes, and the never-dying sinner sinks down under the insupportable load of unpardoned guilt into the bottomless pit of everlasting perdition! There remains no sacrifice for sin; but—fiery indignation, which shall devour the adversary.

A few general reflections shall close the subject. And,

1. Hence let parents learn to be found diligent and faithful in the discharge of their duty towards their children. Watch over them, as those that must give an account, and meet them as witnesses for or against you in the day of judgment. Travail over them in birth, till ye behold *Christ* formed in them the hope of glory. Train them up in the way wherein ye would wish them to walk in future. Reprove with meekness of wisdom; rebuke with tenderness mixed with authority; and exhort with earnestness animated by affection for them, and the importance of the duty ye recommend to them. Ever act with this sacred axiom in view, That he that winneth souls is wise.

2. If the dispensation of the gospel be intended for your *instruction* and *reproof*, then with what temper of mind, disposition of heart, and earnestness of desire should ye statedly attend upon it? Attend with desire to know and to do the will of God. As ignorant

norant come to be taught, and as needy to receive. Bow to God's authority revealed in the scriptures, and submit your judgments and souls to the determination of the Lord God Almighty. In all your attendance upon gospel-ordinances, cultivate the frame and sentiments of *Cornelius*, who, speaking in the name of his family and assembled friends, addressed the heavenly messenger thus, " We are all here present before God, to hear all things that are commanded thee of God."

3. Faith in the report of the gospel, and compliance with it, is not only attended with peace in this life, but affords support and confidence in our departure out of it. What pleasure is it now, to have the testimony of our consciences, that we love instruction, and have not despised reproof, but have obeyed the voice of our teachers, and inclined the ear to them who have instructed us; and with what peace may we hope to be indulged when we remove from this world. There remains a rest for the people of God.—Their end is peace—their course is finished with joy—and life closes honourably in company with God.—Finally,

4. If such are the advantages of being taught of God here, what must it be to be taught by him hereafter? To be led into all truth—see light in his light—contemplate truth no longer in the copy, but in the original.

ginal. Such muſt be truly wiſe, perfectly holy, and completely happy. May this God guide us by his counſel now, and afterwards receive us to glory, for *Jeſus Chriſt's* ſake. *Amen.*

SERMON

SERMON X.

Invigorating Comfort in a dying Hour: or the Compofure of a good Man's Mind in the clofing Scene of Life.

GENESIS xlix. 18.

I have waited for thy Salvation, O Lord.

YOUR attention was lately called to the reflections of a wicked man in a dying hour: We, in our imagination, faw him toffing upon his bed with all the horrors of his foul pictured upon his countenance, and expreffed by his tongue. The review of life was very painful to him, and this was the lamentation he indulged in his expiring moments, *How have I hated inftruction, and my heart defpifed reproof! I have not obeyed the voice of my teachers, nor inclined mine ear to them that inftructed me.* As a contraft to the awful pourtrait which was then prefented to you, we fhall now attempt to exhibit another as pleafing as that was painful. The words of the text contain the language of an eminent believer, expiring under the fenfible fmile of the divine approbation. His confcience science is sprinkled with the blood of the atonement, and his heart condemns him not; but he has confidence in God, and hopes full of immortality.

You see the *man*; you see his hold on heaven; nay, more than that, the very frame and sentiments of his soul in that solemn moment pass in review before us. Here we learn how *Jacob* was employed, and how every good man should be exercised in the close of his journey through this wilderness, viz. in a review of life, and a tranquil expectation of death. The instructions and reproofs of his father *Isaac* had been regarded, he had obeyed the voice of his teacher, and inclined his ear to him that instructed him. Early admonitions had been rendered profitable unto him, and often sent him into the field, while a youth, to meditate on them, and pray over them. In the earlier part of life he had sought the God of his father, and had enjoyed many a visit, many a blessing from him. The salvation of his soul was that concern which had pressed much upon his mind, and when he comes to lie upon a death-bed, and thence to take a review of life, he describes it as a waiting for God's salvation. These words are not to be considered as descriptive of the frame of his mind at this season only, but as expressing more especially the habitual disposition of his mind. His life had been a life of expectation, nor was he disappointed in what he expected; for he now considered himself as going to enjoy salvation. He calls God for his witness—he declares it for the instruction of his surrounding family—and he possesses all the comfort in his own soul, that he *had* lived and now died waiting for the salvation of the Lord.

These cases are held out for our warning and advantage. In a few years, in one or other of these circumstances, each of us will be found. A dying hour will come; and, if reason be then in exercise, will be found more awful or more comfortable according to the general line of conduct that has been pursued through life. The man who now habitually trifles with religion and its great concerns, can have no rational ground to conclude that he shall experience its supports upon his death-bed; nor can he hope that, having treated God as his enemy through life, he shall find him step forward to succour and support him as a friend, at a season when he can no longer rebel against him: Quite the reverse; is there not every ground to conclude, seeing when he called he was refused, and when he stretched out his hand, he was not regarded; that therefore " he will laugh at the calamity of such, and will mock when their fear cometh; when their fear cometh as desolation, and their destruction as a whirlwind; when distress and anguish come upon them." If there be no concern about salvation evidenced through life,

life, what can ye expect when confined to a dying chamber, but to be surrounded by all the horrors of despair and distraction. In that situation you may find no disposition to repent; have no seasons allowed for a reformation of conduct, though upon that presumption all the hopes of thousands respecting an eternity of happiness are founded.

There are two interesting remarks which, while they seem naturally to arise from this contrast between the death of the wicked and the righteous, we wish to recommend to your particular notice. O! that they were written in the deepest recesses of our hearts, and graven as upon the palms of our hands, that so all our principles and all our conduct might be regulated by them.——They are these:—— *That the ways of sin must sooner or later end in sorrow; but that the paths of real religion terminate in peace.* Let every one turn his thoughts inward, and faithfully put the question home to his conscience, Which of these is the habitual course that I am pursuing? Am I like the foolish man, whose case lately passed in review before me, hating instruction, despising reproof, disregarding the voice of my teachers, and turning away the ear from those who would instruct me? or, like good old *Jacob*, am I seeking, pressing towards, and waiting for God's salvation?

The chapter from which the words now to be considered are taken, contains an account

count of the blessings which the Patriarch *Jacob* pronounced upon his several sons when he was dying. At first view the words of the text seem to have no connection with what went before. *Dan* was the last tribe that he had mentioned, and the learned *Ainsworth* supposes that as that tribe was afterwards to be sorely oppressed, partly by enemies without, and partly by their own weaknesses and imprudences, that these words of their dying father were intended to be monitory and instructive to them; signifying, that though he had been grievously persecuted, and greatly exercised with trials, yet the hope he had in God's salvation had born him up under all, and carried him comfortably through. Taken in this view, these words teach us how godly parents should encourage their children to hope and trust in God from what they themselves have experienced in him; and likewise how the children of good men should learn to fly to their father's God in all their trials and difficulties.—But, leaving these remarks, we propose to consider the text in a twofold point of view, viz.

    I. As the dying believer's description of his past life; and,
    II. As holding forth the view he has of approaching death.
After which we shall close with a few reflections.

I. We

I. We propose to confider thefe words *as the dying believer's defcription of his paft life.* " I have waited for thy falvation, O Lord." When the life of a believer is defcribed under the idea of waiting for God's falvation, no doubt feveral things are included under this reprefentation, which are peculiarly worthy of attention. In the general we remark, that thefe words are not defcriptive of the uninterrupted frame of the mind, as if the believer, in every fucceeding moment of life, had this particularly in view; but they reprefent what had been the habitual bent and difpofition of his foul. Thus a faithful fervant who, after living many years in a family, although he may not have the thought of his mafter's intereft continually preffing upon his mind, fo as never to lofe fight of it, yet it becomes fo habitual to him, that he acts as though this were always the cafe; and he cannot act contrary to it.——But to be more particular.

1. When the life of a believer is defcribed under the notion of *waiting for God's falvation,* it fuppofes fuch a fixed and abiding fenfe of his loft condition, as to exclude the idea of all help and hope from himfelf. We fpeak not now of thofe convictions which open to the mind upon the firft difcoveries it hath of the evil of fin, for, deep as thefe may be with fome, and long as they may hang upon the mind of others, they are both fhallow

and

and transient, compared with those which we have now more peculiarly in view. The conviction to which we refer grows with years and experience, and the greater the saint, the deeper is his conviction of the truth of what we now describe. The more bright that light is which shines into his mind, the more clearly he discerns this truth; and the more liberally the grace of *Christ* is communicated to him for his daily support and supply, the more sensible he becomes of his weakness, unless thus supported. The very objection, therefore, which some people produce as an argument that they were never really converted, viz. the growing conviction they experience of the deceitfulness and depravity of their hearts, is really one of those evidences that we would wish them to attend to for the confirmation of it. They that are whole have *no* need of a Physician, so those who feel themselves but a little indisposed, will see but *little* need of him; but such as feel their disorder increasing to an alarming degree, and that more and more every day and hour, these are the persons who find the *greatest* need of applying to him.——It is generally supposed that the Apostle *Paul* wrote his first epistle to *Timothy* three-and-twenty years after his conversion. In that space of time how many visions may we suppose he had been favoured with? How many discoveries had he received? How much happy communion

communion had he enjoyed? The sufferings he had endured, and the service done by him were great. Sinners had been converted—churches had been planted, established, and edified. During this season he had been a fruitful and flourishing plant in the Lord's vineyard; his growth in grace and in the knowledge of the *Lord Jesus* had been abundant; and yet it was at this late date in his experience, when he stiled himself *the chief of sinners*. *This,* said he, *is a faithful saying, and worthy of all acceptation, that* Jesus Christ *came into the world to save sinners, of whom I am chief* He speaks not only of what he *had been* in a state of unregeneracy, but also of what he found himself *then to be* when he was become a father in *Christ,* and the very chief of all the Apostles.—And I apprehend, if the words of our text be allowed to have any meaning, they must hold forth this humbling truth, that *Jacob* thro' life had been followed with the deep and abiding conviction of his great need of salvation.—The very corruptions of a true believer are, perhaps, left to prove him, and to shew him how unable he is to do any thing towards his own salvation. These are the sharp, but successful instruments his God makes use of to cut him entirely off from all expectation of hope or help from himself. In the natural world, the higher the sun rises, the more clear is our discovery of all that had been hid in darkness before;

and,

and, in the spiritual world, perhaps, the nearer salvation approaches to the soul, the more evidently the believer sees and feels his need of it. Instead, therefore, of repining, you have cause to be thankful, if ye have found this abiding conviction attending you and increasing upon you, as your journey through life has advanced; and pray to God that it may never leave you till, with *Jacob*, ye come to the possession of that which ye have been waiting for. This conviction, though painful, is not unprofitable.

2. When the life of a believer is represented as a *waiting* for God's salvation, it intimates, that he is privileged with some happy discovery of that deliverance which his God holds out to him in the word. Waiting for a thing supposes a belief of its reality—a considering it as absent; but a living in expectation of its arrival, and that the enjoyment of it appears very desirable to the mind. Thus the promise which God made to *Jacob*, was a very comprehensive one. *Behold, I am with thee, and will keep thee in all places whither thou goest: for I will not leave thee, until I have done all that which I have spoken to thee of**. *Jacob* had received much out of this promise already: He had been preserved and prospered while absent from his father's tent. The angel of the divine presence had redeemed him from many evils, and both led him and fed him all his life long.

Gen. xxviii. 15.

The

The treasures of providence and grace had both been opened to him: Much he had received already, and yet he saw that there was much more to wait for. He considered the promise as pertaining, not only to the life that then was, but as extending to all that was to come. He viewed an everlasting salvation, as the crowning blessing contained in the promise; and he waited for it. That *Jacob's* promise is now, through *Christ*, made over to all the heirs of *Jacob's* faith, is evident from the testimony of the Apostle of the *Gentiles*. Referring to this, he observes, concerning **God**, that he hath said, *I will never leave thee nor forsake thee* *. What a source of encouragement doth this hold forth to the mind. Under every trial and affliction let us remember that there remains a perfect rest and a perpetual salvation. This is the animating prize—this the inspiring prospect, which a gracious **God** holds out to his friends and followers, under all the present exercise of their faith and patience. They would inevitably faint under the weight of their guilt, were it not that they hoped to see the salvation of their God; and, in proportion to the degree of that discovery they have of their helpless condition, will their God reveal to them, from his word, the glory of that salvation which they are waiting for.

3. This

---

* Heb. xiii. 5.

3. This description of the life of a believer implies in it such a stedfast hold of the divine promise, as tends to promote diligence and activity. It is not an expectation which produces indolence and indifference; but it draws out all the graces into lively exercise. There is an earnest expectation of the blessing and a looking for it. The encouragement which the apostle *Paul* held up to the believing *Romans*, was, that their salvation was nearer than when they first believed †, intimating that there is a near and real connection between faith and salvation; and that, by an habitual exercise of faith upon this salvation as exhibited in the promise, the soul and it are brought nearer to each other. This may be illustrated by a similitude, which is rendered familiar to our view by its frequency. In particular cases, you know, when they want to bring a vessel into our harbour, a rope being first made fast to the shore, is conveyed to the ship. This is received by the mariners on board, then every pull with their hands, or turn of the capstan, bears the ship nearer to the object with which the rope has connected it: So is it by the soul's adherence to, and repeatedly pulling at, the promise, if I may so speak, that the end is received, even complete salvation. *Jacob's* life had been a very active life; but the hope he had of this salvation had been the principle of all that activity: This bore him up

† Rom. xiii. 11.

up against wind and tide, till it brought him into the haven of salvation. He fainted not, but still believed that he should see, enjoy, and be satisfied with God's salvation.

4. When the Patriarch represents the life of a believer, under the idea of hoping for God's salvation, it implies likewise a patient perseverance in the use of those means which God hath appointed, with a view to this end. From the history of this good man we learn, that where ever he removed, there he built an altar unto the Lord, and called upon his name. He could not bear the thought of living a stranger to God's appointments; and every sacrifice he offered tended to enlarge his views, and to enliven his hopes of this salvation. He experienced it good for him thus to draw near to the Lord, and to keep up a correspondence with him as the God of his salvation.—In like manner, brethren, if ye wish to preserve and cherish the lively hopes of this salvation in your souls, ye must keep up a regular attention to all the appointments of *Jehovah,* both in private and in public. Search the scriptures; give yourselves to prayer; set apart proper time for meditation and self-examination; and forsake not the assembling of yourselves together, as the manner of some is. The more regular, diligent, and sincere ye are in the use of these means, the more clear will be your view— the more strong your desires—and the more

delightful your foretastes of this salvation. Waiting upon the Lord you will experience your strength renewed, and that great work of salvation advancing in your souls. Once more,

5. When the life of the believer is described under the notion of hoping for salvation, it supposes that this hope is his grand support under all the trials, disappointments, and discouragements he meets with. He endures, as seeing that which is invisible, and, against hope, believeth in hope. Many things, both within and without, tend to oppose and enervate his hope; such as remaining corruption——fiery temptations——worldly prosperity——daily converse with sensible objects——the imperceptible progress of the interest of religion in the soul——and the declensions and falls of others. But though cast down, hope is not destroyed; like an anchor, sure and stedfast, it entereth into that which is within the veil; or, like the rope which forms a connection between the vessel and the shore, to which we before alluded, though it may sometimes hang loose——may dip into the water——may be hid from our sight, yet the connection still subsists, and the advantages of it eventually appear. This hope of salvation gives support to the mind under the adverse blasts of providence, and enables the soul to outride the severest storm: It renders the heaviest afflictions comparatively

paratively light, and shortens the severest trials.—Such is the account that *Jacob* gives us of the life of a believer. He has such an abiding sense of his lost condition, as to exclude every idea of help from himself; but he is favoured with some happy discoveries of that salvation which is held out to him in the promise—the hold he has of that promise tends to promote activity and diligence. He perseveres in the use of appointed means; and by the hope he has of this salvation, he is born up, and carried safely through all the adverse trials he meets with.—But we have yet,

II. To consider these words of *Jacob, as holding out the view that a dying believer has of death.* " I have waited for thy salvation." Can words more clearly evidence, that such a person looks upon death—as *the period to all his misery*—as *the door which was to admit him to the enjoyment of a full salvation*—and as *that grand ingathering season, when all his graces shall be fully ripened, and lodged safe with his God for eternity?*

1. Living in expectation of God's salvation, the good man makes it appear that he looks upon death as *the period to all his miseries.* Temptations can follow him no further; there he lays down the body of sin and death, to bear the insupportable burden no longer. In a dying hour he resigns every thing but his hope; and that contains a treasure

sure sufficient to enrich him for ever. He is to sigh, to sorrow, to suffer no more; for the days of his mourning are now brought to a conclusion. The root of indwelling sin is now effectually eradicated, its fruit destroyed, and its very being done away. His warfare is ended, the fierce, the tedious, the once-doubtful conflict is to be renewed no more. Death, which to many is the beginning of sorrow and suffering, to him is the end of both: It is the period of his misery, and the port of his salvation. He enters into peace, that he may rest for eternity. *Jacob*, in his dying moments, considered himself as bidding an happy farewell to sorrow: *Esau* had persecuted him; *Laban* had deceived him; his own family had caused him many an anxious thought and many a distressing hour: He had known what it was to be full and to be hungry, to abound and to suffer want; but now, he beheld death in waiting to put a period to all his trials.

2. *Jacob* considered death as the *door which was to admit him to the enjoyment of a complete salvation.* View the good man just going to receive the full answer of all his prayers; to gather the full-ripe fruit of his faith and hope, and to take possession of that incorruptible inheritance, the title to which he had long held in the promise. But a step between him and life eternal—a moment between his waiting soul, and a perpetuity of bliss.

blifs. His heart and his flesh began to fail him, but his hope did not; that was in full vigour still, and brightened the more as the shades of death gathered around him. He considered himself as going to God, without any thing unfriendly in his soul towards him, or apprehending any thing unfriendly from him. The support of the everlasting arms were experienced, and his soul was willing to be separated for a season from the body, that it might find rest in the bosom of his God. The distant intercourse, which had been kept up so long between God and his soul, inspired him with the ardent desire to enjoy greater intimacy, and uninterrupted communion. His expectation had not been in vain—he had waited—and now the chariots of salvation were ready to receive and convey him to the desired country. Nothing now remained to separate between him and the object of his hopes but death, and that he saw and welcomed as the door which was to admit him to the enjoyment of full salvation.

3. This great and good man considered death as *that grand ingathering season, when all his graces should be fully ripe, and himself lodged safe with his God for eternity.* It is in this view that the righteous man is said to come to his grave *like a shock of corn fully ripe*.* After being exposed to many a storm—beset and entangled with many a weed

---

* Job v, 26.

weed —subsisting under many a dark and frowning sky, and weighed down under many a heavy shower, at length it is ripened—is gathered, and housed safe from every danger: So your now imperfect graces will then attain the summit of their growth, and be advanced to nobler services in a better world. Ye shall see God, shall serve him and enjoy him without an intervening vail, an interrupted moment, or the possibility of an end. Faith shall be crowned with victory; hope, with enjoyment; and love, with everlasting delight. In a word, the report of salvation shall then be realized, exceeded, and the blessing possessed. Eternity! a glorious eternity in all its unmeasured ages, will be employed in unfolding, explaining, and enjoying the contents of this great, this significant word SALVATION. On earth it is waited for, in heaven possessed.

From this subject,

1. Learn to reflect upon the death of the righteous. "Mark the perfect man, and behold the upright, for the end of that man is peace." His life was an honour to the doctrine he professed, and his death is a confirmation that there is a reality in religion. What can the world do for its votary when death comes to lay its cold hand upon him? It retires, withdraws all its charms and all its deluding hopes in a moment, and leaves him to grapple with the King of terrors alone.

alone. Not so religion; it steps forward with its friendly aid; it supports him with its comforts in a sinking hour, and shews that precious in the sight of the Lord is the death of his saints.

2. Who would not wish to be in such a frame as *Jacob* was, when he comes to die? It was not peculiar to *Balaam* to wish to die the death of the righteous, and that the last end may be like his. There are two seasons in which the wicked envy the lot of the righteous, viz. when upon their dying bed, and when, like the rich man in the parable, they shall behold their height of happiness from the gulph of misery. At other seasons they are despised—their life is accounted madness and folly: But if ye would wish to have your lot with them at the last, then let them at present be honoured with your approbation and company. Better to take up religion with all its crosses now, than sink at last under the reproaches of your own consciences, and the curses of the Almighty.

3. Examine whether there be a reasonable ground to hope that, when ye come to die, *Jacob's* case will be your case. Consider your latter end—inquire into the state of your souls—learn to die daily—and so to number your days as to apply your hearts unto wisdom. Live in the daily exercise of faith on, and expectation of, this salvation. The wicked

wicked shall be driven away in his wickedness, but the righteous hath hope in his death.

4. There is a close connection between the work of God in the soul and that salvation, which he hath prepared for his people in eternity. He will not forsake the work of his own hands, but will crown it with honour. *Jacob*, you see, could appeal to God as his witness, respecting what had been the frame and disposition of his soul—and God crowned the hope which he had planted and preserved in his soul. He crowned it with salvation. In his hands may we be found living and dying for *Jesus Christ's* sake. *Amen.*

SERMON

SERMON XI.

Hypocrisy exposed.

PROVERBS xxv. 14.

Whoso boasteth himself of a false gift, is like clouds and wind without rain.

THESE words are descriptive of characters almost as common as various, and as flattering in their appearances, but as deceitful in reality as the image by which they are here represented. They, for a season, raise the hopes of those who are most dependent on them, but soon disappoint their expectation. In the present degenerate state of human nature, time and circumstances frequently make it but too evident that men were not what we once took them to be; and he must be almost as great a stranger in the world as the Disciples supposed their unknown Lord to be in *Jerusalem,* who is not already convinced of this. Deeds, bonds, and receipts are required by men in their dealings one with another to guard against fraud and deception. But why? The plain fact is, that the more knowing men are in general, the more suspicion increases, and every precaution is found necessary to guard against imposition. The world is become a mere masquerade; characters are assumed, appearances are put on, and almost every man walks in a vain shew. The seeds of deception are scattered far and wide, and we have hypocrites not only in religious concerns, but in civil affairs likewise. The world has its hypocrites as well as the church. Almost every week's Gazette holds up to public view a number of insolvents, and some no doubt on account of their appearing to be what they really were not. The professions of their lips, and the fair figure they made in life for a season, imposed upon the unwary; but at length the visor dropped, the bailiff entered, the shop was closed, and their name inrolled in the list of bankrupts.

Should any suspect that we transgress the limits of our province in these remarks, there are two things we wish such to notice: The *first* is, that the subject before us is a *proverb*, which, in the general, is full as applicable to the civil as to the religious concerns of men: And, *secondly*, our desire is at all times to point out the degeneracy and depravity of human nature, that men may see the necessity there is for the interposition of a Saviour, and that they must be renewed in the spirit of their minds. The daily conduct of numbers is at once a comment upon, and a confirmation of, of, what the scripture says of man's fallen state; and he that denies this fact seems at once to have closed the eyes both of his mind and of his body. He equally disregards what God says and what men are doing. In words, perhaps, he expatiates upon the dignity of human nature; while they, by their works, are gainsaying what he affirms.

It is no doubt an evidence of sound wisdom to give diligence to know the state of our worldly affairs, much more so in concerns of higher importance. The form of godliness may be assumed by persons who are destitute of its power. There may be a profession of religion where the real principle of it never existed. Some may pretend to stand high in God's favour to whom he will one day say, Depart from me, I know you not. Many who appeared to begin in the spirit have awfully concluded in the flesh. It becomes us, therefore, to maintain a godly jealousy; frequently to examine ourselves whether we be in the faith, and sincerely to refer ourselves to the judgment of him who seeth not as man seeth, and who is as incapable of deceiving any as he is of being deceived. Let us ever keep this in mind, that *whoso boasteth himself of a false gift, is like clouds and wind without rain.*

We may compare a proverb to a curious piece of cut glass suspended in the midst of a large company, and which presents different objects

objects to the several eyes that are directed to it; so a proverb is an object to which different men may look, and from which they may receive instruction, both in their civil and their religious concerns.—But to attend more particularly to the sentence now before us, *Whoso boasteth himself of a false gift, is like clouds and wind without rain.*——In doing this, let us consider,

I. The persons here described.
II. The image by which they are represented. And
III. The instruction or improvement which we should draw from it.

I. *The persons here described,* are those who *boast* themselves *of a false gift.* We pretend not to say whether the sacred penman refers here to persons who pretend that they have it in their power, and that it is their intention to confer something upon others, but in the event prove false to their proposals—or whether he refers to persons who profess really to have attained what they never possessed: However under each of these are to be found characters which claim some attention.

1. There are persons who not only boast that it is in their power, but profess that it is both their desire and intention to lay themselves out for the benefit of others, particularly for their country——their friends——or their

their God, who eventually make it appear that they boasted themselves of a false gift.

The conduct of Statesmen in particular is full to the purpose: Those who have attained the summit of power, are, by their opponents, who envy their situation, represented as inimical to the interest of their country, unfriendly to the rights of men, and aiming at the downfal of liberty, or at the establishment of despotism; while they themselves profess to have no interest at heart but the cause of liberty and of the people. *Absalom*-like, their cry is, O that I were judge in *Israel*, then would I do so and so; but let their ambition be gratified; advance them to the honours which they aspire after, and they also in their turn give ground to conclude, that they seek their own, not the welfare of the community. The event makes it evident, that they had not the power or inclination which they pretended, since they have failed in the performance of that which they had so liberally promised. In profession all are patriots, but few are such in principle and practice. Honour, or affluence, or power is the object of their ambition. This representation is but too evidently confirmed in real life, and the lesson deducible from it is this: " Truft not in men for they will deceive you: Lean not on an arm of flesh:" Remember and rejoice, that it is an invisible power which supports the state, guards

our

our liberties, and defends our perfons and properties. Few periods have made it more evident than that in which we live, that in politics men *boaſt themſelves of a falſe gift*.

And is there not fomething fimilar to this to be found in domeſtic concerns? An imprudent parent, for inſtance, trains up his children as if they were to be heirs to thouſands: The effect of fuch a conduct is, their expectations are raifed, an air of fuperiority is aſſumed, till death arrives, and with one hand removes the parent, while, with the other, it prefents difappointment to his poſterity. In fome inſtances, whole families have been fupported for years, by the expectations which have been raifed by fome rich relation. Fair profeſſions have given birth to hope, and have fupported it when produced; till at laſt an imaginary flight has turned the tide of favour, and changed his delufive fmiles into frowns; or probably death, by executing his office, has at once expofed the true circumſtances of the honoured relation, and evidenced that he boaſted himſelf of a falfe gift. His removal cloaths their perfons with fable, and fills their fouls with difappointment.——Hence learn not to truſt in uncertain riches; but by faith and prayer confign all your concerns to the paternal care of the living God. Such ſhall not be fed with delufive hopes; for they that truſt in him ſhall not be confounded:

Their

Their bread shall be given, and their water shall be sure. No real good will he withhold from them. Such shall be kept in perfect peace, whose minds are stayed upon him, because they trust in him. He will honour the confidence they place in him. Their hope shall not make them ashamed; but the God they wait for, and rely on, will do for them exceeding abundantly above all that they can ask or think.

The same remark holds good in the professions which some people make, respecting the great concerns of God and their souls. They pretend to have a peculiar reverence and respect for religion, and the discoveries and hopes it affords: They readily acknowledge that it is the duty and interest of every man to be concerned for the everlasting safety and happiness of his soul: They assure you that they have very good dispositions this way themselves, and that they feel very strong desires to give more attention to these things than they hitherto have done. Were they but disengaged from such an employment; would Divine Providence but indulge them so far as to raise them above anxious care, or bestow upon them the conveniences and comforts of life, then they would more openly devote themselves to God, and evidence the regard they have for the interests of religion. They assent to all that you can say upon this head as very right, and wish you to believe that it is not the want of a principle

ciple to love and serve God that hinders them; but the want of opportunity. Perhaps the season arrives when their desire is granted; they have all that heart can reasonably wish; but the event proves that they boasted themselves of a false gift. Their hearts remain as strongly attached to the world as ever, and as much estranged from God. They are as cold, as careless, as carnal as before. The business of the world is pursued with the same avidity, and the care of the soul as much neglected, as when they professed only to want the opportunity. But do such at present want either opportunity, obligation, or argument? None of these: The evidence is full and decided against them, that they have boasted themselves of a false gift. Their hearts were never really divorced from the word, or united to the Lord. Thus we fear in a variety of cases, similar to that which has been mentioned, thousands put the awful cheat upon themselves, and endeavour to impose upon others likewise. They purpose much—they promise fair; but their resolutions, like the opening blossoms in the spring, fall to the ground, and leave the tree that bore them in a state of barrenness. Are we now addressing ourselves to any of this character? Ye have pretended, it may be, to fix the time, or to mark out the situation in life when ye would yield yourselves and your services to God. That time

time is paſt, and that condition is attained; but have ye kept your promiſe? Has the engagement been performed? Do ye live as thoſe who are born from above, and who really deſire to preſs into the kingdom of heaven? Inſtead of this being the caſe, probably ye are carnal, ſtrangers to ſerious converſe with God, and unmindful of a future ſtate. All the buſtle you have made about your good principles and ſolemn purpoſes have been but empty boaſtings of falſe gifts. The plain fact is, ye never loved God from the heart; for had ye done that, ye could not have lived thus long without him. Ye never knew the real precioufneſs of *Jeſus Chriſt*, otherwiſe ye had long ere this renounced all as droſs and dung for the excellency of the knowledge of him. Ye never yet ſaw, in a proper light, the dignity, the value, the infinite worth of your ſouls, and the things that relate to your everlaſting peace, or ye could not have trifled with them in the manner ye have done, and ſtill continue to do. Depend upon it, while this is the caſe, whatever convictions ye may have known, ye were never really converted to God. Whatever ſtrong reſolutions ye may have formed, ye were never ſincere in them. Brethren, it is high time for you to conſider how long ye have been deceiving yourſelves. The man who knows what ought to be done, and yet remains inattentive to his preſent duty and unconcerned about it, is more criminal than thofe who are wholly ignorant and thoughtlefs. Convictions flighted will render condemnation much more awful; and that man who thinks he is fomething when he is nothing, is a double cheat. He impofes upon himfelf as well as others.

But while there are fome who profefs to have both the power and the intention of doing good to others, or of caufing their light to fhine before men, there are others,

2. Who profefs that they have attained what they really never poffeffed: And what is this but boafting themfelves of a falfe gift?

Such are they who make a great fhow, in order to appear what they are not, and thus impofe upon them who judge from appearances. Thofe of you who are converfant with bufinefs, frequently meet with perfons of this character, and therefore we need fay the lefs about them.

But is it not truly affecting, that fuch cheats fhould be found in the religious, as well as in the commercial world? Only converfe with thefe people, and you are amazed at their attainments in religious knowledge. You appear to yourfelves meer dwarfs compared with them, and are overpowered with aftonifhment and confufion in their prefence. They are able to explain all the doctrines of the gofpel with propriety, and vindicate them
with

with the most substantial arguments. Probably *Judas* was capable of all this; for he went forth with the other Apostles to preach the gospel, and was not in the least suspected of hypocrisy by any of his brethren; even when their master declared that one of their number should betray him, every one of them suspected himself, rather than the real traitor. In every age there is reason to fear that many who seem rich in gifts, increased in knowledge, and in want of nothing, are, notwithstanding, miserable and poor, and blind and naked. With men they have a name to live; but in the sight of God they are dead. And fair as their profession may be to the eye, they are destitute of the power of vital and practical godliness. Like *Israel*, " they flatter with the mouth, and lie to God with their tongues; but their hearts are not right with him, neither are they stedfast in his covenant *." Such appears to have been the condition of the foolish virgins: They associated with the wise, united with them in the profession of the same faith, and had every appearance of being influenced by the same expectations of the bridegroom's coming: What the one did, the other did; and where those went, these were found. The wise discovered not the least suspicion of the sincerity of their companions; nay, the foolish themselves, in the end seem greatly disappointed. They were deceived—they were undone.

* Psalm lxxviii. 36, 37.

undone. Awful event! it proved that they had mistaken gifts for grace, and had put their profession of faith in the place of the religion of the heart. Their creed stands charged with no errors; but their hearts were not right with God. With the mouth they made confession of their hopes of salvation; but, when the Lord came, it appeared that they had not believed unto righteousness. And what was such a profession but boasting of a false gift? They were all the time disguised hypocrites; and the deception was such, as not only to impose upon others, but themselves also. They do not appear to have entertained any doubt respecting either their present sincerity or their future safety. They were very confident of the goodness of their state, and expressed themselves in the language of the most unshaken assurance. They professed that they loved *Jesus Christ*; and, what is more affecting, they seem really to have thought that their state was safe; but all the time they were boasting themselves of a false gift. Let him that thinketh he standeth, beware that he fall not at last as they did. Gifts may shine upon earth—may be admired by men—and may deceive the possessors; but they will be detected in the close of life. The door will be shut, and the deceiver refused admittance into heaven. But we proceed,

II. To

II. To attend to *the image by which such persons are represented.* They are *like clouds and wind without rain.* The Apostle *Jude* speaks of some in his day, who made a great profession of religion, and were far from being suspected of hypocrisy; yet he represents them also in the language of the text, *as clouds without water carried about with winds**. The image is not more natural than it is common. Specious and hopeful as the prospect may be, it terminates in disappointment. How often have we observed the clouds hanging over our heads, loaded with the treasures that adorn the earth and make it fruitful, apparently ready to pour down that liquid life which gives beauty to the flower, and maturity to our fruits; but in the moment of expectation the winds have risen, have driven the clouds before them, leaving the earth exposed without a shade to screen it from the heat of the sun, or a shower to refresh it when thirsty.—The persons here described, like these clouds, have no command over themselves: They are hurried along before the blast of every temptation; ever about to do good, but never attaining that which they purpose, till, perhaps at length, death bears them intirely away from our view for ever. In themselves they were all promise, all appearance; and in others, they raised hopes which were blasted by the disappointment. How fully is the image of some of the hearers

* Jude, ver. 12.

hearers of the Gospel represented in this glass. The horizon of the religious world is at some seasons almost covered over with these deceitful clouds, but, alas, they come to nothing. Their appearance excites our hopes; their promises encourage our expectations for a time; but temptations scatter them, or death cuts them off and all our hopes concerning them. How necessary therefore to be regarded is the counsel of the Apostle *James*, " Be ye doers of the word, and not hearers only, deceiving your ownselves: For if any be a hearer of the word, and not a doer, he is like unto a man beholding his natural face in a glass; for he beholdeth himself, and goeth his way, and straightway forgetteth what manner of man he was. But whoso looketh into the perfect law of liberty, and continueth therein, he being not a forgetful hearer, but a doer of the work, this man shall be blessed in his deed." * The gift which such a man has is genuine, and the graces he discovers are true. By receiving grace he will desire to serve God acceptably, with reverence and godly fear: His faith will be productive of good fruit, and his purposes will issue in performance. Instead of boasting himself of a false gift, he will be humble and faithful in the possession of that which is true.—Let us now,

III. Endeavour to deduce *the instruction and improvement which this subject holds forth*.

* James i. 22——25.

The

The lessons to be learned from it are various, and we need to have them frequently inculcated upon our minds: For instance, this subject tends,

1. Much to evince and confirm the doctrine of scripture, with respect to the depravity of the human heart. A Prophet assures us, that it is *deceitful,* and deceitful *above all things;* that it is *wicked—desperately* wicked; yea, so desperately wicked, that *none but God* can either *know it* or cure it. What various forms of deceit can the heart of man put on! What fraud can it conceal under the fair professions of friendship; and what vile lusts under the inchanting mask of love! This we see exemplified in the narrative of *Amnon* and *Tamar.** How are men continually deceived, or deceiving one another, by fair proposals, by specious appearances, or by solemn promises. Though few will acknowledge the heart to be so bad as the scripture represents it, yet when they come to trade and barter one with another, almost all men discover the fullest conviction of its truth. The suspicious language and guarded conduct of the buyer, prove what are his views of men; he fears an imposition: But such is the depravity of man's heart that it is capable not only of imposing upon others, but upon himself. Thousands, it is to be feared, have been cheated

* 2 Sam. xiii.

cheated for ever by this worst of all deceivers: And in the parable of the virgins, out of ten professors, our Lord has represented this to be the case with five. Let all who name the name of *Christ* look well to themselves—examine your hearts with an honest diligence——be impartial in your dealings in this important business; and, after all, seriously refer yourselves to the judgment of that God who searcheth the heart and trieth the reins of the children of men. Be concerned to know your true state and your real character. Beware of self-deception; and, as ye value the happiness of your souls, be diligent that ye may be found of God in peace, without spot and blameless. Apply to God with the Psalmist, " to search you and try your hearts, to prove you, and know your thoughts, to see if there be any way of wickedness in you, and lead you in the way everlasting."

2. This subject, properly considered, has a tendency to call off our trust from creatures, and from all undue dependence on them. The language of it in effect is this, Cease ye from man whose breath is in his nostrils, for wherein is he to be accounted of. It clearly discovers the egregious folly of leaning upon any arm of flesh, or building our hopes upon those mutable prospects or delusive promises that frail mortals, like ourselves,

selves, may hold out to us. Men may deceive and difappoint you; but if God be the foundation of your truſt and dependence, he neither can nor will. Men have nothing, are nothing, can do nothing, without him. Glorious as is the natural fun, it ſhines but by his power and permiſſion.——He gives the light, or he veils it as he pleaſes: Bright as is the preſent hour, the next may be overſpread with clouds; fo it is with men, they ſhine to-day, they die to-morrow. This hour the lamp of profeſſion burns clear, probably the next the blaze goes out for ever. Theſe things, however, are not mentioned to make you fuſpicious or cenforious reſpecting others: No, every one that knows himſelf will account others better than himſelf, and put the moſt favourable conſtruction upon their conduct: But we muſt all ſtand before the judgment-feat of *Chriſt*, and then ſhall characters appear to be what they really are.

3. It is likewiſe evident from what has been ſaid that gifts, unleſs accompanied with grace to improve them, are not to be coveted. To others they be profitable; but if they tend to elate and puff up the poſſeſſors, they are exceedingly dangerous. We may be ambitious to pray with the fame degree of correctneſs and fluency that we admire in another, or to ſhine as much in converſation upon the moſt intereſting ſubjects; but let us remember

member with *Paul*, that though we have all knowledge, speak like Angels, or work miracles, if destitute of love to God, we are but a sounding brass and tinkling cymbal. Though gifts be the gold which adorns and beautifies the temple, grace is the temple that sanctifies the gift. Better is it by far to feel the impression and savour of divine truth in the heart, than to be able to make the most lively representation of it with our lips. Covet earnestly then the best gifts, that your faith may be sincere, your knowledge influential, your comforts well founded, your experience solid, and your hopes purifying. Rest not in the externals of religion; but be concerned to grow in grace, to make progress in the divine life, and to be, as it were, absorbed in love to God, and humility before him. Let your ornament be that of a meek and quiet spirit, which is in God's sight of great price. He resisteth the proud, but giveth grace to the humble. The *Pharisee*, when dressed up in all his imaginary excellencies, was rejected, while the poor humbled *Publican* was graciously approved and accepted.

4. This subject, while it tends to expose the folly of dissimulation and hypocrisy, recommends and exalts a principle of sincerity in our dealings, both with God and with men. Remember that all things are naked and

and open to him with whom ye have to do: He seeth not as man seeth, for man looketh on the outward appearance, but the Lord judgeth the heart.——Let then the approbation of God be what ye aim at——and in your dealings with men let integrity and uprightness preserve you.

5. This subject demands both humility and thankfulness from those who have been made partakers of the best of gifts.——What have such but what they have received? Ye are debtors to grace, and cannot honour God more than ingenuously to acknowledge it.—— *Paul* did so, when he declared that by the grace of God he was what he was. Rich as he was in gifts, in knowledge, in usefulness, he attributed it all to grace. Grace shone in him, and through him.——Grace wrought by him and was honoured in his doctrine and life. And are ye made partakers of *Jesus Christ*, of the heavenly gift and calling? What will you render to the Lord, or how will you shew forth the praises of him who hath called you to glory and virtue?——O honour him in your walk——honour him by your conversation and conduct, for herein is your Father glorified that ye bring forth much fruit. Adorn the doctrine of God your Saviour, and shew that the grace of God which bringeth salvation, teacheth you to deny ungodliness and worldly lusts, and to live

live foberly, righteoufly, and godly in the world. Truft in God —triumph in Chrift— and look for falvation: And at laft may we appear to be God's workmanfhip, created in *Chrift* unto good works, and partakers of the heavenly gift, for *Jefus'* fake. *Amen.*

SERMON

SERMON XII.

Gospel Visitations.

ACTS xv. 14.

Simeon *hath declared how God at the first did visit the* Gentiles, *to take out of them a people for his name.*

THE nature of the Gospel, and the design of its being dispensed among a people, are often too little regarded by numbers who statedly attend under it. These words are therefore chosen to shew you—that God has an *end* in sending the Gospel to a people.——That was his end in sending this Gospel to the *Gentiles at first*, is the end which he has *always* in view, and has *now* in sending it to you——and that God's end in this *is always* answered; for the word shall not return to him void, but shall accomplish his pleasure, and prosper in the thing whereunto he sends it.——The end we are informed which God has to accomplish by the Gospel is, to select a people for himself, and thereby to get eternal honour to his name.

The

The words now read as the foundation of our present discourse, are part of the speech delivered by the Apostle *James* in the church of *Jerusalem*.—The occasion which led to it, we are informed, was this: *Paul* and *Barnabas* having continued a considerable time at *Antioch*, endeavouring to confirm the souls of the Disciples in their adherence to *Jesus Christ* and his Gospel, at length a particular circumstance occurred, which not only gave them much uneasiness, but was the means of considerable confusion in that church: Certain judaizing teachers coming down from *Judea* got amongst the members of the church, and boldly asserted, that except they were circumcised after the manner of *Moses*, they could not be saved, *ver.* 1.—From this we remark, that there is a great propensity in the mind of men to look upon mere circumstantials as matters necessary to salvation. By thus magnifying the apparent importance of these circumstantials, the minds even of good men have often been much diverted for a season from subjects of far greater moment; and further, that bigotry always carries a narrow soul.

Paul and *Barnabas* immediately set themselves to oppose these intruders, and to defend the cause of Christian liberty; but as the case was of so delicate a nature, and apparently affected the eternal interests of a great number of that community who had been

been converted from among the *Gentiles*, they prudently resolved to send some of their own number with *Barnabas* and *Paul* to the church at *Jerusalem*, expressly to learn their sentiments upon a subject of such magnitude, *ver.* 2.

As a mark of respect and affection to these venerable messengers, many of the church accompany them a part of their journey. As their road lay through a part of *Phœnicia* and *Samaria*, they declared to all the christians which they met with in every town and city as they passed along, the power of that grace which had been displayed in the conversion of the *Gentiles, ver.* 3. " They caused great joy unto all the brethren."—Here remark— That the conversion of souls to God is a great work.—That work in which the glory of God is much concerned.—And the report of which will always be matter of great joy to all those who sincerely desire to promote the honour of God and the good of men.

Being arrived at *Jerusalem*, they are received with all due respect by the whole body, especially by the Apostles and the Elders of the church. They proceed to give them a general narrative of their travels through *Cyprus, Pamphylia, Pisidia,* and *Lycaonia*, and of all that God had wrought by them, for the honour of his name in those parts, *ver.* 4.

But scarce are they arrived in *Jerusalem*, and even before they have the opportunity to lay the subject of their embassy before the church, they find the same troublesome sentiment begin to operate even there also. Several persons, who, having been converted from the sect of the Pharisees, and joined in fellowship with that church, remarked that, though they greatly rejoiced in the conversion of such numbers from amongst the *Gentiles*, yet they apprehended it needful to circumcise them, and to command them to keep the law of *Moses*, ver. 5. Probably neither the time, nor the warmth of temper discovered by some, would suffer the subject to be fully discussed at that season; the meeting is therefore adjourned for the present, and a time fixed for them to assemble again, to examine more fully into the case.

The appointed season being arrived, the church, with the Apostles and Elders, assemble together. After some debate, *Peter* rises, and freely delivers his sentiments upon the subject thus, " Men and brethren, ye know how that a good while ago God made choice among us, that the *Gentiles* by my mouth should hear the word of the gospel, and believe. And God, which knoweth the hearts, bare them witness, giving them the Holy Ghost, even as he did unto us; and put no difference between us and them, purifying their hearts by faith. Now, therefore, why tempt ye God, to put a yoke upon the neck of the disciples, which neither our fathers nor

nor we were able to bear? But we believe that, through the grace of the Lord *Jesus Christ*, we shall be saved even as they*." He saw, and openly professed, 1. That they that were saved were saved *by Grace*.—Consequently, 2. Not by their observance of the law or rituals of *Moses*.—And 3. That the grace of *Christ* was so abundant, that it was sufficient for the believing *Gentiles*, as well as believing *Jews*.

Peter having closed his speech, solemn silence pervades the whole church, while *Barnabas* and *Paul* repeat again what God had wrought by their instrumentality among the *Gentiles*; probably adding what gave occasion to their present visit to the church of *Jerusalem* †.—Their narrative being ended, *James*, who, some say, was pastor of that church, addresses the assembly upon the same subject, endeavouring to corroborate what *Peter* had before delivered, *Men and brethren, hearken unto me*, Simeon *hath declared how God at the first did visit the* Gentiles, *to take out a people for his name*, &c. From these words we are led to consider the three following things:

 I. The idea under which the preaching of the gospel is here held forth, viz. *As a visit from God*.
 II. The particular intent of this visit, *To take out a people* for himself.

III. The

* Ver. 7—11.——† Ver. 12.

III. The *principle* from which he acts, and the *end* at which he aims in this. It is *for* the honour of *his name*.

The first part of our proposed method is to consider,

I. *The idea under which the preaching of the gospel is here set forth*, "A visit from God." *God*, faith *James, hath visited the Gentiles*. This visit was — by the ministry of his servants — intirely of his grace — with the kindest intentions towards that people — and a visit which is long since over. On each of these particulars we shall dwell more fully in our meditations.

1. Introductory to a visit from persons of any eminence, it is common to send a servant to make known the intention of the visitant. Thus *Paul* and *Barnabas*, in the case before us, had been sent, as servants of the God of grace and salvation, to make known to the *Gentiles* his purpose and pleasure. By their doctrine they were preparing the way for that visit of salvation which the Lord intended to make to the habitations and hearts of this people. They exhorted them to turn from dumb idols, and to adore the living and true God. Their work was not only to prepare the way, but, by their preaching, the Lord prepared a people for his name. And their very appearance in a place was an intimation of intended mercy, and that God had a
people

people in that place to visit with his salvation. Had it been that God had *none* to visit at that place, or if it was not his design to visit them *at that season*, it is more than probable that he would not have sent his servants to them at that time: On the contrary, from what we shall have occasion to remark presently, there is ground to conclude that he would have prevented it. As the morning star therefore ushers in the day, so these Apostles, who indeed were stars in the Lord's hand wherever they appeared, intimated, that the Sun of Righteousness was about to rise, and the day of that people's salvation was at hand. They were messengers of glad tidings, who published peace, and invited sinners to be reconciled to God.

My brethren, you have not these Apostles; but we intreat you to consider these things with some degree of application to yourselves. This is the day of your visitation. The ministers of the gospel are as much under the guidance of a special providence *now* as the Apostles were formerly. They do not come unsent. They appear to inform you, that God is now engaged in the gracious design of reconciling sinners to himself, by *Jesus Christ*, not imputing their trespasses to them. They exhort you to stir up yourselves to lay hold upon the grace which is now brought nigh, and to pay a proper regard to that dispensation of mercy which has visited you. Men and

and brethren, to you is the word of this falvation fent. It is not faid *brought*, left you fhould fuppofe that our appearance amongft you is by the will of man; but this report is *fent* to you by the fpecial appointment and providence of the great God. We appear not in our own name, or on a bufinefs which concerns our own perfonal intereft or advantage only; but, as meffengers from the great Lord of all, we appear to publifh his will, his purpofe, his claims. And as *Jefus Chrift*, while he was here upon earth, fent his difciples, two and two, into every city and village whither he himfelf would come; fo we have to affure you, that this day of great privileges is the feafon in which God draws near to feparate a people for himfelf. Solemn thought! O that every individual amongft you would give it the attention it deferves. This is the feafon in which God comes forth to felect and diftinguifh the happy men, who fhall be honoured to have fellowfhip with him in his heavenly palace for eternal ages. My brethren, it is not a concern of fmall importance what fort of attention you pay to this gofpel. He that heareth the fervant, honoureth the mafter; and he that flights the meffage, infults him that fent it. Thofe who open their hearts to give God entrance, honour the report, and fhall receive the end of their faith in the falvation of their fouls; but he that flights the meffage bars his heart

against

against God, and adjudges himself unworthy of a visit of salvation; and there can be no neutrality in this case, you must either receive or reject the proposal; for this gospel will be the favour of life to life, or of death to death in all that hear it.

2. The visit which God here afforded these *Gentiles*, as indeed all future visits from him, originate intirely with him, and proceed from his mere grace. He manifests himself to those who inquired not after him, and frequently comes without an invitation from his creatures. There are set times to favour particular nations, or parts of those nations; and when the set time is come, he, who reserves the times and seasons in his own hand, opens the channel for the conveyance of the blessing to them. This great shepherd knows *where* to seek his sheep, *when* to look after them, and by what means or instruments to restore, or bring them safe to the eternal fold. Many attempts have been made by good men, yea, even by the Apostles themselves, in some cases, to *force,* if I may so speak, a visit upon a people. Their intention in this, without dispute, was good, and the attempt had something laudable and commendable in it; but such methods have seldom, if ever, proved successful in the event. We find even *Paul* and *Timothy*, on a particular occasion, ready to run unsent, but their master interposed to prevent it. The sacred historian

historian informs us, " When they had gone throughout *Phrygia* and the region of *Galatia*, they were forbidden of the Holy Ghost to preach the word in *Asia*, after they were come to *Mysia*, they assayed to go into *Bithynia*; but the spirit suffered them not*." But it is more frequently otherwise. *Moses* we find was unwilling to go to *Israel*, when God commanded him to announce his purposed visit of salvation to them: *Isaiah* also did not discover the greatest readiness in the day of his commission: And in the case here particularly alluded to, viz. *Peter's* first visit to the *Gentiles*, we all know with what difficulty he was brought to comply with the orders of his Master. A vision must prepare him—an express command must be given him—and, after all, he seems to go about the work with much diffidence and apparent reluctance.

And why has God visited these nations? Why honoured the place of our residence, and at this season, with the gracious dispensation of his mind and will? Has he been found by none who inquired not after him? Has he dealt so with every people, as with the people of this kingdom? Or with every place, as with the inhabitants of this town? O to regard the day of our privilege, as the season of our merciful visitation!—Visits of salvation always originate with God. They are intirely of his grace.

* Acts xvi. 6, 7.

3. The

3. The visit here mentioned was accompanied with the kindest intentions towards that people.——It was to open a correspondence between him and them, which was to last for ever.——To make himself known to them, that they might be enriched with his saving benefits. Before the Apostles were sent to this people, they were without God, without *Christ*, without hope, aliens from the commonwealth of *Israel*, and strangers to the covenants of promise. These Apostles were sent to turn them from darkness to light, and from Satan unto God, that they might receive forgiveness of sins, and an inheritance among all them that are sanctified by faith in *Christ Jesus*. In the nature of things it could not be otherwise; for " How could they call on him, in whom they had not believed? And how could they believe in him, of whom they had not heard? And how should they hear without a preacher? And how should they preach except they were sent * ?" Thus God *sends* ministers, as we have seen, by his special providence.——These ministers are to *preach the gospel*, that is, *Jesus Christ*, and salvation by him.——This gospel is to be *heard* with attention, meekness, and reverence.——This hearing is to introduce or increase the *knowledge* of God and his *Christ*.——This knowledge is to support, nourish, and exercise *faith*.——And that faith turns

* Rom. x. 14.

turns the key of all the promises, institutions, purposes, and providences of God, and *introduces* the soul to the enjoyment of all their important treasures. This, therefore, "is life eternal, to know the only true God and *Jesus Christ* whom he hath sent. And to this knowledge we are introduced by the gospel, and by the gospel this knowledge is still increased. To convert the thoughtless——to pardon the guilty——to instruct the ignorant——to strengthen the weak——to sanctify the impure——and to fill the empty with all the fulness of God: In a word; to bless men upon earth, and to guide them safe to heaven.——These are some of the kind intentions of God, when he visits a people with the dispensation of the gospel.—But, Sirs, have ye these evidences in yourselves, that this gospel has thus visited you? Has it illumined your darkness, subdued your prejudices, captivated your hearts, filled your souls with joy and peace in believing, that ye might abound in hope through the power of the Holy Ghost? Has it come to you not as the word of man, but of God, in power, in demonstration of the spirit, and in much assurance? We add once more,

4. God's visits to those places, to which the Apostle *James* here alludes, are long since over. It was a visit——a gracious visit. But remember it was only a visit. There was

was a very flourishing church at *Antioch*, the city from which *Paul* and *Barnabas* had been sent upon this occasion, which continued for a long time. The famous *Chrysostom* preached in this place in the fourth century. But since that the candlestick has been removed. The place has been convulsed by frequent earthquakes, taken by the *Saracens*, and destroyed by fire. There is now no church at *Antioch*—no city remains— only an heap of ruins sufficient to point out the place which God once visited with the gospel.

Brethren, the day of our merciful visitation will likewise have an end. When God has filled up his purposes, and the inhabitants of this nation and place have filled up the measure of their iniquity, the gracious visitant will withdraw: But wo unto a place and people, when the Lord departeth from them. When he goes, all good retires with him, and the passage is left open for every desolating judgment to enter. To some of us, who are now under the gospel, it may prove a very short visit: Death may soon call upon you and me to quit the sanctuary, and to take up our abode in the darkness of the grave. Be careful, therefore, to improve the opportunities you have. Seek the Lord while he may be found; be willing to learn while he is waiting to teach, and ask of him while he is ready to confer his favours upon those who are unworthy of them. Say to the heavenly visitant, as *Jacob* did upon another occasion, " I will not let thee go, except thou bless me."—Thus having considered the dispensation of the gospel under the idea of a visit from God, we go on,

II. To attend to *the particular intent of the visit*, viz. "To take out a people *for himself.* Here we remark,

1. That this gospel is to be proclaimed and published indefinitely *to all* that come under the dispensation of it. Thus the commission runs. Go out into all the world and preach the gospel to every creature. Ministers are to be as free and liberal in this dispensation, as the clouds are in dropping rain. Every drop is under a divine direction, even what falls upon the ground which bringeth forth thorns and briers, shall, in the event, produce a sweet favour to God. Our commission is to men—to men as sinners—and the sum of it is to proclaim salvation to them. " As *Moses* lifted up the serpent in the wilderness, even so must the Son of man be lifted up: That whosoever believeth in him, should not perish, but have eternal life. For God so loved the world, that he gave his only begotten Son, that whosoever believeth in him, should not perish, but have everlasting life. For God sent not his Son into the world to condemn the world; but that the world through him might be saved *." Eventually there may be found some rejecters of the gospel amongst you.

* John iii. 14—17.

you. However, we have authority now to say, "Men and brethren, to you is the word of this salvation sent," and, " all that believe in *Jesus Christ* are now justified from all things from which we could not be justified by the law of *Moses*. Beware, therefore, left that come upon you which is spoken of in the Prophets, Behold, ye despisers, and wonder, and perish; for I work a work in your days, a work which ye shall in no wise believe, though a man declare it unto you *." The only remedy is now proclaimed and published among you.

2. The intent of this gospel being preached, is to make a separation for God. He has promised to bear testimony to the word of his grace, that it shall not return to him void, but accomplish that for which he hath appointed it. This gospel is the grand instrument of separating the church from the world. It always has been so from the first day in which it was published, and will be so to the end. In all places where this is published, men arrange themselves in the view of that God who seeth their hearts, according to their proper and respective characters. They that believe, take their side, and they who do not believe, take theirs. Mixed as this assembly is in our view; in the sight of God there is no confusion: There are amongst you believers and unbelievers.—The Lord is even now seeking out his friends, and separating the precious from the vile. Solemn thought!

* Acts xiii. 39, 40.

thought! The separation is now begun. It may not be altogether visible to us at present; partly through the exterior conformity of sinners, in this day of privileges; and partly through the many imperfections which still accompany the best of men; but that false covering will one day be removed. Then it will appear that God has been setting apart them that are godly for himself; and their godliness will be the evidence of it. And is it so, that this is the day in which the solemn separation is making? Then let each one put such questions as these to himself: Am I likely to be separated *for,* or *from* the Lord? To be distinguished as a favourite or as a foe? Have I believed—do I believe the report of the gospel, and believing it, do I fly for refuge to the hope which it sets before me? Do I approve of *Jesus Christ;* of his doctrine, his institution, his precepts, and his method of saving sinners? Or am I offended in him, and unmindful of it; Do I behold and believe in him as the wisdom of God and the power of God; or, is he as a root out of a dry ground, without form or comeliness in my esteem? Is it my desire not only to be pardoned, but saved from all mine iniquities, and to be sanctified in body, soul, and spirit; or, am I rolling sin as a sweet morsel under my tongue, and hating holiness at my heart? In fine, have I taken God to be my God—*Christ* for my treasure—the word

for

for my guide—holiness and heaven for my end; or, is the reverse of all this the case with me? Brethren, give diligence to make your calling and election sure, that at last you may be found of him in peace. Be earnest with the Lord to take away all your iniquity, and to sanctify you thoroughly.

3. The end of such visits God has always in his eye, and the event, with respect to him, is certain. This we are assured, that though many be called few are chosen; but God knows, with the greatest certainty, all the fruits and effects which will result from the preaching of the gospel in this, and in every other place. Hence we find, that when *Paul* first preached the gospel at *Corinth*, he was much opposed, the name of that *Jesus* whom he preached was blasphemed; a few indeed believed, but the major part of the people were quite averse to the gospel. While things wore this discouraging aspect, a vision appeared to him by night, saying, " Be not afraid, but speak and hold not thy peace; for I am with thee, and no man shall set on thee to hurt thee; for *I have much people in this city**. The Lord knoweth them that are his; and from the beginning knew who would believe, and who reject him and his benefits. His word cannot return to him void. His work is all before him, and he knows the souls which he has to visit with salvation during the continuance

* Acts xviii. 9, 10.

tinuance of the gospel in this place, town, and nation.—We add, once more,

4. Those who will be left at last, will be left without excuse. How inexcusable, suppose ye, will they be found who have attended to the gospel with no serious concern to know, understand, and profit by it! Neglecting so great a salvation, how can they escape, or excuse their inattention to it, and unconcernedness about it! Should any say, but how can they do otherwise? Is not faith the gift of God? It is; but we venture to pronounce those men inexcusable who do not endeavour to improve and profit by that conviction which arises from their own experience. We would say to such, you have attended long under the gospel, but it has been all in vain. Such will be your condition still without extraordinary aid. But how should you act upon this conviction, if you acted as reasonable men; yea as your very children would act in similar circumstances? What child, after trying and trying again at the request of a parent to lift some considerable weight, and all in vain, would not cry out for the parent's aid? And what parent would, in such case, withhold his assistance? But if " ye being evil, know how to give good gifts to your children—how much more will your heavenly Father give the Holy Spirit to them that ask it?"—But *Christ* pronounced those inexcusable who rejected him and his doctrine,

trine, and afferted that it would be more tolerable in the day of judgment for the inhabitants of *Tyre* and *Sidon*. We have the fentiment of eternal truth fully expreffed upon this head: " Becaufe I have called, and ye refufed; I have ftretched out my hand, and no man regarded; but ye have fet at nought all my counfel, and would none of my reproof; I alfo will laugh at your calamity: I will mock when your fear cometh—Then fhall they call upon me, but I will not anfwer; they fhall feek me early, but they fhall not find me. For that they hated knowledge, and did not chufe the fear of the Lord: Therefore fhall they eat of the fruit of their own ways, and be filled with their own devices*."——It yet remains that we confider,

III. The *principle* from which the Lord acts, and the *end* at which he aims in this. It is *for* the honour of *his name*. *He takes out of them a people for his name*. That is, he acts thus,

1. That he may have a people who fhall believe in, reft on, and honour the name of *Jefus Chrift*. Salvation is in none other; for " there is no other name under heaven given among men, whereby we muft be faved." The Lord has declared that he will caufe this name to be remembered unto all generations; therefore fhall the people praife him.

* Prov. i. 24—26, 29, 31.

him. Becaufe this *Jefus* made his foul an offering for fin, he fhall fee his feed, and the pleafure of the Lord fhall profper in his hand: He fhall fee of the travail of his foul, and fhall be fatisfied.

2. The name of the Lord is honoured in them, as they are his workmanfhip created in *Chrift Jefus.* The change effected in them is all of God, and intirely of his grace. It is he that has made them to differ from what they were formerly. He called, convinced, quickened them, and works in them both to will and to do of his own good pleafure. It is he that makes them willing in the day of his power, and fhews forth the riches of his grace in their juftification, adoption, prefervation, and fanctification. Are they adorned with the fruits of righteoufnefs: It is he that hath wrought all their works in them? The change he has been effecting upon the hearts of men from generation to generation, has been like the lighting up of fo many beacons one after another, to fhew men their danger and the remedy; and to evidence his care to guard them againft the one, and to excite them to attend to the other.

3. This feparation is made with a view to glorify his grace, power, and holinefs, in the pardon, prefervation, and falvation of the whole church: Thus runs the language of our pardoning God: " I will cleanfe them from all their iniquity, whereby they have finned

sinned against me, and I will pardon all their iniquities whereby they have sinned, and whereby they have transgressed against me. And it shall be to me a name of joy, a praise and an honour before all the nations of the earth, which shall hear all the good that I do unto them *. It is to the praise of the glory of his grace that we are made accepted in the beloved. He will come to be glorified in his saints, and to be admired in all them that believe. Then shall the church appear the fulness of him who filleth all in all."

To conclude. From this subject may we be led to bless and praise the Lord, that ever the separating wall was broken down between the *Jews* and the *Gentiles*. Long were the visitations of divine mercy continued with, and almost confined to, that people. But they grew proud of their peculiarity: They treated the heavenly visitant with ceremonious formality and indifference: At length they excluded him from their principal city, and with wicked hands they crucified the Lord of life and glory. He submitted to the indignity, but soon he revived to punish it. Their city was left to them desolate when he withdrew, soon after they were driven from it, and ever since have they been smarting under the marks of his just displeasure. He has now, for a long time, been going amongst the *Gentiles* to seek from amongst them

* Jer. xxxiii. 8, 9.

them a people for his name. By the ministry of the gospel he is come even unto you. Behold, he now waits to be gracious. He stands at the door and knocks, declaring that if any man hear his voice and open to him, he will come in and sup with him, and privilege that man to sup with himself. May we all be sensible of the grace discovered in the proposal, be disposed to receive the word with all readiness of mind, and this be the language of every one of us, " Lord remember me with the favour thou bearest to thy people, and visit me with thy salvation." Amen.

SERMON

SERMON XIII.

Profeſſing Chriſtians warned by the diſperſed *Jews*.

LAMENTATIONS i. 18.

The Lord is righteous, for I have rebelled againſt his commandment: Hear, I pray you all people, and behold my ſorrow: my virgins and my young men are gone into captivity.

IF we allow the government of *Jehovah* over the univerſe, and over man in particular, it is natural for us to conclude, that he can be at no loſs for means to convey his will and pleaſure to them as the ſubjects of his government: And as he *can,* it ſeems neceſſary in the very nature of things that he ſhould do it, ſeeing that where there is no law there can be no tranſgreſſion. The method that he takes to do this, we may conclude, will always be the moſt ſuitable to the ſeaſon or occaſion when it is revealed: For he who is infinite in underſtanding, and who ſees all things as they really are, can be at no loſs for inſtruments, and he will chuſe and fix upon ſuch as are beſt calculated to anſwer

the

the end designed. And where, or by whatever method he reveals his pleasure respecting the line of duty, or his displeasure against the conduct of any of his rebellious creatures, it is the duty of all those who love and fear him, cheerfully to listen to the one, and with caution to avoid the other. Now the usual methods earthly sovereigns have taken to discover their will to their subjects, have been either the promulgation of laws requiring obedience, or the inflicting of punishments upon notorious transgressions, as a caution and preventative. Something analagous to this is to be traced in the conduct of the Almighty towards his creatures; tho' in these respects earthly sovereigns have probably imitated him rather than he them. The will of God is comprehended in the sacred pages of the Old and New Testament: There every thing relating to the worship of God, the duty, interest, and obligation of men are so clearly revealed, that he that runs may read, the most simple may obtain information, and the most daring cannot easily pervert the meaning. Subjection to God, love to him, and dependence on him; together with submission to his will, obedience to his authority, and faith in the record that he hath given of his Son; this is the sum of what is required, and this appears both right and reasonable; just for him to claim, and equitable for man to yield. Sin

is

is either a transgression of this reasonable rule, or a want of conformity to it. He that offendeth, though but in one point, is obnoxious to the divine displeasure: He justly deserves to be treated and punished as a transgressor; for though God delights in mercy, is slow to anger, and ready to pardon, yet the honour of his government requires that some examples of displeasure be exhibited for the benefit of others; nor can more suitable persons be fixed upon than those whose advantages and obligations to love and to serve him have been peculiar. A remarkable instance of this kind we have in the *Jewish* nation. Early were they distinguished by the separation of their progenitor *Abraham*; and long indulged with the sovereign and peculiar marks of the divine favour; great were their privileges and advantages compared with all the surrounding nations: Rich was the treasure that was deposited amongst them: His law in their hands—His presence in their sanctuary——His pleasure respecting future times exhibited to them under the thin veil of solemn institutions: That veil so thin that we are almost astonished at the blindness of their minds which saw not to the end of the things which were to be abolished. But though thus privileged, thus enriched, thus remarkably distinguished, they closed their eyes against all the evidence; they shut their hearts against the promised Saviour; they sinned

sinned away the day of their merciful visitation; murdered the great Deliverer that their God had provided for them; rejected the counsel of God against themselves; and plunged not only themselves but their posterity into such calamities as they have not been able to extricate themselves from, for more than seventeen hundred years. In them we behold the evil of sin and the consequences of unbelief. In their punishment and preservation we see what God hath wrought. We see them oppressed, yet preserved; scattered amongst many nations, yet kept distinct from each, from all of them: a warning to every eye which beheld them, and to every person who compares their past with their present condition. The words which we propose now to consider were originally delivered by the Prophet *Jeremiah*, as representing the *Jewish* nation in person. And though they may originally have a much higher date than the last and general dispersion of the *Jewish* nation, yet may easily be accommodated as descriptive of their condition in the present age. True, this is not the language of their lips, but is it not the language of their appearance amongst the different nations? *The Lord is righteous, for I have rebelled against his commandment: hear, I pray you, all people, and behold my sorrow: my virgins and my young men are gone into captivity.* These words we propose to consider as descriptive,

I. Of

I. Of the *Condition*:
II. Of the *Confession*: And,
III. Of the *Caution* of the *Jewish* nation, held forth to us, and to all the nations among whom they are dispersed.

We consider the *Jews*, in their present dispersed condition, as the heralds of the divine Majesty, to confirm the truth of Revelation, to warn all, to whom the Gospel is sent, of the sin of unbelief, and to display to the eye the execution of all the judgments denounced against them in God's word. But we wish you to understand that the intent of this discourse is not to excite your enmity against that abandoned people, but to draw forth your pity towards them, and your prayers for them. You are here called to listen to them, and to learn what God is now speaking by them, and through them, to you. From the exalted privileges they once enjoyed, but enjoy no longer, you are called to learn the great duty and necessity of attending to the things that belong to your peace. May almighty power and grace sanctify what we have now to lay before you to these valuable and important purposes.

I. The *Condition* of the *Jews*, as a nation and people, is pictured in very strong language in the passage before us: *My virgins and my young men are gone into captivity.* Affecting representation! Let us endeavour as much as possible

possible to realize the idea. Suppose then all the young, the vigorous, the active of the inhabitants of this nation removed: Parents bereaved of their children: All of them borne away from our view except the aged, the decrepit, and the infirm. None left to till our fields, to prune our orchards, or collect our harvests. In that case, what would remain but disorder, barrenness and poverty, famine and death? We should behold gray hairs declining by slow, but sorrowful steps to the silent grave, joy banished, the reign of peace and plenty ended, sorrow and sadness, misery and wretchedness consummate. No hope—no helper—none to alleviate distress; and to increase the real evils we felt ourselves, the painful reflections which would press the mind with the imaginary distress and disgrace of our children in captivity. "Is my daughter yet alive, would the aged mother say? O that she were now present to comfort me in my fast declining days! Rather, O that I had never born her to be the subject of such distress and dishonour!" While the aged father of a once-flourishing family would lament his condition in such expressions as these: " Once I had sons, and flattered myself that they would, at this season, have proved comforts to me. Were they present, how would they alleviate the burdens of declining age, and minister to my necessity. Had they been here I should not

have

have known the want of bread: But, probably they have already breathed their laſt, under the grievous hands of cruel tyrants; however not a gleam of hope remains that I ſhall ever—ever ſee them more till the morning of the reſurrection."——But we apprehend more to be included than expreſſed. This ſeems to be the meaning of the words, that their young men and maidens, old men, and thoſe who ſtooped for age, were delivered up by the hand of Providence to the enemy. The once fruitful land was turned into barrenneſs, the holy city polluted and broke down, and the ſeed of the renowned *Abraham* ſcattered amongſt the nations.

But not to expatiate upon the calamitous condition of a people thus forſaken of their God, permit me to indulge a reflection or two under this head which may prove of more general utility. From this repreſentation we remark,

1. That young men and maidens are the hope, and ought to be the helpers of declining age. In you, my young friends, are bound up the expectations, the happineſs, and, in ſome ſort, the health of your aged parents. It is your province (under God) to ſmooth their rugged path to the grave, and render their paſſage into eternity more eaſy and delightful. Like *Lamech*, the father of *Noah*, they have already predicted, and frequently comforted themſelves with ſuch a thought

thought as this concerning you: "This fame shall comfort us concerning all our work, and the toil of our hands." And will ye by a cruel conduct put a negative upon the prophecy, blast their prospects, and crush their pleasing hopes? Shall your hands strew their paths with thorns, and your impiety or unkindness bring down those hairs, which have grown gray in your service, with sorrow to their graves? Shall they have to lament over you, as *David* did over his undutiful *Absalom*, when he cried out, "O my son *Absalom*, my son, my son *Absalom*, would God I had died for thee, O *Absalom*, my son, my son!" * What! will ye, by an unkind and unchristian conduct, strike the dagger of distress into those very breasts from which ye have drawn your lives? Shall cruelty and rebellion be all the return for their care and kindness? No, my brethren, honour the God of your fathers, and let every tender office of filial sympathy and support evince how much you are desirous to answer their hopes, to crown their expectations, and to solace their sinking frame. Remember how much you stand indebted to them; how long, with unremitted care, they have watched over you; with what tenderness and perseverance they have ministred to your wants; and with what heart-felt importunity they have recommended your case to God as their best friend; and shall their prayers be in vain—their instructions in vain--
their

* 2 Sam. xviii. 33.

their hopes—their expectations in vain? O no, prove that you love them—that you tenderly love them——that your happiness is inseparably united with theirs——and that the same faith that dwells in them dwelleth also in you.——Our other remark is this,

2. That sin renders every situation and every enjoyment uncertain, even to those who are in the days of youth. Sin separates not only between God and the soul, but between the transgressor and every outward comfort. It turns a fruitful land into barrenness, intails a curse upon every comfort, and sometimes ejects the transgressor not only from his father's house, and the house of God, but from his country also. To you, my young friends, the lines have fallen in pleasant places: It was once so with the tribes of *Israel*; but, for their irreligion and impiety, they were ejected from those pleasant places, and sent into captivity. In their case you may see, that God will not hold them guiltless who rebel against him; and that disobedience to godly ancestors may shorten your days. God is here acknowledged to be righteous in sending their virgins and their young men into captivity; for though it may imply some neglect in their education, which their parents had to bewail, yet it seems to refer more expressly to their own conduct as the cause of it.—So, however great the privileges of this our land may be, how soon

may the injured donor of them reclaim the grant? Judgments are subservient to his call. Our removal, from place to place, is under his direction, and death itself acts agreeably to his orders. Early piety is a real ornament; it comes from heaven; and, like a blooming spring, cheers the hopes of the beholder. Provoke not the Lord then by your conduct to change your liberty for slavery, and gospel-light into darkness; but, on the contrary, shew that ye love and honour the God of your fathers, and that as they fall by death, it is your desire and purpose to fill up their places. May a gracious God, in his mercy, ever avert from them the unutterable pain of this cutting reflection, *my virgins and my young men are gone into captivity.* Look upon the *Jews,* consider their case, and as ye would avoid their condition, avoid their crimes. Their country was once singularly favoured with the smiles of providence and grace, as ours is now; but what an affecting change has sin produced! The former inhabitants are now removed, and their country left almost desolate. But from their condition we turn,

II. To the *confession* of the *Jewish* nation. This consists of two parts: *First,* an acknowledgment of their crime; and, *secondly,* of God's equity in their punishment.

1. The sin they acknowledge is, that they had *rebelled against the commandment of* Jehovah.

vah. The original, with the margin of the bible, is, if possible, more emphatic. *I have rebelled against* the mouth *of Jehovah*. The sin of the *Jews* was not barely a transgression of the law of *Moses*, but of that whole revelation of mercy which the Lord was pleased, in such a peculiar manner, to vouchsafe to them. His laws they had broken—his prophets they had slain—and when God's own Son had assumed flesh——when He, who had spoken to their fathers upon *Sinai's* mount in so much pomp of majesty, descended to speak with them face to face, as a man with his friend, they stopped their ears, hardened their hearts against him, and with wicked hands seized and crucified the Lord of life and glory. Thus they put away the word of life from them, and plunged themselves and their posterity into all the awful judgments that had been predicted by *Moses:* He had foretold his advent, and directed them how to conduct themselves towards him when he should appear: " The Lord thy God," said he, " will raise up unto thee a Prophet from the midst of thee, of thy brethren, like unto me; unto him ye shall hearken. According to all that thou desiredst of the Lord thy God in *Horeb*, in the day of the assembly, saying, Let me not hear again the voice of the Lord my God; neither let me see this great fire any more, that I die not. And the Lord said unto me, They have well spoken that which they have spoken:

spoken: I will raise them up a Prophet from among their brethren, like unto thee, and I will put my words in his mouth, and he shall speak unto them all that I shall command him. And it shall come to pass, that whosoever will not hearken unto my words, which he shall speak in my name, I will require it of him."* *Jesus Christ* then is the divine Oracle; for no man knoweth the Father but the Son, and he to whom he is pleased to reveal him. He delivered the law——spake in and by the Prophets——and promulged the Gospel. See, therefore, that ye refuse not him that speaketh from heaven; not to hearken, not to believe, not to obey, is to rebel: It is to reject the authority of the Sovereign *Jehovah*, and to give the lie to eternal Truth. And rebellion against the mouth of *Jehovah* lays the soul naked and exposed to the weightiest judgments of his arm.——This then has been the silent confession of the *Jews* for near eighteen hundred years. You may almost read this sentence upon their very foreheads, *We have rebelled against the mouth of the Lord,* and are sent out as wanderers into the nations, to warn every one that sees us that they guard against our sin and folly. But what are eighteen hundred years compared with everlasting ages! and if the remedy now proposed to you in the Gospel be rejected, you will have to take up this bitter reflection for eternity: *I have rebelled against the mouth*

* Deut. xviii. 15——19.

mouth of the Lord.——Such is the confession of the crime: But this is not all. They acknowledge,

2. The equity of the divine conduct in their punishment. *Jehovah is righteous.* The *Chaldeans* first, and the *Romans* afterwards, as instruments in the execution of the judgment, might be severe, but the Lord was righteous. He had inflicted no more upon them than what they deserved: Against his mouth they had rebelled, and therefore, in their extremity, he refused to hear their cry: They had slighted his servants and slain his Son, and therefore he delivers them up into the hands of their enemies; but he did not punish them more than their iniquities deserved—nor was righteousness shewn only in what he did, but in the accomplishment of what he had spoken. The denunciations of woe predicted by *Moses* and the Prophets have been, or now are, inflicted on that stubborn people. Their God has cast them off, and they are become wanderers amongst the nations, because they did not hearken unto him. Is not the truth of this before our eyes almost every day? *Moses* had foretold, that upon their disobedience they should be removed from their land*—— be scattered amongst the people from one end of the earth even to the other †——there they should become an astonishment, a proverb, and a by-word ‡——and that their plagues should

---

* Deut. xxviii 63.—† ver. 64.—‡ ver. 37.

should be wonderful, great, and of long continuance *. And what a display of God's righteousness is now set before us in the accomplishment of those dark sayings. God is righteous when he taketh vengeance, no less than while he distributes his favours. He can do no wrong, and what he hath said he will do, and what he hath spoken he will bring to pass, whether it be the denunciation of woe or the accomplishment of a promise. Proceed we now briefly to consider,

III. *The Caution of the* Jewish *nation held forth to us, and to all the nations among whom they are dispersed.*—Hear, *I pray you, all people, and* behold *my sorrow.* There is something to be *seen,* and something to be *heard* by us, in this dispensation of the Almighty towards them.

1. There is something to be *seen.* This is the vision which the God of nations is pleased to set before our eyes while the trumpet of the Gospel is sounded in our ears. Let us behold their sorrow—and in order to this,

Look into their History. What distress in all its horrors! What destruction in all its magnitude is presented to our view by their own Historian *Josephus!* Not to detain you with the repetition of particulars, from his account we learn that the number of those who were known to be slain, during their last conflict, was no less than one million three hundred and fifty-seven thousand six hundred and

* Deut. xxviii. ver. 39.

and sixty men; and not even to pretend to guess the thousands who were butchered in cold blood, he informs us of ninety-seven thousand who were sent into captivity. Such were the devastations of war; and to those may be added the thousands also devoured by famine and pestilence.——Behold their sorrow then as delineated in their history.

See it likewise in *the appearance of their country*. Where is now the once fair and fruitful land that flowed with milk and honey, and smiled under the protection and blessing of the Almighty? What is its condition now? It is troden down of the *Gentiles*, and become so barren, that some have even staggered at the account the Scripture gives of it while in its vigour: It is now a land of slavery and superstition: Its vineyards blasted; its vallies barren, its hills no longer cloathed with verdure. The kidney of the wheat and the blood of the grape, once renowned in prophecy, are scarce to be found. There, despotism is enthroned and industry has retired: There, according to the account of modern travellers, the truth of prophecy stands confessed; and there, is to be seen, in the most awful characters, how the Lord turneth a fruitful land into barrenness for the iniquity of them that dwell therein.

Would you behold their sorrow? It is to be seen in their *present condition*. O degraded condition! Where is their altar, their high priest,

priest, or their temple? By their general conduct ye see them breaking the very law they profess to honour; ye hear them blaspheming the name of that God they pretend to reverence, and while they bear the guilt of ancient generations, they are adding to it by their own criminal conduct. They appear as if doomed by the Almighty to confirm the truth of that Gospel they revile, to all that will attend to their present condition. In them we have the testimony of *Jesus* confirmed, and the truth of what he predicted continually passing in review before us.—— But,

2. There is something also to be *heard* in this solemn dispensation of Providence: This in effect is the address of that deluded people: " Hear, we pray you all people, for in us there is a voice from God to you: We appear as messengers from him to warn you that ye fall not by the same example of unbelief." It may not be unprofitable here to inquire what those sins were by which God's ancient people forfeited their privileges, and drew down upon their heads these awful judgments. And we shall find that pride of privileges—false conceptions of the writings of *Moses*—confidence in their descent from *Abraham*—secular views of the *Messiah*'s kingdom—and the rejection of *Jesus Christ* and his salvation, are the sins which they stand particularly charged with.

They

They were *proud* of their great *privileges*. True, to them God had granted the peculiar revelation of himself; amongst them he had erected his palace, displayed his power, and manifested his presence: To them were committed the lively oracles of God: And to them likewise pertained the adoption, the covenants, and similar advantages. Of these things they grew vain—they exulted that they were the temple of the Lord—looked upon others with disdain, and pronounced them accursed. Thus they went on till at last their house was left desolate, and the protection of Providence withdrawn from them and their country.—It must be confessed that God has not dealt with every nation as with our own—We have his word in our hands, the ordinances of his worship in our sanctuaries—his ministers to shew us the way of life, and invite us to be reconciled to God. Pardon, peace, and salvation are proclaimed.—It is the day of our merciful visitation—but presume not on these privileges, they are moveable—they call for your humble acceptance and instant improvement, otherwise God can take them from us, and send them to a people that will bring forth fruit.

False conceptions of the writings of Moses was another fault of the *Jews*. The letter they observed, but looked no farther—nay, even that they twisted and moulded to their own fancy: And, ignorant of God and his righteousness,

ousness, they went about to establish their own righteousness. Touching the righteousness of the law they accounted themselves blameless, while enmity to God, pride, rage, covetousness, yea cruelty pervaded their hearts. Pleased with the shadow, they turned their backs upon the substance, and sought to please God by the multitude of their sacrifices, rather than from the principles of humility, faith, and hope in the promise with which they ought to have offered them. Brethren, by the deeds of the law no flesh can be justified in the sight of God: It is not by works of righteousness, but by mercy that we are saved. All dependence upon self must be disclaimed and renounced, in order that we may stand accepted in the Beloved. God's law requires truth in the inward parts, and his Gospel an intire and unfeigned submission to the righteousness of *Jesus Christ*.

Confidence founded on their descent from Abraham was another of their sins. "We have *Abraham* to our Father:" But did his faith dwell in the heart while his blood circulated in their veins? Did they rejoice as he did to see *Christ's* day? Did they, like him, embrace the promised Deliverer? Were not a persecuting *Ishmael*, a prophane *Esau*, an accursed *Achan* also children of *Abraham?*—Lean not therefore to birth-privileges: What though ye had those for your parents who were eminent for faith, zeal, and practical obedience,

the

the greater is your sin at present, and the heavier will be your condemnation at last, if ye tread not in their steps and copy not their example. If this be the case, those that begat will disown you, and appear against you in the great day.

Secular views of the Messiah's kingdom was another part of their crime: A temporal prince and worldly glory was all that they looked for. When *Jesus Christ*, therefore, appeared, and declared that his kingdom was not of this world, they were offended in him.—See that ye copy not after them—rest not upon external rites and ceremonies; but remember that God's kingdom consists in righteousness, peace, and joy in the Holy Ghost.

The rejecting of Jesus Christ filled up the measure of their iniquity. O beware that ye fall not after the same example of unbelief. Your situation is such that ye must either receive him or reject him; it is impossible to be neuter: He that is not for him is against him; and they that are for him will open the heart to give him entertainment, and consecrate their lives and all their powers to his service. May the Lord make us all willing in the day of his power, for *Jesus'* sake.—Amen.

SERMON

SERMON XIV.

Modern Miracles.

PSALM cxlvi. 8.

The Lord openeth the eyes of the blind: The Lord raiseth them that are bowed down: The Lord loveth the righteous.

THE words to which you have now been referred, are highly characteristic of the power and grace of that God who worketh wonders: They have been already realized and exemplified in the conduct of the great Redeemer when here upon earth. "By him the eyes of the blind were opened, the ears of the deaf were unstopped, the lame man leaped as an hart, and the tongue of the dumb proclaimed his power or sung his praise." These miracles were indubitable evidences of his divine nature, and to these miracles he referred the disciples of *John*, to prove that he was the *Messiah*. We live in an age in which we are not surrounded with such external proofs of the divinity and authority of this Saviour. The blind still remain blind, and the crooked still are bowed down:

down: But has the evidence entirely ceased? Or has the Lord left himself without witnesses in these later ages of the world? Neither of these is the case. We have *that* evidence of which, perhaps, these miracles were only emblematical. What our Lord then wrought upon the bodies of men was comparatively but sketching the outlines of what he intended to effect upon their souls; and we trust that many of you have that evidence of which these miracles were but the shadow, not only before your eyes, but in yourselves; and as we go along we hope to have it in our power, both to refer to you, and refer you to yourselves in confirmation of this truth, that *The Lord openeth the eyes of the blind: The Lord raiseth them that are bowed down: The Lord loveth the righteous.*

The Psalm before us is opened with an exhortation to praise the Lord: This exhortation is directed to all in the general, to himself in a particular manner. *Ver.* 1. *Praise ye the Lord: Praise the Lord, O my soul.* The Lord is worthy to be praised for what he is in himself, and for what he has done, and still continues to do, for his church. Angels incessantly praise him, for they see further into the propriety of doing it, and are better capacitated to express his honour: But God is exalted above all blessing and praise: Even the highest order of angels feel themselves every way unequal to the undertaking.

The Pfalmift, in his own name, and in the name of the whole church of believers, introduces the refponfe to this claim in the fecond verfe. To this divine employ he refolves to confecrate the fervice of his life; yea, and more than his life, he refolves to perpetuate the praife of his God with his being.

Probably the mufic to this Pfalm was originally compofed fo as to be performed in different parts, and fung by different perfons or companies. In all the folemnity of found one opened the fong, faying, *Praife ye the Lord: Praife the Lord, O my foul.* Another was heard to return this anfwer: *While I live, will I praife the Lord: I will fing praifes unto my God, while I have any being.* A full chorus then proclaimed the imbecility and mortality of earthly potentates, *Put not your truft in princes, nor in the fon of man, in whom there is no help. His breath goeth forth, he returneth to his earth: in that day his thoughts perifh.* Another introduced his fong defcribing the power, veracity, rectitude, providence, compaffion, and grace of that God on whom his confidence is placed.—*Ver.* 5—9. *Happy is he that hath the God of Jacob for his help, whofe hope is in the Lord his God: which made heaven and earth, the fea, and all that therein is: which keepeth truth for ever: which executeth judgment for the oppreffed, which giveth food to the hungry: the Lord loofeth the prifoners: the Lord openeth*
the

the eyes of the blind: the Lord raiseth them that are bowed down: the Lord loveth the righteous: the Lord preserveth the strangers; he relieveth the fatherless and widow: but the way of the wicked he turneth upside down.—— Then the whole company united in one grand chorus, in publishing the gracious, providential, and everlasting dominion of *Jehovah*. Ver. 10. *The Lord shall reign for ever, even thy God, O Zion, unto all generations Praise ye the Lord.* Such, probably, was the manner in which this Psalm was originally performed: And thus performed by all the sons of *Asaph*, assisted by all the musical instruments employed in the temple, it must have appeared inimitably grand.——But pleasing as such a performance must have been to the ear, that pleasure will be found far more profitable and abiding, if we can find the notes of this song, not only transcribed but realized in our own happy experience. *The Lord openeth the eyes of the blind: The Lord raiseth them that are bowed down: The Lord loveth the righteous.* Let us consider these words as they are descriptive of the three following things:

I. The evils removed from the people of God, viz. *Ignorance* and *Oppression*.
II. The great Author of this deliverance, *the Lord*.

III. The

III. The principle from which he acts in doing this, and in confirmation of which he does it, viz. *His love, the Lord loveth the righteous.*

There is a kind of tautology in the text, which, to a good man, will appear both pleasing and profitable. *Jehovah* is thrice introduced, but never without propriety and apparent necessity. The Psalmist seems as if afraid that either he or others should lose sight of him in any part of the verse, for he knew how prone the human mind is to do this. While therefore this repetition seems to throw additional sublimity into the poetry, it adds also clearness and perspicuity to the sentiment. Here all is represented as of God—our light—our liberty—our felicity for time and for eternity, are all traced up to him as their spring and origin.—But that we may prosecute the method already proposed, we shall consider this divine sentence as descriptive,

I. *Of those evils removed from the people of God, viz.* Ignorance *and* Oppression.

1. *Ignorance* is one of the evils they labour under, and from which the Lord is pleased to deliver them. This is expressed in the text: *The Lord openeth the eyes of the blind.* Our mental perception is liable to dimness, and a variety of other disorders, no less than the natural organs of vision. We see things imperfectly, in false lights, with great confusion;

fufion; or, probably, have no perception at all of those things which to others appear exceedingly plain and evident. In confirmation of this we may advert to many of the leading truths of Revelation—to God's dealings with his children, and to some of the dispensations of his providence.

In spiritual things how often have we to complain, and that justly too, of great dimness, or the entire want of perception? How has sin blinded men to God's method of saving sinners by *Jesus Christ* alone, and to the glorious manifestation of his grace in that astonishing device. They have a kind of consciousness that some sort of satisfaction must be made to divine Justice for crimes which they have committed; but they look for it no higher than themselves. With considerable diligence and pains they go about to establish their own righteousness. They pray—fast——give alms to the poor——and mortify their bodies, perhaps to the injury of their constitution. To what is the mistake owing but to their ignorance of God—of what his law requires—of what *Jesus Christ* hath done and suffered, and of what they really are in themselves? " Being ignorant of God's righteousness," says the Apostle, " they seek to establish their own:" But by the Gospel and Spirit of *Jesus Christ*, the Lord enlightens the understanding: He shews to man his righteousness; discloses the way in which he can

be

be juſt and juſtify the ungodly; and makes it evident to him that the whole is by grace, through faith, and according to the riches of his mercy. The eyes of the blind are opened to ſee the beauty of holineſs, the glories of *Jeſus Chriſt*, and the harmony of all the attributes of *Jehovah* in the pardon and in the juſtification of the believing ſinner. It is quite a new proſpect which is laid open to the mind; and he that unvails the proſpect, enables the ſoul to perceive and admire it. It now appears to be a ſcheme worthy of God in all its parts; honourable for him to unfold and glory in, and worthy alſo of being admired, contemplated, and fully approved by the believing ſinner: In this caſe the eyes of the blind are opened to ſee that there is ſalvation with the Lord, and that this ſalvation is free, great, and everlaſting.

There is much ignorance in God's people reſpecting the reaſon why he permits ſin to dwell in them: They feel the remains of depravity, which is their complaint and burden; nor do they always ſee the reaſon of this. Perhaps they draw falſe concluſions from it, and are ready to ſay, " Was I the Lord's, it would not be thus with me."—— Hence *Paul* beſought the Lord again and again to remove the inſupportable burden under which he laboured: By the anſwer returned, the eyes of his mind were ſo far opened, that he was content to bear, and even

even gloried in his infirmities, that the power of *Christ* might rest upon him. And though I am apt to think, that those must have been some bodily infirmities, seeing they were made the subject of glorying through the power and grace of *Christ*; yet it may be in some measure accommodated to the remains of depravity, as appears more plainly from the 7th chapter of his Epistle to the *Romans*. He saw that sin was suffered to remain, in order to keep him humble, watchful, and dependent; to keep his faith leaning on the promise, and his soul depending on the power of *Christ*.— To lead him to converse more with that Saviour in his several offices, to make him sensible of the great duty of prayer, and to keep his soul alive in the discharge of that duty.— Were sin entirely done away, you would have eternal cause to praise the Physician of your souls; but you would have no further occasion to apply to him under that character. Were your enemies all slain, you would no longer need the Captain of your salvation. Were your souls completely sanctified, you would have no further occasion to apply to the unsearchable riches of divine mercy. The Lord, therefore, shews his people that he has very wise ends in view, in thus permitting sin to remain in them and annoy them so much. It is not to reconcile their minds to sin, or to render it less loathsome and evil in their sight. No; but to make *Jesus Christ* more precious to them—to keep them more humble before him—to mortify Satan more completely—to induce them to follow more earnestly after righteousness——and to bring them to long more for heaven.

There is great ignorance in the minds of good men likewise, with respect to the important contents of God's word. The wisest and best of men often find reason to pray, that the Lord would open their eyes to behold the wonderful things contained in his word; for they find that they know but in part. Often are the divine precepts out of view when we most need their counsel; or the promises, when we most require those comforts and supports which they contain. Perhaps there have been instances in which a precept or promise brought to the view of the mind at those particular seasons, was as if the Lord had opened the eyes of the blind. It was a word in season, as it discovered that to be your duty or privilege which you had no more conception of before, than a blind man has of those objects which, tho' present, are rendered invisible to him. Hence the Lord promises that he " will bring the blind by a way they know not, and lead them in paths that they have not known; will make darkness light before them, and crooked things straight: These things will he do unto them, and will not forsake them *." He will cause them to hear as it were a voice behind

* Isai. xlii. 16.

behind them, saying, This is the way, walk ye in it, when he sees them ready to turn to the right hand or the left; and this direction shall be from his word. From a conviction of this amazing ignorance, even in the minds of the best of men, we find the Apostle praying for the *Ephesian* church, that the God of our Lord *Jesus Christ*, the Father of glory, would give to them the spirit of wisdom and revelation in the knowledge of himself: The eyes of their understanding being enlightened, that they might know what was the hope of his calling, and what the riches of the glory of his inheritance in the Saints, and what the exceeding greatness of his power towards them who believe according to the working of that mighty power which he wrought in *Christ* when he raised him from the dead, and exalted him to his throne of glory †. Thus is the Lord pleased graciously and gradually to remove this ignorance from the minds of his people. For even after he has begun to open the eyes of the mind, like the poor man in the gospel, they see things but very imperfectly; men as trees walking.

There is much remaining ignorance in them also respecting his providential dealings both with themselves and others. Often are they led entirely to misinterpret his conduct, or to put false constructions on his dealings with them. Their forefather *Jacob* was not the only one who said, " all these things are against

† Eph. i. 17, &c.

against me." Many of his children have concluded the same, and with much less apparent ground of probability. Some of you, perhaps, think that your trials are of a peculiar nature; that never were any so bewildered, so perplexed, so crossed as you are. And though you have often been convinced of the error of such rash conclusions, and led to acknowledge that this was your infirmity, yet now you apprehend there can be no possibility of mistake in the case. The Lord having brought you into a wilderness, all appears confusion around you, and you see no way out of your present difficulty; but is the Lord's arm shortened? Are you so shut in that he cannot bring you out? Or have you forgot all his former appearances for you? The rough road in which he formerly led *Israel*, though they had often murmured against him for leading them in it, was, in the event, found to be the right path. Ignorance lies at the bottom of all our murmurings and complaints against God's providential dealings with us. We see not the connection of things; how comforts are connected with crosses, and the most lively pleasures with our heaviest sorrows. Viewing things as separate and distinct from each other, we have no kind of conception how they are to work together for our good; and this is often productive of much confusion and distress. Our help is at hand, but till

the

the Lord open our eyes, like *Hagar*, we see not the source of our comfort.

2. *Oppression* is another evil under which God's people labour, and from which they, at seasons, suffer much: But *the Lord raiseth them that are bowed down*: Under this branch we might again refer you to the burden of sin, and to the burden of corruption; but having glanced at these already, we shall only mention here the burden of worldly cares. Under their heavy pressure, perhaps, your spirits are almost broken, and you feel yourselves ready to sink. You scarce know which way to turn, or what to do. Sensible you are, however, that unsupported you must inevitably sink: Nor does it appear only probable in your view, that this may be the case, but almost certain. How to get disintangled and unincumbered, you know not. It appears impracticable; like *Elisha's* servant, you seem to yourselves to be altogether encompassed with hosts of difficulties, which bear a threatning aspect; but, like him, you see not your helper and deliverer. *Elisha* interposed, saying, *Lord, I pray thee open his eyes, that he may see*. And the Lord opened the eyes of the young man, and he saw; and behold the mountain was full of horses and chariots of fire round about *Elisha**. Though bowed down with many an anxious fear, and accumulated trials, the Lord is able to lift you up. He that has delivered you in the past,

* 2 Kings vi. 17.

past, is able to deliver you still; and he has promised strength for the day, and that light shall shine out of obscurity. In every fresh difficulty, say, therefore, "Thou hast been my help, leave me not, neither forsake me, O God of my salvation."—He can pour light into the darkest understanding, and strengthen those who are most oppressed; for, "he giveth power to the faint, and to them who have no might he increaseth strength." *Ignorance* and *Oppression* are evils under which many of God's people labour.——We proposed to consider the words,

II. As descriptive of *the great author of this deliverance*. This the text three times assures us, is *the Lord*. And the reasons we may conclude are such as these—that self may be abased—that all the honour may be taken from every instrument employed in the deliverance—and that the whole may be attributed, without reserve, to the Lord.

1. The Lord is here asserted to be the author of this deliverance, *that self may be abased*. There is a propensity in man too much to depend on, or give honour to himself; but the Lord will suffer no flesh to glory in his sight. Whatever light, O professors, ye have into divine truth, whatever discoveries ye have into God's ways, or whatever liberty ye find in his service, remember it all comes from him. In yourselves you are poor, dark, bewildered creatures. Unenlightened by him, you see no more, and can do no more than
the

the blind. Unaffifted and unfupported by him, you will fink under every trial, however fmall, and will be found infufficient for any undertaking. What have ye that ye have not received; and if it be received, how vain is it to glory, except it be in the liberality of him who confers every favour upon you? Lean not, therefore, to your own underftanding. Say not my own arm hath done it; but as *Jehovah* is the author of the whole of your deliverance, and of all your help, let him have all the glory.

2. The Lord is reprefented to be the fole author of this deliverance, that fo all *the praife may be taken from every inftrument employed by him in this work.* He may ufe inftruments in removing this darknefs from the mind, or in fupporting you under your various trials; but there is no other honour due to them, than to a prop which fupports a finking building. It is very ufeful in its place, but it owes all its ufefulnefs to him who placed it there. Thus of Minifters; who is *Paul,* and who is *Apollos,* but minifters by whom ye believed? If others be enlightened, comforted, or edified, it is by *that* light, and by *thofe* comforts wherewith they alfo have been comforted of God. "Therefore," fays the Apoftle, "let no man glory in man, for all things are yours, whether *Paul,* or *Apollos,* or *Cephas,* or the world, or life, or death, or things prefent, or things

to

to come; all are yours, and ye are *Christ's*, and *Christ* is God's*."—We add,

3. Hereby the whole honour is *claimed for, and attributed to, the Lord.* His glory will he not give to any; but he requires it of all, and expects to receive it from his own people in a peculiar manner: And, therefore, under a constant sense of your ignorance, look up to him for light; and under an abiding conviction of your weakness, look to him for support. This is to honour God—to own him as the author of all that has been done for you, and to depend upon him to perfect that which concerneth you. " He that offereth praise," saith the Lord, " glorifieth me; and to him that ordereth his conversation aright will I shew my salvation." But, agreeable to what we before proposed, we have yet to consider the words of the text as descriptive,

III. *Of that principle from which he acts in doing all this, and in confirmation of which he does it,* viz. His love. The Lord loveth the righteous. They may be afflicted; may be exercised with a variety of trials; and yet at the same time loved of him; for " whom the Lord loveth he chasteneth, and scourgeth every son whom he receiveth." Under this part of the discourse, we shall just glance at two things:

1. *The Lord loveth* his people, and therefore *will he* open the eyes of the blind, and lift

* 1 Cor. iii. 21, &c.

lift up thofe that are bowed down. This is the reafon—the principle—the caufe why he will do it. He loves them; and therefore he will fhew them his love. He loves them, and therefore will he fupport them, or raife them up when they are caft down. He is gracious, becaufe he will be gracious. It is not any fitnefs in the object that induces him to do this, but the favour that he bears to his people. Thus *Mofes* afcribes all thefe privileges and favours which the children of *Ifrael* received to this principle of love which the Lord bare towards them. " Yea," fays he, " he loved the people; all his faints are in thy hand: And they fat down at thy feet; every one fhall receive of thy words *." The Apoftle alfo, under the New Teftament difpenfation, traces all fpiritual bleffings to the fame fource. " God, who is rich in mercy, for his great love wherewith he loved us, even when we were dead in fins, hath quickened us together with *Chrift*, and hath raifed us up together, and made us fit together in heavenly places in *Chrift Jefus* †." His love is the reafon from which we may conclude that he will do this. And,

2. The Lord loveth his people, and therefore *he has done this for them.* He *has* opened the eyes of the blind—*has* lift up them that were bowed down—and why has he done all this, but to prove his love towards them? Had the Lord intended to deftroy them, he would

* Deut. xxxiii. 3.—† Eph. ii. 4—6.

would not have acted thus towards them, or shewn them such things as these. Has he therefore, in some measure, shone into your hearts to give you any saving discovery of his glory in the face of *Jesus Christ?* There read the evidence of his love towards you. And has he supported you, and strengthened you with strength in your souls? In a word, has he wrought a sincere desire in your hearts to know and do his will?—Led you to love and long for holiness; brought you to see the preciousness of *Jesus Christ*; to approve of him in all that he is; to rely upon his promised grace and strength; and to desire to grow up into him in all things? These are the evidences of his love. Ye, therefore, are the Lord's witnesses, that *he openeth the eyes of the blind; raiseth up them that are bowed down; and loveth the righteous.*

And is that God, with whom we all have to do, such a gracious and wonder-working God? And is it our privilege to hear his wonders thus proclaimed? And is he now amongst us under the present dispensation, as much as when the Psalmist penned these words? Then approach him all ye blind, for there is encouragement for you to apply to him, and it is now your duty. This wonder-working God is waiting to be gracious. He will be found of those who seek him in truth, and will manifest himself to those who inquire after him in sincerity. You have

heard

heard what is the character of this God; and let him hear your importunate requests for his needful benefits. Let him see your readiness to accept his favours, and to be healed of him.

Once more: To deny the work of God, is to dishonour him, and to plunge ourselves into the deepest distress. Though you have not attained what you wish; though you desire the full ripe fruit, yet despise not the buds and blossoms. Ye were once totally blind to the glory of God, the grace of *Christ*, and the suitableness and efficacy of gospel doctrines; but now ye see, though it be very imperfectly, and like the glimmering of the sun between the parting clouds. Yet be thankful. Your path, like the dawn of the opening morning, shall shine more and more unto the perfect day. Cast your burden upon the Lord, he will sustain you. Lean upon his arm, and he will bear you up in all your journey through this wilderness. His power is infinite, and his love immutable, and he will confirm and display both, in bringing all those who trust in him to behold him in his glory, and to see and prove how much the Lord loveth the righteous. That this may be our happy and everlasting privilege, God grant, for *Jesus's* sake. *Amen.*

SERMON XV.

God glorified, by Inſtruments of his own forming.

ISAIAH xliii. 21.

This people have I formed for myſelf, they ſhall ſhew forth my praiſe.

GREAT is the grace which is diſplayed in theſe words! aſtoniſhing is the deſign, and pleaſing the reflection which they preſent to our minds! In ancient hiſtory we read of a prince, who, from the ſummit of his palace, beholding the metropolis of his extenſive empire, exulted thus: " This is *Babylon* the great—*Babylon*, which I have built for the houſe of my kingdom, by the might of my power, and for the honour of my majeſty."* He beheld the riſing domes, the ſolemn temples, the numberleſs palaces of his lords; his heart bounded at the proſpect, and his ſoul was inflated with pride. Small cauſe, however, to be proud, had he recollected that theſe buildings were inhabited by a nation of ſlaves, and thoſe temples filled with ſuperſtition and idolatry. In the sentence

* Dan. iv. 30.

sentence just read you have a far more noble potentate, even the King of kings himself, reflecting upon the work of his hands, and rejoicing in the review of it. Beholding the triumphs of his grace, the accomplishment of his sacred purposes, and the wonders of his power, he expresses his complete satisfaction. His labour is not found in vain, his exertions are crowned with the designed success, and the production exactly corresponds with the plan laid down. With pleasure he reviews his workmanship, and already anticipates that chorus of praise which will perpetuate the honour of his name through eternal ages. That God who cannot be deceived—who seeth the end of all things from the beginning—and who never had a design which miscarried through neglect, or any unforeseen occurrence, is here described as looking upon his people with complacency and delight.—His language is, *This people have I formed for myself*, not probably *they may*, or certainly *they ought*, but *they shall shew forth my praise*. With God effects are certain, and success is sure.

The chapter where the text is found opens like the clear shining of a serene morning after a dark and stormy night: Instead of bursting clouds or descending tempests, the rising sun gilds the joyful east, and the gentle breath of morn scatters every trace of the preceeding hurricane. The last chapter closed with denunciations of the moſt tremendous judgments: This opens with as pleaſing proclamations of the moſt gracious promiſes. The Lord aſſures his people that he will no more utterly forſake them, and that deliverances ſo miraculous ſhall be wrought in their behalf, as would almoſt obſcure and efface the remembrance of all that he had ever done for them.

In the two firſt verſes of the chapter the Lord aſſerts his intereſt in this people, not barely upon his general claim as univerſal Creator, but on account of their redemption and vocation; and aſſures them of his preſence with them under all their trials and afflictions. " Thus ſaith the Lord that created thee, O *Jacob*, and he that formed thee, O *Iſrael*, Fear not; for I have redeemed thee, I have called thee by thy name, thou art mine. When thou paſſeſt through the waters I will be with thee, and through the rivers, they ſhall not overflow thee; when thou walkeſt through the fire, thou ſhalt not be burnt; neither ſhall the flame kindle upon thee." They are reminded of what, as a people, he had done for them, and he promiſes yet to load them with additional favours, as evidences of the unalterable nature of that love he bare to them.—*Ver*. 3, 4. " I am the Lord thy God, the Holy One of *Iſrael*, thy Saviour: I gave *Egypt* for thy ranſom, *Ethiopia* and *Seba* for thee. Since thou waſt
precious

precious in my fight, thou haft been honourable, and I have loved thee; therefore will I give men for thee, and people for thy life." He further affures them, that although their feed might be fcattered amongft the nations for a feafon, he would, by his providence and grace, bring them back, and engage them to return and feek the Lord.—*Ver.* 5—7. "Fear not, for I am with thee: I will bring thy feed from the eaft, and gather them from the weft: I will fay to the north, Give up, and to the fouth, Keep not back: bring my fons from far, and my daughters from the ends of the earth." This introduces a bold challenge to all the nations of the *Heathen* to produce fuch evidence of the wifdom, power, and interpofition of their idols as *Ifrael* had to produce in honour of their God. *Ver.* 8—13.—On this follows a prediction of the ruin of *Babylon*, a promife of deliverance to the *Jews*, and a reference to what their God had formerly done when he brought their forefathers out of *Egypt:* All which is mentioned by way of encouraging their faith at that feafon, *ver.* 14—17. But what were *Ifrael's* deliverances, firft from *Egypt*, afterwards from *Babylon*, when compared with that which God now promifed to work for them? Great as the wonders were that he had wrought, they would hardly admit a comparifon with that *new thing* which he was about to introduce, viz. the Redemption and Salvation of finners sinners by the Lord *Jesus Christ,* especially as displayed in the calling and conversion of the *Gentiles.* In former works his power had been gloriously displayed; in this his wisdom and grace were to be no less exalted.——— *Ver.* 18———21. " Remember not the former things, neither consider the things of old. Behold I will do a new thing: now shall it spring forth, shall ye not know it? I will even make a way in the wilderness, and rivers in the desert. The beasts of the field shall honour me, the dragons and the owls: because I give water in the wilderness, and rivers in the desert, to give drink to my people, my chosen. This people have I formed for myself, they shall shew forth my praise." The leading articles held forth by these words to our particular attention are these three, viz.

 I. That it is the prerogative of God alone to form the souls of men for his service and enjoyment.
 II. That in this act of special sovereign grace he has always respect to himself; that is, to the display and manifestation of his own glory as the *end.*——And
 III. That from this, as from all his other works, he will eventually derive a glorious revenue of praise.

And while this triumphant language of the heart-forming God is the subject of our meditation, may we be found severally looking
up

up to him by fervent prayer, either that he would form us for himself, or favour us with the comfortable evidence that already we are his workmanship, created in *Christ Jesus* unto good works.

The first thing we proposed to attend to in this discourse is,

I. *That it is the prerogative of God alone to form the souls of men anew, both for his service here, and enjoyment hereafter:* " This people have I formed for myself." We apprehend it may not be unprofitable, under this head, to take notice both of *the subjects of his workmanship,* and of *the work itself.*

1. The *subjects* of his workmanship are sinners of *Adam's* family, or, as we hinted in the introduction, sinners of the *Gentiles* in particular. A people, at one time, apparently unnoticed and uncultivated, lying under all the disorders and disadvantages of the fall. Sin has destroyed the once-fair and glorious image in which man was created. Sin has thrown every thing out of order, not only in the world at large, but especially in the nature and constitution of man. His powers are all debilitated—his passions debased—his affections deranged—his attention diverted from its proper object—and his mind led captive by every delusive vanity. Sin has unmade the man which God created, and his posterity are no longer what their forefather originally

originally was. Man was created in knowledge, righteousness, and true holiness; now the darkness of ignorance pervades the mind of his posterity, irregular appetites direct all their pursuits, and sin reigns in the heart to bring forth fruit unto death. The image of God is lost, and the heart of man is become the seat of ignorance, vanity, and confusion.

But these remarks, though just, we apprehend are too general; permit us, therefore, to call your attention to a nearer and more particular view of these subjects of the divine workmanship. Behold and wonder at human nature as degraded by sin. It has precipitated man, once the head of this lower world, and who then wore the image of God as his brightest ornament, from the height of honour, almost to a level with the brute creation: Nay, degraded him so low, as to rank with the most fierce, or more stupid of animals. This seems to be intended by the strong metaphoric language expressed in the preceding verse. "The beasts of the field shall honour me, the dragons and the owls, because I give waters in the wilderness, and rivers in the desert, to give drink to my people, my chosen." And is this great Artificer able to subdue dispositions so savage? Can he tame men who have been fierce as dragons; or bring those who, like owls, have long been the inhabitants of darkness, to rejoice in the clear shinings of gospel-light, and

bask

bask under the beams of the Sun of righteousness? Will he destroy the enmity of rebellious hearts; cause the obdurate neck cheerfully to bow to the Saviour's yoke; or make those who have loved darkness to rejoice in the light of the Lord? All this he is not only able, but has promised to do; and the pleasing wonderful effects of gospel-light and of sovereign grace are described under this very image in the same prophecy. " The parched ground shall become a pool, and the thirsty land springs of water: In the habitation of dragons, where each lay, shall be grass with reeds and rushes. And an highway shall be there, and a way, and it shall be called the way of holiness, the unclean shall not pass over it, but it shall be for those: The way-faring men, though fools, shall not err therein. No lion shall be there, nor any ravenous beast shall go up thereon, it shall not be found there; but the redeemed shall walk there. And the ransomed of the Lord shall return and come to *Zion* with songs and everlasting joy upon their heads, they shall obtain joy and gladness, and sorrow and sighing shall flee away*." How descriptive are these words of the power, the astonishing power of renewing grace! It surmounts the greatest difficulties, subdues the most stubborn heart, causes even dry bones to live, and enables transgressors, once dead

---

* Isai. xxxv. 7, &c.

in trespasses and sins, to arise and to adore. Sin hath rendered the world we inhabit a wilderness, a desert, a dry and barren land; but where the waters of the sanctuary reach, wherever the river of mercy flows, there God has honour, even from persons who before were savage as the beasts of the forest, fierce as dragons, or stupid as the owl. Such were some of you, but now renewed, even in the spirit of your minds; ye have your fruit unto holiness; old things are passed away, and behold all things are become new. Once ye were not a people, now the people of God; once ye had not obtained mercy, but now have obtained mercy.

We may therefore derive encouragement from this consideration, viz. That power belongeth unto God, and that nothing is too hard for him to do. He can humble the most stubborn heart—renew the most depraved will—exalt the most debased soul—and bring order out of all that confusion which sin has introduced into the world. This God has power to bring every thought into subjection to himself, to subdue the most violent corruptions, and to break the firmest bonds of sin. The residue of the spirit is with him; and as this should be matter of comfort to every believer on his own account, so of encouragement likewise, respecting those who lay near to him in the bonds of friendship and the ties of blood. The baseness of the materials

terials is no impediment in the way of this work; on the contrary, if possible, it tends the more to display, and gloriously to exalt the power of that God who produces the admirable change. The excellency of the power is seen to be of God and not of man. But,

2. The *work* itself claims our attention. *This people have I formed for myself.* How great is the change! compared with what they were formerly, it may well be said that old things are passed away, and all things are become new. By renovating grace, the Lord forms this people for himself. They are his workmanship, created in *Christ Jesus* unto good works. They partake of a divine nature, being united to that living head who is both God and man in one person. *Christ* is formed in them, for they were predestinated to be conformed to his image who is the firstborn amongst many brethren. This important change is represented in the Old Testament under such language as this, taking away the heart of stone, giving them an heart of flesh, putting his spirit within them, and writing his law upon the mind. In the *New*, they are said to be renewed in knowledge, righteousness, and true holiness after the image of him who created them. The whole of the work is the Lord's, and his grace, wisdom, and power are to be admired and honoured in it. To him they are indebted for what they are; and for every be-

nefit and blessing received. A great change hath passed upon them; but who hath made them to differ from what they once were, and still had been, but for this God? Or what have they which they have not received? Every good gift, and every grace by which they are distinguished, is from above, and cometh down from the Father of lights, with whom there is no variableness nor shadow of turning. To this source the Apostle of the *Gentiles* taught the *Colossians*, and in them all succeeding professors to ascribe it. " Giving thanks unto the Father, who hath made us meet to be partakers with the saints in light; who hath delivered us from the power of darkness, and hath translated us into the kingdom of his dear Son*." But is there ground, brethren, for you to hope and conclude that this great and necessary change has passed upon you? Having fled for refuge to the hope set before you, are ye daily putting on the Lord *Jesus Christ* as your righteousness, strength, and ornament? This is that necessary and important change, without which ye must for ever remain strangers to true peace upon earth, and be for ever excluded from the kingdom of God and glory. The evidences of this change are many: Persons who once saw no beauty in *Christ*, and who felt no need of such a Saviour, now account him infinitely precious, altogether lovely, wonderfully, yea exactly, suited to their various

* Col. i. 12, 13.

rious wants. Men who were once impure, now pant after holiness; and, seeing their unworthiness, build all their hopes of heaven upon the free mercy of God, and the complete satisfaction and merit of *Christ*. Like new-born babes they desire the sincere milk of the word, and discover a prevailing wish to grow in grace, and in the knowledge of our Lord and Saviour *Jesus Christ*.

But when it is said this people *have* I formed for myself, it is not to be understood as though the work were already completely accomplished. That will not be the case, till all the ransomed of the Lord shall be brought safe to the heavenly *Zion*. God is here represented as seeing the things which are not, as though they were, and as beholding the end from the beginning. We remarked before, that the words of our text, as connected with the preceding verses, refer to the call and conversion of the *Gentiles*. Now, though this prophecy was delivered several ages previous to that happy event taking place, yet the great *Jehovah* here speaks of it, as though it were already accomplished, *This people* have *I formed for myself.* With him to will and to do, to purpose and to perform, are so closely, so infallibly connected, as, in effect, to be the same. In the forming of this people he not only imparts every grace to them, but he is careful to preserve and cultivate those graces already implanted.

implanted. And though there be much to do for, and in, this people, indeed in each of them in particular, so long as they continue in the world; though there be many to bring in who are yet unborn, yet this great work of salvation is in his hand who will perserve and perform it till the day of *Jesus Christ*. It is the work of that God who will bring forth the top-stone with shoutings, grace, grace unto it. This people shall be brought to behold his face in righteousness, seeing he that hath wrought them for the self-same thing is God. This work, though it be progressive, is no less certain. Hear how the great Artificer speaks himself upon this subject. "Before the day was, I am he; and there is none that can deliver out of my hand: I will work, and who shall let it *." " Ask me of things to come concerning my sons, and concerning the work of my hands command ye me †." In the view of such declarations, every good man may rejoice with the Psalmist, and say, " The Lord will perfect that which concerneth me; thy mercy, O Lord, endureth for ever, forsake not thou the work of thine own hands ‡."

How pleasing, composing, and encouraging is the thought which every real believer not only may, but ought to indulge upon this view of the subject! Such may say, I am now under the forming hand of a covenant and gracious God: One who is ever watching

* Ver. 13.—† Isai. xlv. 11.—‡ Psalm cxxxviii. 3.

watching the opportunity, and waiting for the feafon, to do me good: One who has folemnly engaged himfelf by promife to make all things work together, fo as fully to accomplifh that defirable end. He may fee proper to exercife me with a variety of trials—may bereave me of fome of my outward comforts—may fhift me from veffel to veffel; but his whole defign is to purge me from my drofs. Should I not then cheerfully and implicitly bow to his fuperior and unerring wifdom, cordially believe his purpofed love, and confign myfelf and all my concerns to his fatherly care? He intends me no wrong; he afflicts not willingly, and he knows, far better than I do myfelf, what will eventually be for my good. Certainly it is my duty to lift up my heart with my hands to this God in the heavens, that he may take it, and form it to his own pleafure.

Whatever God may call you to do or fuffer, be earneft with him to work in you both to will and to do of his own good pleafure. With *Eli* bow to his fovereign authority, and fay "it is the Lord, let him do what feemeth him good." Is it not your ardent wifh to be formed for himfelf? Yea, however trying the procefs may be, what is there that ye would not be willing to part with, to comply with, or to be, provided at laft ye may be privileged to ftand complete in the whole will of God? Yield then yourfelves selves to the Lord—Lie paffive in his hand, compliant with his will, as clay upon the wheel of the potter, that he may turn you, mould you, yea form you to his own mind. In a work of fuch importance he will neither be directed nor contradicted. He is acquainted with his own defign, and will accomplifh it. He will work, and none fhall hinder him. Plead with him, therefore, to take away all your iniquity, to make you partakers of his holinefs, and finally to bring you to behold his face in righteoufnefs. Nothing tends fo much to compofe the mind under perfonal afflictions, domeftic trials, or the various croffes we meet with in the world, as this confideration, that we are creatures under God's forming-hand, and that this God has nothing elfe in view, in all his dealings with his children, but to purge their drofs, to put a brighter polifh upon their feveral graces, or to advance his benevolent defigns refpecting them. But while thefe words prove that *it is God's prerogative to form the fouls of men for his fervice and enjoyment*, they no lefs teach us,

II. *That in this act of his fovereign grace he has always refpect* to himfelf; *that is, to the manifeftation of his own glory, as the end*. This people have I formed *for myfelf*. The fcriptures invariably teach us to reflect upon God as having made all things for himfelf—a lower motive than this he never acted from—

an

an end inferior to this he never yet chiefly proposed to himself; but of this he is best able to speak, and to him we would refer you, presuming that he will engage your closest attention. These are his words, " I will say to the North, Give up; and to the South, Keep not back: Bring my sons from far, and my daughters from the ends of the earth, even every one that is called by my name; for I have created him for my glory, I have formed him, yea, I have made him*. It is for the manifestation of his own glory that he forms souls for himself. Particularly,

1. It is for the manifestation of the astonishing and unsearchable riches of his *grace* that he forms this people. And how glorious is the grace manifested in this great work! To conquer and captivate sinners with no other design than to conform them to his own amiable image, and to bring them to his kingdom! Astonishing grace! How glorious does it appear in the pardon of sin, in the sanctification of the soul, and in the support, supplies, and consolations of the people of God. Would ye know what grace can do? See it exemplified in a real character, or displayed in all its force and energy? With pleasure we refer you both to the example and description of the Apostle. This is the language, " I thank *Jesus Christ* our Lord who hath enabled me, for that he counted me faithful, putting me into the

* Ver. 6, 7.

ministry, who was before a blasphemer, and a persecutor, and injurious. But I obtained mercy, because I did it ignorantly, in unbelief: And the grace of our Lord was exceedingly abundant, with faith, and love which is in *Christ Jesus*. This is a faithful saying, and worthy of all acceptation, that *Jesus Christ* came into the world to save sinners, of whom I am chief. Howbeit, for this cause I obtained mercy, that in me first *Jesus Christ* might shew forth all long-suffering, for a pattern to them which should hereafter believe on him to life everlasting*." Nor,

2. Is the glory of the divine *power* less conspicuous in this work. How powerful must that word be which can penetrate even an heart hard as adamant! How omnipotent must that arm be that can enthrone grace in that very heart where sin has reigned; can preserve it, though encompassed with so great opposition——opposition deeply rooted, and long protracted in its efforts! Yet this grace can finally present the soul thoroughly purged from all its dross, and completely polished with the highest lustre of holiness. *Kept by the power of God*, this will be the pleasing astonishment of every saved soul on its entrance into the heavenly *Zion*. *Kept by the power of God*, will be inscribed upon all the mansions of the redeemed in the heavenly palace; and *kept by the power of God*, will be the free confession, and the delightful song of eternity. What astonishing

* 1 Tim. i. 12—15.

ing power will then be manifested in the formation, the preservation, the perseverance, and perfection of the glorified throng! The God of power will then be glorified in all his saints, in a manner and in a degree which he never was before.——The same remark may be applied,

3. To the *wisdom* of God. This attribute of *Jehovah* shall likewise be gloriously manifested and honoured in this great undertaking. Wisdom, the most astonishing wisdom, will then appear to have exerted itself in the whole dispensation of the gospel, sending it to this or that people in particular—directing ministers in the ordinary dispensation of it—sealing it upon the hearts of men, and thus sanctifying and supporting them to the day of *Christ Jesus*. The wisdom of God will no less appear in fixing upon the means of bringing sinners to *Christ*, ordering every thing relative to their course, over-ruling all things for their good, and raising them from the depths of human misery to the summit of heaven's honours. Such must have reason for ever to exclaim, " O the depths of the riches, both of the wisdom and knowledge of God! How unsearchable are his judgments, and his ways past finding out *! And when the grand designs of eternal wisdom are completed, all his redeemed people will unite in saying, *He hath done all things well*.——But it yet

* Rom. xi. 33.

yet remains that we glance at the third thing proposed, viz.

III. *That from this, as from all his other works, the Lord will eventually derive a glorious revenue of praise.* " They shall shew forth my praise." The success was certain to himself when he entered upon the great design, but the event shall prove that it has fully answered all that he expected or intended from it. Here we would briefly remark,

1. That it is not only the duty, but the desire of that people whom God forms for himself *to praise him in the present life.* All the honour of the work they ascribe to him; and to him they cheerfully own their obligation. All those sacred privileges with which they are honoured, they consider as so many incentives to promote his praise, agreeable to the Apostle's observation, " Ye are a chosen generation—a royal priesthood—an holy nation—a peculiar people, that ye should shew forth the praises of him who hath called you out of darkness into his marvellous light *."

2. It will be the happy disposition, and the delightful employ, of God's formed people, *eternally to give unto him the honour due on that account.* Now is he forming the instruments which are intended to celebrate his praise in eternity; and, from the expence he has been at, as well as the length of time employed in preparing them, what a jubilee of praise may we suppose will be heard when all shall be ready! In our own country and

* 1 Pet. ii. 9.

and age preparations have more than once been made to celebrate the renown of the immortal *Handel*. The day was fixed, and the event, we have been informed, not only anfwered, but every way exceeded expectation. But what will be the honour and the triumph of *that day*, when the Herald of the King of kings fhall cry, " To the North, Give up, and to the South, Keep not back: Bring my fons from far, and my daughters from the ends of the earth; even every one that is called by my name, for I have created him for my glory—I have formed him, yea, I have made him."

We proclaim, therefore, the fummons this day. Prepare—prepare to meet your God—confecrate your beft fervices to him—ftudy his glorious character—bow to his authoritative pleafure—fall into his gracious hands—begin his praifes here—and prepare for the nobler celebration of his honour in eternity. Look up to this God *now* to form you for himfelf. The forming feafon will foon be over, and remember that " there is no work, device, or repentance in the grave, whither we are all going." Be ye therefore ready: Addrefs yourfelves to him who now fitteth upon his throne, making all things new; and, when he fhall appear, may an abundant entrance be adminiftered unto us into his everlafting kingdom. *Amen.*

SERMON

SERMON XVI.

Happy Mediocrity: Or, an humble Plea presented to the universal Proprietor.

PROVERBS xxx. 7, 8, 9.

Two things have I required of thee, deny me them not before I die. Remove far from me vanity and lies; give me neither poverty nor riches, feed me with food convenient for me: Lest I be full, and deny thee, and say, Who is the Lord? or lest I be poor, and steal, and take the name of my God in vain.

THE chapter before us is ascribed to *Agur*, the son of *Jakeh*. Some suppose it to be only a name assumed by *Solomon*, and that no other than himself is intended; but this seems highly improbable, both from his descent and from his prayer. His father's name is particularly mentioned, and the petitions offered here by no means suit with that condition in which *Solomon* was placed by the hand of divine providence; who he was we presume not to say

say farther than what is related of him in the first verse of the chapter. Evident it is from the context that he was a wise, humble, and eminently good man. We find him freely acknowledging his ignorance respecting the unsearchable greatness of the divine Majesty, and the wonderful works of his hand.—— *Ver. 2, 3, 4. Surely I am more brutish than any man, and have not the understanding of a man. I neither learned wisdom, nor have the knowledge of the Holy. Who hath ascended up into heaven, or descended? Who hath gathered the wind in his fists? Who hath bound the waters in a garment? Who hath established all the ends of the earth? What is his name, and what is his Son's name, if thou canst tell?* He professeth the most unfeigned esteem and reverence for the word of God.——*Ver. 5, 6. Every word of God is pure: he is a shield unto them that put their trust in him. Add thou not unto his words, lest he reprove thee, and thou be found a liar.* He then relates what was the daily and the importunate prayer of his soul. But previous to our review of the prayer, we would make a few general remarks on the introduction to it, which is contained in ver. 7. *Two things have I required of thee, deny me them not before I die.* From which we remark,

That God is to be owned by all his intelligent creatures, as the great proprietor and disposer of all things. He doth whatsoever he pleaseth not only in the armies of heaven, but amongst the inhabitants of the earth. Riches and poverty are alike at his difpofal; he appoints and commiffions them at his pleafure, configning this to one, that to another as he pleafeth. The earth is the Lord's and the fulnefs thereof; the filver and the gold, yea crowns and fceptres belong to him. He formeth the light and createth the darknefs; he makes peace and creates evil; he, even he, doth all thefe things.* He fixes the boundaries of every man's habitation, and allots that meafure of plenty or of poverty which his fovereign pleafure fees beft for each of them. Poverty and riches are here reprefented as proceeding alike from God. He affigns to every one his portion, and deals forth with infinite wifdom the evidences of his pleafure. He gives or takes, adds or diminifhes, according to the rule of an infinite underftanding.

We remark further from this introduction to *Agur's* prayer, *that importunity and perfeverance in prayer is a great duty.* " Two things have I requefted, deny me them not." He follows the application—cannot bear a denial, is all importunity to obtain. He prays, and he looks up, fo that his eyes may be faid to exprefs the language of his foul as much as his lips. Like the Patriarch, he cannot, will not, let the Lord go till he has conferred the bleffing upon him. *I have defired, deny me not.* Earneftnefs and importunity become

* Ifaiah xlv. 7.

us when necessity spurs us on, and the blessings of God are to be obtained: As one observes, " A lazy suitor begs a denial," and formality in prayer puts a negative upon the very petitions we present. " Ye ask and have not, because ye ask amiss." Pray in prayer. Wrestle for the blessing. It is worthy of all the ardour with which ye can pursue it. It comprehends both grace and glory.

Once more: *In all our addresses to a throne of grace, a dying day should be kept in view.*— " Deny me not before I die." God's blessings are the life of the soul; these denied, the soul languisheth. We faint, we are undone for ever without them. View yourselves as upon the borders of your graves every time that ye bow before the throne of mercy. The remark of a good man, whom I lately conversed with, was much to this purpose. He observed, " that the gradual approach of his trials had, he trusted, prepared his mind for that great change which seemed to be at hand.——That for some time past he had habitually gone to a throne of grace, and retired from it as though it were the last time that he should have the opportunity to go to, and that he had found himself calm and serene in the idea that this might be the case."*

Happy, desirable frame! May we so wrestle

---

* The person here alluded to died in about four days after this, in the full exercise of reason and of grace. It might be truly said of him that his end was peace, and that his course was finished with joy.

and plead as those who are pursued by death, and have eternity in view. Every approach to the throne of grace is a step nearer to the throne of judgment. There must be a last visit for each of us to make there, and may every visit be improved by us as though it were the last opportunity that we may have, to ask for, or to receive grace: Be importunate to obtain *that* before a dying hour which is not to be had after it. These things being remarked, we propose more fully to consider,

I. The prayer itself.
II. The reasons upon which the petitions are grounded.

We shall then close the subject with a reflection or two.

I. We propose to consider *the prayer of Agur*, which is, *Remove far from me vanity and lies; give me neither poverty nor riches; feed me with food convenient for me.* The sum of this prayer consists of three parts, which may be arranged under these three words, *Remove—Withhold—Confer.*

1. *He pleads that vanity and lies may be removed far from him.* By vanity and lies some understand the same as poverty and riches; others, that sin, in its various approaches and appearances, is intended. Certain it is, that though sin assumes the most specious appearances in its approach and temptations, yet it always

always issues in deception and disappointment. It promises pleasure or advantage, but terminates in pain and misery. To the mind of a good man sin appears the greatest of all evils. It is that which he both dreads and deprecates. Having been repeatedly deceived by it, he intreats the Lord to remove it far from him. We shall consider the believer in this petition as supplicating for pardoning grace—crying for preventing goodness—and acknowledging his own weakness.

When he says remove far from me vanity and lies, may not the words be considered as a *supplication for pardoning grace?* In how many instances have we been deceived and imposed upon by sin! How long have some of us been living under the deception! But the soul, awakened to a sense of its state and danger, sees that it has been so long lying under a load of guilt and a sentence of condemnation. Sin is hated—is confessed—the conscience is burdened—and the soul implores pardon and forgiveness; and to pardon sin is, in the language of scripture, *to put it away*, or *to remove it from the soul as far as the east is from the west:* For this desirable blessing burdened sinners plead. They see and feel their need of that inestimable favour. Their prayer is, " Take away all iniquity, receive us graciously and love us freely." Sin is that intolerable burden which, unless removed, must inevitably sink them into the depths of despair and ruin. The pardon of sin, therefore, is the first and grand business which the awakened sinner has to attend to at a throne of grace. He sees that he has followed after lying vanities; that he has been wretchedly deceived; and that unless sin be removed, the separation between God and the soul must be everlasting. Were this important truth seen in its proper light, believed as it ought to be, and felt in all its vast importance, with what earnestness, Brethren, should we plead for the pardon of sin every time we go to the throne of mercy, our cry would be, " Lord, remove far from me vanity and lies."

But is not *preventing goodness*, as well as pardoning mercy, implored in this sentence? When he requests that the Lord would remove from him vanity and lies, it is the same as if he had desired, with the Psalmist, to be kept back from presumptuous sins, lest they should gain the dominion over him. We need every moment to be kept far from the object of temptation; and it is a mercy in God to remove that far from us, which the folly or the deceitfulness of our hearts would otherwise prompt us to follow to our ruin. To be kept from the evil that is in the heart, and not to be led into temptation, are petitions never to be forgotten. No more would be necessary to ruin the most wise or eminent professor, than to suffer or permit those objects of temptation to come full into his way to which his depraved nature is moſt inclined. When this is the caſe the piety of a *David* is ſtained, the wiſdom of a *Solomon* changed into fooliſhneſs, and the ſtrength of a *Sampſon* is reduced to weakneſs: But as parents lay thoſe things out of the way which they apprehend might be prejudicial to their children; ſo the Lord, to evidence his regard to his family, removes far from them vanity and lies. Were not this his conduct, how much more frequently ſhould we be allured by falſe appearances than we are, and impoſed upon to our great diſtreſs, if not to our utter deſtruction. A gracious God looks all around, yea kindly goes before his family, that he may remove every difficulty and danger out of their way.

Surely nothing can more fully expreſs the ſoul's *acknowledgment of its weakneſs* than the words now before us, " Pardon and prevent," ſays the ſinner, " for I ſee that I am neither able to remove the guilt of ſin by any methods I can deviſe, or to reſiſt the leaſt temptation to ſin, unleſs ſuccoured and aſſiſted by thee. In me, that is in my fleſh, dwelleth no good thing." What an acknowledgment is this that both the juſtification of the ſinner, and the preſervation of the ſoul in a ſtate of acceptance, is all of God! It is he that forgiveth all our iniquities, and healeth all our maladies. He pardoneth, and he preſerveth the ſoul for his name's ſake. O how ſhould we ruſh upon temptation, and
completely

completely ruin ourselves, did not he prevent us with the blessings of his goodness! Look back, O ye followers of the Lord, with gratitude and with astonishment, and see in how many instances he has withheld you from sinning against him! With the cords of love he has graciously held you in; or mercifully hedged up your way, when you were ready to rush upon your ruin.——And were he even now, after all the warnings you have had, all the evidences of the deceitfulness of sin, and all the grace ye have received—were he now for a single day or hour to forsake you, how wretched, how miserable would ye be! O, plead with him to hold you up, and to hold you back; for therein consists both your safety and your honour. Without him ye would trifle and presume, and fall and be snared and taken. By this time, it is hoped, ye begin to see the propriety of the first petition in *Agur's* prayer, and are led to make it your own. We need the Lord's interposition continually, both to prepare us for the way, and to take up the stumbling-block out of the way of the people.

2. The next plea is, that God would be pleased *graciously to withhold whatever might be injurious to the soul's best interest: Give me neither poverty nor riches.* This petition is by no means to be understood as prescribing to the Holy One of *Israel*; nor was it poverty or riches, strictly considered, that he deprecated,

cated, but those disagreeable effects or evils which are generally connected with them. Poverty, with the presence and blessing of God, may be a profitable situation; and riches, where wisdom and grace are given to improve and to enjoy them, may render a person more happy and more extensively useful. Either of them he could bear with God, but with neither of them without him.

Poverty is therefore pleaded against on account of those anxious thoughts, those perplexing cares, and those grievous temptations which generally attend it. Poverty often draws the veil over God's faithfulness to his promises, hides comfort, anticipates misery, obstructs our way to a throne of grace, and keeps the soul upon the rack. Little do the sons of plenty imagine into what distresses and perplexities many of their fellow-creatures are plunged. Promises and Providences seem to jar in their experience, and the tempestuated soul is ready to say, " It is in vain to wait for the Lord any longer." Distrustful and dishonourable thoughts of God are frequently the progeny of poverty.——The usual supply suspended——every stream apparently cut off——the purse exhausted——an empty board—a craving appetite—perhaps a numerous family crying for bread, while every demand is as a dagger to the heart of an agonizing parent.—From such evils who would not wish to be delivered; and yet even in such a

situation

situation grace has often shone, and infant piety has sometimes begun to discover itself. A remarkable instance of this kind is related by the great and good Mr. *Carryl*, from his own knowledge; and after an author of such repute we dare repeat it: " I remember," says he, " a woman who had a child about eight or nine years of age. Once they were reduced to such a strait, that hunger began to pinch them sore: At length the child looking earnestly at the mother, said, *Mother, do you think God will starve us?* No, said the mother, I hope not. *But if he do*, added the child, *yet we must love and serve him still*. Such language argued her to be more than a child in grace." *

Riches also are deprecated so far as they tend to draw away the heart from God: *Neither give me riches.* Riches often blind the eye, so that the possessor sees not his mercies— they enervate the hand, so as to prevent its doing the good that it ought—they intoxicate the mind, and keep it groveling in the dust— they beget covetous desires, false confidence, the love of the world, and expose those who possess them to envy, to danger, to the illwill of relatives, and sometimes to death.— *Agur* wished to avoid the certain cares, incumbrances, and evils which riches generally bring with them. Trust not then in uncertain riches, they often draw the heart from God,

* *Carryl* on *Job*, vol. I. p. 16. Fol. Edit.

God, retard the soul in its course, and distract the mind with a variety of forehand contrivances.

What the good man here wished for, was a sufficiency without superfluity; that happy mediocrity which neither exposes a man to anxious care, nor deprives him of the smiles of God and the sense of his presence. He wished to be fixed not so low as to be continually enveloped in the fogs of chilling fears, nor so high as to be exposed to the adverse winds of temptation. A supply, but not a superabundance, was what he requested in his way to heaven. Support is what we all stand in need of, and having food and raiment, that is every thing convenient and sufficient, therewith we should be content. A staff (as one observes) may assist the traveller in his way to the city, but a bundle of them would only prove a burden to him. Be not anxious then to be rich, but leave the Lord to choose your inheritance for you.

3. The other petition is, That the Lord would be pleased to grant him a sufficiency. *Feed me with food convenient for me:* Feed me, just as a parent does his child, or as a bird her young. This request implies both *submission to God's choice, and satisfaction with it,* as also *an humble and habitual dependence on his Providence.*

It implies *submission to God's choice, and satisfaction with it.* " Feed me with food convenient for me." All the children of God are not fed alike, nor could they all bear it: Some have milk, and others ftronger meat. To fome he fees it moft convenient to give them but little at a time, while others have greater plenty beftowed upon them at once: But their heavenly Father knows what is beft adapted to each ftate, and to every conftitution of the whole family. Refign thyfelf then, O believer, to the fuperior judgment of the heavenly Parent. What if he appoints bitter herbs for thy provifion, it is either to purge out fome peccant humour, or to ftrengthen thee under fome weaknefs. Thou haft juft *that* which thy God fees to be beft for thee; and though thou mayeft, yet he cannot be miftaken. Learn contentment with his will. A little, with his blefling, is enough. What if it be not fo coftly, fo delicate, fo palatable as might be wifhed, it is what he that loves thee, and what he who ftudies thy real intereft with the greateft exactnefs, fees and knows to be moft convenient for thee. Commit then thy way to the Lord, and while he gives you your daily bread, be fatisfied with your portion.

An humble and habitual dependence upon his Providence is alfo included in the petition, *Feed me.* He who has fed you to-day will alfo feed you to-morrow, while you confecrate to him the ftrength derived from the laft fupply, and look to him for more, that you
may

may use it in the same way: And remember that God, who fed the Patriarch when he wandered alone, fulfilled his prayer in providing for his family afterwards upon his return. The sacred historian tells us that "*Jacob* vowed a vow, saying, If God will be with me, and will keep me in this way that I go, and will give me bread to eat, and raiment to put on, so that I come again to my father's house in peace, then shall the Lord be my God."* The Lord honoured his faith, and so answered his prayer, that returning, as he expressed it, with *two bands*, he and all his family were amply provided for. The Lord has encouraged us to pray to him for our daily bread, and to depend upon him continually: And to have an eye to the gracious, constant provision made for us by a kind and bountiful benefactor, is one mean to engage the heart to love and praise the Lord. Cast then your care upon the Lord, trust also in him, and verily thou shalt be fed. Thy demands, should they increase ever so much, cannot exhaust his treasures; " for the earth is the Lord's and the fulness thereof." It was God's ancient promise to *Israel*, that they should be watered, even as a gardener watereth his vines with his foot. The meaning of it was this: That as in those parts the gardener with his foot trod out a channel or gutter, which led from every vine, up to

* Genesis xxviii. 28.

a grand refervoir for water, fituated in the higher part of the vineyard, by which means every plant was fupplied from thence.——So the Lord waters all the trees of righteoufnefs, thofe parts which are of his planting: And in proportion to the number of plants that there are in each vineyard, (under the image we mean families) he will both mark out, and open the channels of conveyance to them.

Having now confidered the prayer itfelf, we pafs on,

II. To *the reafons upon which thefe petitions are grounded.* Thefe are found in the *ninth verfe*, "Left I be full and deny thee, and fay, Who is the Lord? or left I be poor and fteal, and take the name of my God in vain." You will fee, as was hinted before, that it was not fo much the different ftates here referred to, as the evils and dangers connected with them, which the good man here prayed againft.—— He faw,

1. That the rich were in danger of forgetting God, and of viewing things as flowing to them in an ordinary way. Sometimes they are unmindful of the fpring from which they are fupplied; they lofe the relifh of their comfort, and abufe their mercies. Fullnefs often produces infenfibility, ftupidity, loathing, and impiety: Thus *Jefhurun* firft waxed fat, and then kicked. Ye that are in affluence have need to requeft of God to keep

your

your eyes open to your mercies, and your hearts deeply affected with a sense of them. Let not their Author be denied. The goodness of the Lord should constrain you to gratitude, to own your obligations, and to profess your allegiance. *Moses* saw occasion to warn *Israel* of their duty in this respect.——
"When", says he, "thou hast eaten, and art full, thou shalt bless the Lord thy God for the good land which he hath given thee: Beware that thou forget not the Lord thy God, in not keeping his commandments, and his judgments, and his statutes, which I command thee this day: Lest when thou hast eaten and art full, and hast built good houses, and dwelt therein; and when thy herds and thy flocks multiply, and thy silver and thy gold is multiplied, and all that thou hast is multiplied: Then thine heart be lifted up, and thou forget the Lord thy God." *

2. *Agur* saw that poverty also had its dangers: That such were in danger of taking that which was not their own, and thereby bringing a disgrace upon their profession.—— This he represents as taking the name of his God in vain. Hunger will break through every barrier, and even a good man may, in circumstances of distress, be tempted to steal; some have not only felt the temptation, but have been permitted to fall into it. Mr. *Perkins* mentions the case of a good man who, being very poor, was reduced to such an extremity

* Deut. viii. 10——14.

tremity for the support of his family, as to steal a lamb from a neighbouring rich man. He did this—a part of it was dressed—meal-time came when he sat down with his family—he attempted, as had been always his custom, to ask a blessing upon their provision—but he was not able—he burst into tears—rose from the table—hastened to the proper owner—acknowledged his fault—and promised that if it were ever in his power he would make restitution. The good Lord preserve us from such trying circumstances, and not suffer us to be led into temptation, but deliver us from evil!——But we close all with a reflection or two from the subject; and,

1. How different is the prayer of many from that of *Agur*. Give me riches is the cry of one, nothing less will satisfy me—and me honour, says another, for riches without that is not sufficient for me. To be poor is to be miserable, says the first; and to be destitute of the honours of this world, is to be wretched, says the other: Happiness is conceived by these to be comprehended in the one or in the other; but says the good man, Give me neither, for happiness I see lies between these extremes. Neither silver nor gold can satisfy me; no, nothing but the light of God's countenance. This man's portion is not in the creature, but in the God of every creature. He soars above the creation, and seeks his good where alone it is to be

be had. The heart muſt be weaned from the world before it will be ſatisfied with any thing but the world.

2. If poverty, on account of the evils with which it is connected, is to be prayed againſt by every good man, then every prudent care is to be taken, by every exertion of diligence and induſtry, to guard againſt it. Be active in your ſeveral callings, ſetting the Lord always before you, labouring as under his eye, and looking to him for direction, aſſiſtance, and a bleſſing. Indolence is injurious both to the mind and the body; it is reproachful to a profeſſion of religion; it often entails wretchedneſs upon a family, and is a robbery committed upon ſociety.— The active man redeems time, promotes his health, ſerves his family; and, if that activity proceed from a principle of grace, he imitates Angels, and *Jeſus Chriſt*, and God. Where poverty comes with a divine commiſſion, we may hope for the ſupport of the everlaſting arms, and the comforts of the divine preſence under it; but if it originate from our own indolence or imprudence, we may expect to feel it in all its weight. May we be diligent in buſineſs, fervent in ſpirit, ſerving the Lord, and in every ſtate learn to be content: may we deſire to be uſeful here, and finally to be admitted into that world where poverty will be for ever removed, and where the

riches

riches of glory shall be possessed without the mind being in the least injured by them.—— Rich in faith, may we give glory to God, and finally be glorified in his presence through *Jesus Christ*. *Amen*.

SERMON

SERMON XVII.

God the Refuge of his Saints.

PSALM lxxi. 3.

Be thou my strong habitation, whereunto I may continually resort: thou hast given commandment to save me, for thou art my rock and my fortress.

WHAT a pleasing mixture of humble prayer and holy confidence is presented to our view in the words now before us. While it claims our most serious attention, it calls for our strictest imitation. The faith of *David* was fixed upon that God to whom his prayer is here preferred. He believed that *Jehovah* had purposed to save him—that in virtue of that purpose the command was already gone forth for the execution—and that the event would certainly take place, for what can resist the will of Omnipotence? And yet he considered prayer as neither unnecessary nor improper on this occasion. He pleads to be admitted to the full view of the happiness of such a condition, and to rest upon God as his refuge and security.

Two things are evident respecting the season to which this Psalm particularly alludes. It was composed in a time of great trouble, and when the Royal Psalmist was far advanced in life: His strength was greatly impaired, his natural vigour much declined, and grey hairs indicated that he had not long to live: Hence he prays that God would not cast him off in the time of old age, or forsake him when his strength failed, *ver.* 9. At this season the good man met with a very severe trial, and what greatly added to the weight of the trial was, that it arose from the son of his own bowels. *Absalom* seems to have seized the advantage of his father's illness, and basely employed every artifice to steal away the affections of his subjects from their sovereign. So great was the success that accompanied the unnatural attempt, that at length he presumes to sound the trumpet of rebellion, erects the standard of revolt, and the people flock around it: so soon was the scheme ripe and brought to maturity, that others proclaim it to the king before his suspicions were so much as excited. No army collected to stem the torrent of rebellion—the wisest counsellor in the cabinet gone over to the interest of *Absalom*—weakened with age, and enfeebled by his late indisposition, the afflicted monarch is obliged
to

to abandon his palace, the capital, and even a confiderable part of his houfhold. Think, O ye parents, what muft *David* have felt on this occafion; his domeftic felicity interrupted, his honours, nay more, his very life in danger, and by his own fon. The fword drawn, perhaps, with the black intent of fheathing it in the bowels of an affectionate parent. Ah *Abfalom!* it had penetrated too deeply already, and pierced to his very foul.— But how does this great man conduct himfelf under fo trying a difpenfation? Doth he break forth in the language of defpair, or imprecate curfes upon the head of a rebellious fon? Neither of thefe: Meekly he bows to the fovereign pleafure of the King of kings: He places both his honours and his life before his footftool, that he may difpofe of them at his pleafure: He is all refignation, and what his heart indites his lips exprefs. Thefe words, *the will of the Lord be done,* expreffed the frame and temper of his mind; or, more exactly, as the facred hiftorian copied them from his lips: " If I fhall find favour in the eyes of the Lord, he will bring me again, and fhew me both his ark and his habitation: But if he thus fay, I have no delight in thee; behold here am I, let him do to me as feemeth good unto him." * The trials which *David* met with were like fo many meffengers fent from his God to call him

* 2 Sam. xv. 25, 26.

him nearer to himself. They invited, nay pressed him to the bosom of his gracious father. They excited desire, drew forth faith, promoted confidence in God, and enabled him to direct his prayer and to look up.

In the first verse of the Psalm we find him proclaiming his confidence in God, and requesting that he might not be put to confusion: *In thee, O Lord, do I put my trust, let me never be put to confusion;* as if he had said, should that be the case, the distress, the disappointment, indeed, will be mine, but the dishonour must fall upon thee, my God; but do not abhor me for thy name's sake, do not disgrace the throne of thy glory; remember, break not thy covenant with me.*

The Psalmist having in the general expressed his dependence and desire, proceeds to a more particular request for deliverance and salvation in the *second* verse: *Deliver me in thy righteousness, and cause me to escape: incline thine ear unto me, and save me.* How brief, and yet how expressive are these petitions: *Deliver me—cause me to escape—save me.* How earnest, how importunate is he in the request, *Incline thine ear;* and how substantial the argument upon which he founds the desire! *Do it in thy righteousness:* As if he had said, " Display thy equity in judgment; defend thine honour, and confirm thy truth by protecting and delivering me from all mine enemies." In the words of the text he enlarges

* Jerem. xiv. 21.

more

more fully upon the concluding petition of the preceding verse. There he had pleaded for salvation; but was it only a salvation from the rebellion and rage of his son *Absalom* that he requested? That, no doubt, he desired, but further than that, even to a spiritual and eternal salvation, we apprehend, he looks in the words now before us: " Be thou my " strong habitation, whereunto I may conti- " nually resort: thou hast given command- " ment to save me, for thou art my rock and " my fortress."——In the words we have,

I. The view that the Psalmist had of God, and of his interest in him upon this oc- casion: " Thou art my rock and my fortress."

II. The petition he presents to God, grounded upon this view he had of him: " Be thou my strong habitation, where- " unto I may continually resort."

III. The encouragement he found to hope for a favourable answer: " Thou hast " given commandment to save me."

In the words we have to notice,

I. *The view that the Psalmist had of God, and his interest in him:* " Thou art my *rock* and my *fortress.*" These words, though placed at the close of the verse, seem to claim our first attention.

That

That we may more fully enter into the spirit and beauty of the two images here made use of, it will be necessary steadily to keep in view the situation we have supposed the Psalmist to be in at the season here referred to. By the rebellion of *Absalom*, it is natural to suppose the whole state was shaken, the throne seemed to totter, and even the royal city was no longer a place of security. In a concussion so violent, the eyes of *David* are directed to the Lord: He looks up to him as his *rock*, and he flies to him as his *fortress*. While the very earth seemed to tremble beneath him, and all things appeared in a state of agitation around him, he seems to have reasoned thus: " O, my soul, how mutable, how uncertain are all the honours of the present life.——On earth every refuge seems to fail thee, but in God there is all the stability of a *rock*, and the security of a *fortress*. *This* God is still my friend: He will support me in this trying season: He will environ me with his everlasting arms, and secure me from the threatening danger. But striking as these images may appear to us; happily calculated as we may apprehend them to convey to the mind the most comfortable conceptions of the perfections of *Jehovah*, engaged for the security and salvation of his favourites; yet in *Judea*, a country which abounded so much with rocks and fortresses, these images would appear,

pear, if poffible, far more fignificant and expreffive.——But to come to the words,

1. *David* viewed and addreffed God under the idea of a *rock*. This is a character by which he is frequently known in fcripture; being ftiled the *rock of Ifrael*——the *rock of ages*—and the *rock of falvation*. Now, under the image of a *rock*, the *ftrength*, the *immutability*, and the *eternity* of *Jehovah* feem to be prefented to our view, and impreffed upon our minds. Founded upon this rock, the church has ftood for ages unconquered by rage, invincible againft oppofition, and fuperior to every foe: Supported by the ftrength of Omnipotence, incircled with the arms of immutable affection, and borne up a monument of all the glorious perfections of the Deity, it ftands uninjured by all the fly attacks of art and error, as well as the more open affaults of infidelity and perfecution.— It ftands the miracle of Chrift's power, the proof of the imbecility of men, as well as of devils, to effect its deftruction. Upon this rock the church is built, nor fhall the power of earth or the policy of hell prevail againft it: And ftand it muft, feeing both the purpofes and promifes of *Jehovah* are engaged for its fupport.

If then, under all our fears and weakneffes, we be led to this rock, we fhall experience fupport and ftability. Here the believer ftands fecure: When preffed with the moft

heavy

heavy trials, and tossed with shaking dispensations, this rock is sufficient to sustain him. The immutable, the everlasting *Jehovah* fainteth not, neither is he weary. Here *David* found support in the season of trial; and he that was *David's* rock is still without variableness or shadow of turning: He is the same now that he was then; as able, as willing, as ready to support you as he was to sustain him: His power is not diminished, nor his purpose altered. God is a rock, his work is perfect; for all his ways are judgment; a God of truth, and without iniquity, just and right is he.* The frequent falls of rain may wash down the tops of the more lofty mountains into the lowly vallies, and thus, while they sink the one advance the other; but rocks are parts of the creation which undergo no change through length of time, or by the rage of storms. Well the powerful, the immutable, the eternal *Jehovah* is the rock of *Israel*, and founded upon that God who is possessed of these perfections, the humble believer stands superior to every storm, and shall outlive them all.

2. *David* also viewed and addressed *Jehovah* as his *fortress*. Now this image tends both to heighten and enlarge the idea. In a rock we have the representation of natural strength; but a *fortress* supposes the addition of something which tends to improve and to complete the natural strength of the rock upon which

* Deut. xxxii. 4.

which it is founded; so is it in the case before us. The omnipotence, the immutability, and eternity of God are (if the expression may be allowed) his natural strength; but the bare discovery of these perfections in God doth not constitute him our *fortress*. In order to our taking encouragement from these his natural perfections—in order to our finding support from, and security in them, there needs an addition. What I mean is, there wants a discovery of the divine will—a declaration of his pleasure and purpose—a promise that he is resolved to exert these his perfections in our behalf.—In a word, a solemn engagement to complete and accomplish our happiness and salvation: It is this, and this alone, that constitutes him a *fortress:* This discovers his wisdom, power, grace, promise, and truth, engaged to succour, to defend, and deliver all those who put their trust in him. God hath spoken in his holiness.—Faithful is he that hath promised.— He cannot deny himself—and he will not deceive or disappoint his people. His counsel must stand, and he will do all his pleasure according to what he has declared in the promises of his word; and he who formed the one and speaks the other is immutable. We see then that both the natural and the moral perfections of Deity are here united, and stand solemnly engaged for the support and security of all those who have fled for refuge to this grand object of hope set before them in the Gospel.

Before we entirely dismiss this particular, the situation of *David*, upon this occasion, demands more particular notice. It was truly pitiable on *two accounts*, and in each of them he was a proper representative of every believer. In *himself* he was very weak, partly through age, and partly through his late indisposition; and in this weak state he was called to engage in a very trying and unequal conflict: But though weak in himself, his God was a *rock* to support him; and though surrounded with enemies, and unable to resist them in his own strength, God was his *fortress*. In like manner, under all his natural weaknesses, his sinful infirmities, as well as against all his spiritual enemies, the soul that relies on a Covenant-God is supported. Out of weakness he is made strong; the power of *Christ* rests upon him, and while his grace proves sufficient for him, his strength is made perfect in weakness. Of himself he is no way equal either to duty or difficulty, but he can do all things thro' *Christ* who strengthens him, and all his sufficiency is of God.

3. In that God, whom he had represented under these images, he claims particular interest: Thou art *my* rock and *my* fortress. Should it be inquired upon what ground was this confidence founded? The answer is ready; upon the free and gracious promise
of

of God—his former kind and wonderful appearances for him—the frequent, solemn, and unfeigned surrenders he had made of himself to God—and the present frame and disposition of his mind. The Spirit of the Lord had drawn out his soul in faith and prayer—his hopes were fixed, his expectations raised, and his confidence established; and from all this he concluded that his God would not fail him, but would realize all *that* to him that was represented under the idea of a rock and fortress:—And from this we learn that true confidence of a soul's interest in God is not founded upon any transient impressions on the mind, nor does it arise from any lively flights of fancy, but from the word of God directed to us, from the work of his Spirit in us, and from the appearances of his grace and providence in our behalf. They are evidently of God who are thus led by his Spirit.——Proceed we now,

II. *To the petition which the Psalmist presents to God, grounded upon the preceding view that he had of him, and of his interest in him:* " Be thou my strong habitation whereunto I may continually resort." The whole of the language, you will observe, is metaphorical. Before he had spoken of God as a rock and a fortress: Here, under the notion of an *Habitation.*—— Under this branch of the discourse we shall glance both at his request, viz. that God would be *his habitation*—and likewise at the properties of this habitation.

1. He pleads that God would be his *habitation*. Turned out of an earthly mansion, through the unnatural conduct of his son, forced out of his chamber when he was sick, and excluded the sanctuary, his request is, that God would be his habitation. Now endeavour to unite in your idea age, indigence, and infirmities, and then you will behold in *David*—a king—a tender parent—and a friend of God, stripped of every honour, of every comfort, except what he found in God, and driven from his dwelling by a proud, profligate, and wicked son. Perhaps this is one of the most striking pourtraits of royalty in distress that the page of history ever exhibited: But the mind of *David* was carried above and beyond all these things: His eyes, his heart, his voice were all directed upwards: His prayer was, *be thou my habitation*. From this then learn, that God himself is the proper habitation of believers. In him they find rest, and to him they naturally turn in a time of trouble. The trials of this world drive the Christian to his God, just as a thunder-storm drives us to our habitation for shelter: On the contrary, the smiles of the world, and prosperity in it, like a clear summer's day, tempt us to wander further and further from our home. The immutable *Jehovah* has been the habitation of his people

in all generations. From him they have always derived their rest, their safety, and their comfort—to him they have applied in all their trials, and have always found him ready to receive them, and well furnished for their support and satisfaction. God is the home, the habitation of his people when exposed and destitute.

2. The *properties* of this habitation are not to be passed over in silence; as described in the text they are these two: It is a *strong* habitation—and *easy of access* at all seasons.

Be thou my *strong* habitation. To assist you in forming some suitable conception of the strength of this habitation, we must refer you to what has been said in the former part of the discourse: The image, as taken from the natural world, has something peculiarly happy in it to point out the absolute security of the real Christian. Nay, *three* images seem necessary, and are happily selected, in order more fully to express the design of the sacred penman.—To collect the whole into one view before you; suppose first a lofty *rock*, raised up and supported by the power of God; upon the top of this rock a *fortress* erected by one of the most skilful engineers that ever drew a plan, or saw it carried into execution; and defended by some renowned commander with a chosen band of brave and resolute soldiers: Within this fortress suppose further an *habitation*, the residence of a poor feeble mortal, for whose

whose sake all this provision is made, and for whose security all this force is employed.—How secure, how composed may we suppose such a person to be!—Such are the images made use of in the passage now before you. Such the shadows of the security of the friend and favourite of the Almighty: But remove all these shadows, and the Reality of all this representation is to be found in God. He is, he ever was, and will continue to be, the strong habitation to which his people may resort: In himself, (with reverence I speak it) in himself he is as incapable of any natural decay as he is of being overcome by any created power. The scripture, when it presents us with a representation of the security of the church and people of God, either holds it forth under the most significant metaphors, or in the most nervous and expressive words that language can furnish. These words of the Psalmist are a sufficient evidence of the former, and as a specimen of the latter, I need only refer you to *Paul's* address to the church at *Coloſſe*, chap. iii. verse 3. *Your life is hid with Chriſt in God.* The security, as the great Dr. *Doddridge* remarks, is double: " The life of the Christian," says he, " is here represented as an invaluable *jewel*, and under a double *security*, reserved *in heaven*, and laid up *with Chriſt in God*; secure, therefore, as the abode of Christ with the Father, or as the fidelity and immutability of the
Father

Father himself could make it." *—But to proceed.—As God is a *strong habitation* to the believer, so

Another property of this habitation is, that to such it is easy of access at all seasons: *Be thou my strong habitation, whereunto I may continually resort.* Such are always welcome to approach their God, and they may do it with confidence. He is ready to receive and to succour them in all their trials and difficulties. " God is their refuge and strength, a very present help in every time of trouble."† " In the day that they call he will answer them, and strengthen them with strength in their soul." ‡ He will supply all their wants, succour them in all their trials, and never leave them nor forsake them. In every age God has been the refuge and the strength of all the family of the faithful, and he is the same still, without variableness or shadow of turning. Knocking at his door ye shall find ready entrance, and he will take you under the protection of his power, while he entertains you with the riches of his grace and mercy: Hither then resort at all seasons: Flee for refuge to the hope set before you, and remember that those that come to him he will by no means cast out, but will receive them graciously.—It yet remains that we attend,

III. *To the encouragement the Psalmist had to hope for a favourable answer:* " Thou hast given

---

* Doddridge in loc.—† Psalm xlvi. 1.—Psalm cxxxviii. 3.

given commandment to save me." The command was already gone forth, nor could he entertain a doubt of its being punctually executed. Three things are to be noticed under this head—the *person* commanding—the *command* itself—and the *subject* to whom it related.

1. The *person* commanding, *Thou*. There was no need to multiply words to inform us whom he intended, the whole tenor of the address kept the mind fixed to the object. Evident it is that he had been all along immediately speaking of God, and dealing with him: But here again the idea must be heightened in order to give us a more perfect representation of the character he wished to describe. He had already represented his God under the idea of a *fortress,* now he describes him as the *commander* of that fortress. Intimating, no doubt, this comfortable truth, that the great Lord of all exerts all his perfections, and influences, inclines, and directs all his creatures to succour, to defend, to honour, to deliver, and to save the people who place their confidence in him. The great proprietor and governor of universal nature has himself graciously undertaken the defence of the church, and of every individual believer.

2. The *command* is also to be noticed: *Thou hast given commandment to save me.* Do ye inquire to whom the command is given? The

The answer is, to all his servants. Angels are constituted ministering spirits, sent forth to minister to the heirs of salvation, and to see that all things work together for their good. His purposes give birth to the command—his promises hold it forth continually—and his providence takes particular care that it be carried into execution. This then is the comfort held forth to *Zion* and to all her children; and this draws forth their souls in supplication. *Their God hath commanded their strength*; and therefore they plead, *Strengthen, O God, that which thou hast wrought for us* *. How expressive are these words of the *ease* wherewith God can save his people! He need only speak, and it is done. And how descriptive are they likewise of his *unlimited authority!* If he command, no created power can resist his sovereign pleasure, but must yield to it and submit. Consider we also,

3. The *subject* of all this care, who is so particularly alluded to in the command. *Thou hast given commandment to save* me. Weak, helpless, unworthy as I may be in myself, yet thou hast graciously espoused my cause, interested thyself in my behalf, and engaged to save me. From this we learn, that the eyes of the Lord run to and fro throughout all the earth, to shew himself strong in the behalf of them that fear him †. Thousands of angels stand before him, and ten thousand times

* Psalm lxxiii. 28.—† 2 Chron. xvi. 9.

times ten thousand fly to execute his orders, or accomplish his commands in the succour or salvation of his servants*: Nay more, their trials and their enemies too are both under the command of that God, who worketh all things according to the counsel of his own will. The wrath of men shall praise him; all things move according to his direction, and the intended event shall be accomplished; the top-stone brought forth, and the work of salvation completed to the glory of his Majesty; for, their God *has commanded to save them.* From the whole we infer,

1. That while we continue in this world, it is in vain to hope to be exempt from trouble: *David*, though a King, and a man eminent for real religion, yet had his trials; but faith in God will raise the mind above their distressing effects. The friend of God *dwells on high; his place of defence is the munition of rocks; bread is given him, and his water is sure* †. He has such support as the world knows not of.

2. From this we infer, that complete rest and permanent security are only to be found in God. There *David* sought and obtained them: But how great a loss do we sustain by the superficial views we have of the divine perfections. O study the character of God, as the grand relief in every time of trial.

3. What reason have those to bless God for their trials, when those trials have been

* Dan. vii. 10.—† Isai. xxxiii. 16.

the means of driving them to himself. It is good for you that you have been afflicted in your person, family, or circumstances: These things, perhaps, have brought you to serious thought; have directed you to your only refuge; have given you to taste *that* in God which was not to be obtained from the creature. Even when your heart has been overwhelmed, you have been led to that rock which was able to yield you both support and security. You have seen your danger, fled to the remedy, and obtained the comfort.

4. When there will be no more occasion for the *fortress* to resist the enemy, God will be the *habitation* of his people to all eternity.—In him they will find everlasting rest, perpetual entertainment, and never-failing satisfaction. He, that has been their dwelling-place in all generations, shall be their rest and their all for ever. Sorrows shall be ended, trials ended, conflicts ended; but they who have endured those sorrows, trials, and conflicts, shall enter into rest, and drink of the river of his pleasures. That this may be our privilege, God grant for *Jesus Christ's* sake. *Amen.*

SERMON XVIII.

The Soul voluntarily humbled under God's sovereign and saving hand.

---

1 PET. v. 6.

Humble yourselves, therefore, under the mighty hand of God, that he may exalt you in due time.

THESE words, you will perceive, contain an inference, and point out a duty of the real christian, deduced from the opposite character to which the apostle had referred in the verse preceding the text. He there introduces to our view the great God, armed with omnipotent power, yet furnished with all the treasures of superabounding grace. On the one hand of this infinitely glorious, and infinitely amiable Being, he places a *proud man*, or rather all the sons of pride; on the other, the *humble soul*, or all of that character who are sensible of their ignorance, impotence, and wants. The conduct of each of these towards that glorious Being, is also described, as also his towards them. Pride is represented as the life of sin; the opposite,

to

to that subjection of mind and conduct, which is due from creatures to their Creator; the ever-fruitful source which opposeth every thing in God, every thing done by him, every thing that proceeds from him. Pride is the parent of enmity, the principle, the very soul of rebellion against God. From this source hath proceeded all the contempt, and all the contradiction which God hath met with from his creatures, ever since the entrance of sin into the world, down to the present moment. Sinners, through the arrogance of their hearts, and the pride of their countenance, will not submit to God. His commands they trifle with—his counsels they reject—his authority they disown—and his yoke they endeavour to shake off. Against this principle God has set himself resolutely and without intermission. None ever yet hardened themselves against him and prospered. In every age great numbers have fallen in the contest; but, instead of being warned by their weakness and folly, others have filled their place, and the same principle has stimulated them to the same conduct. Now, against all these proud men, God has set himself in the conduct of his providence, and the threatnings of his word. Though long opposed, he fainteth not, neither is he weary in the conflict. Hitherto he has prevailed, and must eventually prevail; for *God resisteth the proud*. He first expostulates with their folly

folly—then he checks their rage a little—proves their weakness again and again—frustrates their attempts—and, when no other method will do, laying his hand upon them, he sinks their bodies into the grave, and their souls into hell. God and they did not agree in this world, nor will they be reconciled in the next; for that same principle of pride which wrought so forcibly in them upon earth, will actuate them also in hell; and therefore God will resist them for ever.

On the other hand you see a person open to conviction, sensible of his wants, his weaknesses, and unworthiness; convinced that in him, that is in his flesh, dwelleth no good thing, contented to be indebted to God for every saving benefit. He thirsts for God, even for the living God—is willing to be nothing, so that God may be all and in all. Humbly he bows to God's will, submits to his grace, loves his character, desires to be conformed to him, nor can he ever be satisfied till he awake up in God's likeness. In a word, he is humbled at God's footstool—approves of what he requires—pleads that his glory may be advanced—and is enlightened to see how this can be accomplished in the sanctification of a creature so unholy—in the salvation of a subject so unworthy as himself. He approves that God should be in all things what the word declares him to be; that he should both have what he requires, and do

what

what he sees to be right. He meets God with a meek and an humble heart, and gives him honour, by giving him confidence, believing that he will perform all *that* which he hath spoken to him of. So that this Being, who is all terror, all opposition, all contrariety to the proud sinner, is all grace, all kindness, all affability, all compliance to the humble soul. To such his blessings flow freely, liberally, constantly. The one is like an impediment in the course of a river, which opposeth, and is opposed, till, at length, it is quite worn away in the contest: The other is like a channel ready cut and just opened, which receives, embraces, and is filled to the very brink from the flowing stream. *God resisteth the proud, but he giveth grace to the humble.*

Such is the representation which is set before you by the Apostle in the preceding verses; and if ye pay that attention to it which it deserves, it will be an instructive representation to you. It addresses itself to every eye, while this necessary instruction is, by the Apostle, whispered into every ear. *Humble yourselves, therefore, under the mighty hand of God, that he may exalt you in due time.*

We might have realized the whole of the representation that has been given in the case of *Joseph* and his brethren. They were proud men; set themselves to oppose the purposes of God, and the plan of his providence:

dence: But the Lord refifted and prevailed againſt them. *Joſeph* was humble; his mind bowed in fubmiſſion to the will of God; and thought, for a feafon, he was brought low, very low indeed; yet, in due time, the Lord exalted him to be the deliverer of thoufands, and an inſtrument, in his hand, in conveying falvation to the church in every future age. But to come to the text; thefe words hold forth *three* very inſtructive leſſons for our confideration.

I. The ſtate, fituation, or condition in which we are, as creatures, *under the mighty hand of God.*
II. The incumbent duty of each of us as thus fituated, which is *to humble ourſelves under his hand.*
III. One particular end that we ourſelves ſhould keep in view, and humbly expect and wait for at the hand of God, viz. *that he may exalt us in due time.*

And may the reafonableneſs and the advantages of fuch a conduct appear to each of us in fuch a light, that we may fully comply with the apoſtolic direction. May we view it as our privilege, as well as our duty, to be under the hand of God.

I. As creatures, our *ſtate, fituation, and condition* is here repreſented, as *being under God's hand.* See his hand, we do not; feel it, it, we may not; but this is the condition of every individual of mankind. And what is the lesson we are taught by such a representation? A lesson the most humbling and interesting, viz. that, as creatures, we are in a state of *subjection* and subordination to God—that he has *ability* to accomplish his great designs with respect to each of us; and that as he *can*, so he certainly *will* effect the whole of his pleasure.

1. Our being under the hand of God is a very striking evidence and demonstration of that state of *subjection* and subordination in which we are placed with respect to him. It is he that hath made us and not we ourselves; we are his people. Different as our stations in life may be, the richest are not exempt, nor the poorest excluded from this subjection. Even the hearts of Kings and the persons of the wicked are in the hand of the Lord, and he turns them, uses them, or restrains them at his pleasure. Sin, indeed, has deranged the order on our part, but has by no means relaxed the authority on God's part. As clay ye are under the hand of the potter, and he has an indubitable right to do what he will with his own. It is in vain to murmur at his will—to rebel against his providence—to cavil at the sovereignty of his grace—or to resist his authority. Let the potsherds strive with the potsherds of the earth, but wo unto the man that striveth with his Maker.

Maker. If he be our sovereign, we ought to obey his will, and be submissive to his providence and grace; and instead of accounting this a grievance, let us esteem it our greatest privilege. His hand is upon you for support, for protection, for salvation; only resign yourselves to him and to his wonder-working hand. Resistance and ruin are not more closely connected than true subjection and complete salvation. Laying his hand upon you, therefore, the great God now claims you for his own; and will any of you dare to say, " No, I will not be subject to this God, I will not be indebted to him for my salvation." Rather, with that great and good man *David*, say, " Truly, Lord, I am thy servant, even thy servant and the son of thine handmaid. I will be the Lord's for ever." Ye are not your own, but are indebted to God for your very existence, with all its powers, its supports and comforts: And we have now to inform you, that his hand is upon you, and, as thus situated, we claim you for his servants. O bow to the authority, and bless the sovereign, shielding hand of the great *Jehovah* Whether sinner or saint, believer or unbeliever, a rebel or a subject, we can assure each of you that ye are under the hand of God: Under that same hand that humbled the pride of the haughty *Pharaoh*, that drove *Judas* to his own place, and has overwhelmed thousands of of the sons of pride with an everlasting destruction. Ye are under that hand which will either form you for himself, that ye may shew forth his praise, or separate you from his blissful presence for eternal ages. Let each of us, therefore, take up this reflection, "From this representation, it appears, that I am a creature under the hand of God. Escape from it I cannot, resist it I may, but not with impunity. That hand will either crush me to eternal death, or save me with an everlasting salvation. Lord, turn thy hand upon me, and let it prove my security, even while it evidences my subjection. Purge away my dross, create in me a clean heart, O God, and form me a vessel to thy honour and praise."

2. Our being placed under the *mighty* hand of God is expressive of his *ability* to accomplish his great designs with respect to each of his creatures. For a single moment endeavour to stretch your thoughts through earth and heaven. Reflect upon the thousands, and thousands of thousands of angels which surround the throne of Deity, or fly through worlds innumerable to execute his pleasure. Cast your attention upon the different nations of this earth and their numerous inhabitants, and then, in order to form some conception of the majesty, authority, and matchless power of God, fix your attention upon this one assertion of sacred truth,

He doth what he pleaseth in the armies of heaven and among the inhabitants of the earth; none can stay his hand, or have a right to say to him, what doest thou. Power belongeth unto God; and, would you judge of the extent or greatness of that power, know that all these creatures are *under* his hand *as subjects*; are *in it* as *instruments* for the conducting and completing of his vast designs. His hand must be a mighty hand, seeing it is armed with sovereign, unlimited, everlasting power. Only reflect upon the awful, the tremendous judgments which his hand has inflicted, or upon the great, the wonderful deliverances effected by it, and then remember his arm is not shortened, nor is his hand less mighty now than formerly. Could we either look through the mansions of heaven, or the regions of hell, the might of God's hand would stand confirmed in our view by millions of instances, the most awful or astonishing. His hand must necessarily be a mighty hand, for he is able to save and to destroy. And,

3. As he *can*, so he certainly *will* accomplish the whole of his pleasure. With creatures to will and to do are different powers, or perfections. They bear a very inadequate proportion to each other. Neither sinners nor saints can do all that they wish or incline to do: And this is one undeniable proof of the imperfect state in which they are at present;
but

but *he* that is perfect—he, whose perfections and attributes are all equal, with him to will and to do, are exactly commensurate. What he inclines to do, that he effects with the greatest ease and certainty. Hence he introduces himself to the attention of his creatures, speaking in this authoritative language, *My counsel shall stand, and I will do all my pleasure.* This God is resolved to be glorified in each one of you. The humble believer will readily say, and let him be glorified—eternally, completely glorified in my sanctification and salvation: But be ye willing or not willing, God will be honoured, either in the eternal salvation or condemnation of each individual. He will be glorified when he comes to take vengeance on them that know not God and obey not the gospel.——We now go on,

II. To consider *the incumbent duty of each one of us as thus placed under the mighty hand of God,* this is *to humble ourselves under it.* Our being under the mighty hand of God is a case of necessity: We can no more avoid that, than we could avoid being born in England, or being of such a complexion or stature: But to humble ourselves under his hand, is to be active in the surrender of our persons, our judgments, and our concerns to the pleasure of the Almighty, saying with *Eli,* " It is the Lord, let him do what seemeth him good." *Humble yourselves,* that is, resign and give up yourselves to the direction

tion and difposal of the Lord, that he may work in you and by you all the good pleafure of his will.——Now, refpecting this requirement, we remark—That it is a duty, to the exercife of which we are called *daily*—upon fome *particular occafions*, and for the *accomplifhment of that work*, which we muft defpair of ever being accomplifhed, except by his own hand.

1. It is the *daily* duty, and will be the daily defire of every good man to humble himfelf under God's mighty hand. By prayer, with fupplication and thankfgiving, he comes to God daily to place himfelf, his connections, and concerns under his directing and difpofing hand. To him he directs his prayer, and looks up for protection, for profperity, and with earneft defire for God to work all his works in him. He feels himfelf happy in a ftate of dependence, and efteems himfelf honoured in being under the direction and conduct of *One* who can require nothing unreafonable, and has power to effect the greateft things by the moft infignificant inftruments. He would not be his own, was it left to his choice; his defire and determination is to be the Lord's. Senfible how reafonable it is that every thought fhould be brought into obedience to *Jefus Chrift*, and that every member, power, and paffion fhould be confecrated to the fervice of God: And confcious at the fame time how infufficient

ficient he is to effect all this of himself, or even the smallest part of it, he daily humbles himself under God's mighty hand in such petitions as these: "Undertake, O Lord, for me. Work in me all the good pleasure of thy will, and the work of faith with power. Bring down all the strong-holds of sin, and build me up in faith, in holiness, in full conformity to thy sacred will." Thus he comes to God daily with a sincere desire to be moulded into the image of *Jesus Christ* and his gospel. Without faith in *Jesus Christ* ye can do nothing, when contending against sin, or pursuing holiness. His power alone can eradicate your corruptions, support you under your weaknesses, and confirm and establish the several graces of his spirit in your hearts. In short, his grace alone is sufficient for you, and his strength must work all your works in you, or none of them will be found acceptable. But is this your habitual conviction, and this your daily conduct as the effect thereof? Are you coming to him daily with the desire that he would not forsake the work of his own hands, but would perfect that which concerneth you? Are ye daily devoting yourselves to God, to his service, submitting yourselves to his government and conduct, placing your souls before him that he may erase the character of the old man, and upon them draw the image of his son? Are ye desirous to live, not to yourselves,

selves, or for yourselves, but wholly for the Lord? Do ye lay yourselves at God's feet and under his hand, that he may mould and form you to his pleasure? Every good man goes to God daily, desirous to learn his will, to follow the leadings of his providence, to subject his mind to his pleasure, and to supplicate his direction in all things. His prayer is, " that which I see not, shew thou me, and make me what thou wouldest have me to be." And as this is the daily work of the believer, so,

2. There are also *particular occasions* in which he is called to this duty, and desires to be found in the practice of it. Thus, for instance, doth the Lord lay his hand upon his person, his property, or his family? He bows to his sovereign pleasure. His language is that of *Job*, " Naked came I out of my mother's womb, and naked shall I return thither; the Lord gave, and the Lord hath taken away, blessed be the name of the Lord." Such a person views himself as holding every comfort in a state of dependence upon the divine pleasure; and that no one can take from, or add to, his comforts, but under the permission or direction of that glorious Being, who either extends or contracts his hand as he sees best. Thus was it with *David*, when he was called to relinquish his palace, to retire from his family, and to withdraw from those sacred privileges which
were

were dear to him as his own soul; humbly he submits to the disposals of his sovereign hand, saying, "If the Lord delight in me, he will bring me back again; and if he say I have no pleasure in thee, lo, here am I, let him do with me what seemeth him good:" Or, is his way hedged up, as with thorns? Does a cross accompany every undertaking in which he is engaged? His schemes are frustrated—his efforts prove ineffectual—his endeavours return unsuccessful, still he desires to submit to that hand which never crosses in vain, and which is able to over-rule outward crosses for the soul's advantage.—In seasons also of persecution for the cause of God, when called to suffer, the humble believer bows to the hand of God, and places himself under it, that he may receive either protection or support from it. If he suffers for righteousness sake, he accounts himself not only happy, but honoured, seeing the spirit of glory and of God resteth upon him. In a word, at all times, and upon all occasions, he desires to bow to the will of God, and to submit to his pleasure in all things.— Once more,

3. We are happy to humble ourselves under the hand of God for *the accomplishment of that work* which we must for ever despair of being accomplished except by his own hand. Ye will readily perceive that I have respect to that grand work, your *sanctification* and *sal-*

vation. In that concern we have no other resource, no other remedy but to place ourselves under this hand, despairing, for ever despairing of all help or hope from ourselves. What but that power which is equal to every undertaking, can subdue such strong corruptions—bear down such high thoughts—eradicate evils so deeply rooted, or stablish, strengthen, and perfect graces so weak, desires so languid! Would ye not despair of ever attaining perfect holiness or perfect happiness, were it not for the gracious engagements of the God of salvation? While ye look to yourselves, every thing is discouraging; but when ye have respect to God's mighty hand, and reflect upon the mighty works which have been wrought by it, then ye can with confidence rely upon him who declares that he will cleanse you from all your iniquities, and perfect that which concerneth you. Reflecting how gloriously his mighty hand hath been exerted and displayed in the works of creation, providence, and redemption; and how in each of these instances the most glorious order has been brought out of the most wild confusion, ye dare still believe that this mighty hand is able to sanctify you wholly in body, soul, and spirit. Nay more, ye see that no power, short of this power, is able to effect so great, so necessary, so desirable a change. Ye submit, therefore, to this mighty hand, that ye

may

may be created in *Christ Jesus* unto good works—renewed in the spirit of your minds—sanctified through the truth—perfected in holiness—and finally presented without spot, blemish, or any such thing before the presence of his glory with exceeding joy. Your duty, your interest, your privilege is to rely upon *Jesus Christ* as much for the sanctification, as for the justification of your souls. This work is one of the great concerns of the real Christian, and remember ye are exhorted, in the words succeeding the text, to cast all your cares upon him who careth for you. Let us now attend,

III. To that *particular end we ourselves should keep in view, and humbly expect and wait for at the hand of God,* viz. "that he may exalt us in due time." Under this branch of the subject we observe *three* things,

I. That there is ground to expect this glorious event from *his own express declarations.* In all his dealings with his people, in all his dispensations towards them, God has their good in view. Does he afflict them? It is not willingly, but either to take away sin, or to make them partakers of his holiness. If he sees them humbled before him for their sins, he cheers their soul with discoveries of his pardoning mercy. If humbled on account of languid frames or formal duties, he lifts up the soul by fresh communications of his quickening grace: And when

distressed,

distressed, because of constitutional sins, he elevates the soul by displays of his Almighty power, and its engagements to subdue them. Thus their good is the end at which he invariably aims, and to which he claims our attention and faith.

2. The process may be long, for the trial of faith, before the exalting season arrives: But the trial of your faith being more precious than gold when it is tried, shall be found to praise, honour, and glory at the appearing of *Jesus Christ.* There must be time and opportunity for all things to work together for good; and the nearer the exalting season approaches, the greater may be the trial. Thus *Israel* in *Egypt* were brought low. The hand of the tyrant grew more and more heavy. Salvation was promised, but every fresh demand, every renewed order from their task-masters seemed to place it at a still greater distance; but when pride had attained its summit, and faith could bear no more, then the Lord made bare his arm—he delivered—and he exalted them.

3. The exalting season will come when God will put an honour upon his saints, and upon the confidence they have placed in him. He will be glorified in them, and by them: And in that day it will appear that the meanest, the most humble believer was not too low for God to be exalted in. Many of you, no doubt, are well acquainted with
the

the Perſian fable, which ſeems well calculated to illuſtrate the preſent ſubject. It relates that a drop of water falling one day from a cloud into the wide extended ocean, broke out in this reflection: " Alas! what an inſignificant creature am I in this prodigious collection of waters! I am leſs than the leaſt of all the works of God!" Scarce was the reflection concluded before an oyſter opened its ſhell and ſwallowed the drop: There it lay long incloſed——was conſolidated at laſt into a pearl—fell into the hands of a diver—paſſed from hand to hand—till at length it reached the ſovereign, and was ordered to be placed on the top of his diadem.—Believers are God's jewels—they are now forming—the day approaches when he will claim and ſeparate them for himſelf—and, when poliſhed and properly arranged, they ſhall appear a royal diadem in the hand of their God.

And now permit me again to bring forward the repreſentation with which we introduced this diſcourſe. Ye ſaw God as it were reſiſting the proud, but giving grace to the humble. Which of theſe is your picture? Which of them your character? Have ye ſubmitted to the righteouſneſs of God, or are ye going about to eſtabliſh your own righteouſneſs? Reſiſtance is in vain. Grace or omnipotence will prevail. Caſt down, therefore, the weapons of hoſtility. Our God waiteth to be gracious. He loves, he honours

honours the humble; with such he promises to dwell on earth; and such alone shall dwell with him in heaven. O bow then to the hand that waits to bless you. With pleasure fall under it now, that at last ye fall not into it to your everlasting confusion. May that hand be our shield, our support, our security for *Christ's* sake. *Amen.*

SERMON

SERMON XIX.

Dark Dispensations illumined: Or, present Twilight ushering in a glorious Day.

ZECH. xiv. 6, 7.

It shall come to pass in that day that the light shall not be clear nor dark; but it shall be one day, which shall be known to the Lord, not day nor night: but it shall come to pass that at even-time it shall be light.

THERE are many things very dark and inexplicable in the prophecies of scripture, especially in those which refer to future times, and to events which are not yet accomplished. Into subjects of this nature, men of a curious turn of mind may endeavour to pry. Invention may fabricate a variety of conjectures, and fancy stamp them with the signatures of her sanction, as the most indisputable of realities: But modesty becomes us while we gaze upon subjects in their own nature so profound; for the times and the seasons God has reserved in his own power. Our only assistance, at present, in under-

understanding and explaining the prophecies that relate to future ages, must be obtained from a due attention to those prophecies and their accomplishment which are already fulfilled: Perhaps, in such cases, the patience of faith is our greatest duty, and modesty of expression our highest wisdom. Not that such parts of scripture are without their present use; nor must we pass them over as if unconcerned in them. All scripture is given by inspiration of God, and instruction or edification is to be derived by us from every part of his word; even we who are now alive may derive profit from such parts of the divine oracles as well as those who shall inhabit this world one hundred or five hundred years hence. To explain scripture is one thing; to draw improvement from it is another. Much more light is found necessary for the former than for the latter: In the one case we need a direct light falling upon the subject, and illuminating it, just as the sun does the world in a summer's day: In the other there is the same light afforded, but it falls obliquely upon the object, it only just glances upon it as the same sun does upon this part of the world in the winter season. In the perusal of some parts of the prophetic scriptures, even wise and good men may find their minds in a situation similar to the mind of *Peter*, after *Jesus Christ* had washed his feet: He saw not the propriety

priety of what had been done—he understood not the meaning thereof.——His Lord told him that he must wait for the explanation till a future season: But seeing *Jesus Christ* washed his feet, and expresly said, "That except he washed him, he had no part in him," *Peter* believed that it meant something very important, and desired to receive all the advantages of his cleansing power: "Lord," said he, "not only my feet but my hands and my head."

In the chapter before us, if not in the very words of the text, there are some things as hard to be understood as any of those parts of *Paul's* epistles to which *Peter* alludes.

The taking of *Jerusalem* by the *Romans* is supposed to be the subject treated of in the beginning of this chapter; *Behold the day of the Lord cometh, and thy spoil shall be divided in the midst of thee: For I will gather all nations against Jerusalem to battle, and the city shall be taken, and the houses rifled, and the women ravished, and half of the city shall go forth into captivity, and the residue of the people shall not be cut off from the city.* *—— Previous to the destruction of *Jerusalem*, in virtue of the predictions and precepts of *Jesus Christ*, we are told that the Christians went forth to a place called *Pella*, where they were preserved. The city itself was destroyed, and the far greater part of its inhabitants were cut off and led into captivity. These Christians, therefore,

therefore constituted the true Church and people of God. They were the subjects of that *Jerusalem* above, which is the mother of all believers.

Scarce are the *Jews* scattered, before the *Roman* empire begins to persecute the followers of Christ; the Lord steps forward as the protector and defender of his people. The *Roman* Empire is broken to pieces—the *Jews* are more extensively dispersed—even the true followers of Christ are astonished and flee:—But the event tends to a more full and extensive manifestation of the character and glory of the God of salvation. *Then shall the Lord go forth and fight against those nations, as when he fought in the day of battle. And his feet shall stand in that day upon the mount of Olives, which is before Jerusalem on the east, and the mount of Olives shall cleave in the midst thereof toward the east and toward the west, and there shall be a very great valley; and half of the mountain shall remove toward the north, and half of it toward the south. And ye shall flee to the valley of the mountains: for the valley of the mountains shall reach unto Azal: yea, ye shall flee like as ye fled from before the earthquake in the days of Uzziah king of Judah: and the Lord my God shall come, and all the saints with thee.* * God can rend the mountains of opposing empires, and open vallies for the reception of his timid or persecuted people. The most violent persecutions of his church

Ver. 3, 4, 5.

church have generally terminated either in the further advancement of his glory, or in the wider spread of the Gospel of his grace. Perhaps, with a view to something of this nature, it is added, *And it shall come to pass in that day that the light shall not be clear nor dark; but it shall be one day which shall be known to the Lord, not day nor night: but it shall come to pass that at even-time it shall be light.* We propose to consider these words as descriptive,

 I. Of the present state and condition of things, both in the world and in the church: *In that day the light shall not be clear nor dark.*

 II. Of God's inspection, arrangement, and management of things during this twilight state: *It shall be one day which shall be known unto the Lord, not day nor night.*

 III. Of that happy and glorious end with which the present state of things shall be concluded: *At even-time it shall be light.* We shall then close with a reflection or two from the subject.—— Let us therefore, as proposed,

 I. Consider this passage as *descriptive of the present state and condition of things, both in the world and in the church.* "In that day the light shall not be clear nor dark." The Sun of Righteousness is risen with healing under his wings. Light is come into the world, even the true light which now shineth. This light, though perfect in its own nature, is rendered partial through fogs, mists, and intervening clouds, which weaken its influence. The light which we enjoy under the present dispensation of the Gospel is not so obscured as it was under the Ceremonies, or by the superstitions of the *Jewish* Church, nor yet so clear and glorious as it will be in that desirable season, when the light of the knowledge of the glory of God shall fill the earth as the waters cover the sea: Not that there is any imperfection in the revelation of the mind and will of God with which we are now favoured; for we apprehend that the church, while upon earth, will have no more occasion for a new revelation from God, than the future inhabitants of this world will need an additional sun. Dark and gloomy as some of our days may be, could we soar above our atmosphere, the sun would be seen shining in all its splendor, bright as when in the meridian of one of our clearest summer-days.—Clouds and darkness originate from a lower source, and are the natural and necessary effects of the imperfect state in which we are at present placed; even in the natural world our light is neither clear nor dark. And something analogous to this we shall find to be the case, if we take a view—of the dispensation of the Gospel in the world—of that knowledge

knowledge and experience which good men are able to attain in the present state—or of the dealings and dispensations of Providence respecting them.

1. The light will appear to be neither clear nor dark, if we reflect upon *the dispensation and spread of the Gospel in the world at this day.* Upon the inhabitants of this nation, whose fathers once sat in darkness and the very shadow of death, the true light now shineth. Many have been raised up and sent forth by Providence throughout our land, to proclaim the unsearchable riches of *Christ* to sinful men; to invite them through this Saviour to be reconciled to God, and taste that he is gracious. Perhaps, since the day when the light of the Gospel first shone upon the nation, the truth as it is in *Jesus* was never more faithfully dispensed, or had a greater number to publish it than at this season, both in the Established Church and out of it.— And seeing *Christ* is preached, let it be where and by whom it may, as it is our duty to rejoice, so we do rejoice: But God hath not dealt with every nation as with this, nor has he manifested himself in all the parts of this favoured country in an equal degree. Some kingdoms are yet left under total darkness—others have only a few glimmerings of true light——from some parts of the world where the light of truth once shone, it hath been excluded by the inhabitants, or withdrawn
from

from them in displeasure: Clouds have intervened to prevent its beams from falling upon some nations—while, from other parts of the world, the shades of darkness have been dispelled to make way for this heavenly visitant. He who commandeth the sun to shine upon one city or village, and not upon another, for reasons best known to himself, and reasons neither to be investigated nor explained by us, acts the very same part respecting the dispensation of the Gospel. We find the Apostles of *Christ* themselves attempting to preach the Gospel in places where the Spirit either forbad or suffered them not. Some have remarked, that out of seven hundred and thirty millions of *Adam's* posterity, who are now supposed to inhabit this earth, not more than an hundred and twenty-two millions of them profess Christianity in any form. Of this number, part, we know, are Christians *by compulsion*—a greater part are such *by custom*—and we fear a far greater part still *can give no reason at all why they profess to be Christians*. It is probable, therefore, that they appear a very little remnant indeed, compared with the bulk of mankind, in the view of that God whose prerogative it is to distinguish characters with certainty.—Even in the true church, in the best of Christians, what ignorance and weaknesses, what imperfections and disorders discover themselves! The rays of sacred truth are, through ignorance, obstructed, misapprehended, or misapplied. Sin darkens the understanding of all in a greater or less degree, and truth is discovered by the best of men but in part, and operates upon them only in measure.——Thus it appears that the dispensation and spread of the Gospel, not only in the world but in the church, is justly represented as a day in which the light is neither clear nor dark.——The same remark holds good if we take a view,

2. *Of the knowledge and experience of this Gospel, which even the wisest and best of men attain in this life.* They have the light, and they have been savingly illuminated by it. Their " God hath shone into their hearts to give them the light of the knowledge of his glory in the face of *Jesus Christ:*" But though this discovery be special, and shall finally issue in their salvation, yet they know but in part, and see through a glass darkly. Particular truths, at seasons, sparkling before them just like stars in the heavens in a frosty night. These objects, though discovered, are seen at a distance, and viewed only on one side. In the present state of things they can no more bear to see all the truth as it is in *Jesus*, than their bodily eyes can gaze upon the sun shining in its strength: Or, were they permitted to see the whole truth for a moment, they could not long endure it. Such happy seasons are soon over—and the discovery soon forgotten. The pleasure, or the profitable impressions

impreffions which that manifeftation then made upon their mind are foon erafed, nor can they recall it, would they give the whole world to obtain their defire. In the minds, even of good men, darknefs and light ftruggle for the maftery; the light difcovers the darknefs that is in them, and that darknefs, for a feafon, obfcures the light. Their fenfations and frames often vary and oppofe each other. Corruptions and a principle of grace—hopes and doubts refift, and alternately prevail; when they would do good, evil is prefent with them. "The law in the members wars againft the law of the mind: and the flefh lufteth againft the fpirit, and the fpirit againft the flefh, fo that they cannot do the things that they would." The light of truth fhines, though imperfectly, upon their underftandings. Such fogs of darknefs and deception furround the mind in the prefent ftate, that we find an eminently holy man pleading with the Lord to fhew him the truth, and to examine into the ftate of his foul: "Open thou mine eyes, that I may behold wonderful things out of thy law—Search me, O God, and know my heart; try me, and know my thoughts, and fee if there be any wicked way in me, and lead me in the way everlafting." Ye profeffed followers of *Jefus*, long as I have been in the fchool of your divine Mafter; many and great as your opportunities and advantages have been,

when

when your attainments are impartially examined, may it not be said that your light is neither clear nor dark? You neither take in all the comforts you ought, nor can ye yield up all claim to them. No; ye would not give up even the imperfect and glimmering hopes ye have of reaching heaven at last for the world; nor yet have ye attained to that confidence which would greatly contribute to advance both God's honour and your own comfort. Your light is neither clear nor dark.——The same remark may be applicable,

3. *To the dealings and dispensations of divine Providence,* even with respect to God's own people. Their "light is neither clear nor dark." Prosperity and adversity——smiling and adverse Providences—crosses and consolations——expectations and disappointments compose their motley experience. They have to sing of mercy one day, perhaps the next to tell of heavy and distressing judgments. Often when they would converse with God about his providential dealings with them, they find themselves enveloped with darkness. His purposes and his procedures respecting them are very obscure: Sometimes, like *Israel*, they are in doubt whether the Lord be engaged on their side or not; by and by they are so situated that every doubt is entirely removed, and they are fully confident of the Lord's guidance and support.

Now, the intentions and promises of God respecting them seem just ready to be accomplished, and one march more will bring them to *Canaan*, when presently they are led back almost to the borders of the Red-Sea. Thus God to-day indulges us with a spiritual comfort, and strips us of a creature-support to-morrow. He smiles——He frowns——He raises you up—and again sinks you down; and in all these changes you no more know what he is doing with you, than *Jacob* did when the bloody garment of his *Joseph* was presented to him, or than *Job* did when his God had stripped him of his property—his family—his all, and placed him naked upon the dunghill: But as in their cases, so in yours, he will hereafter shew you the reason of his conduct: " Clouds and darkness may be round about him, but justice and judgment are the habitation of his throne. His way is in the sea, his paths in the mighty waters, and his footsteps are not known;" but he has the whole plan perpetually before him. Infinite Wisdom is capable of judging what is best for you. Your God does not act upon peradventure, but with the greatest certainty. You may be permitted to walk in darkness, and have little or comparatively no light respecting his providential dealings towards you; but he seeth the end from the beginning. Through this life you may be called to walk by faith, not by sight; but in
the

the end light shall be thrown upon all the way in which the Lord has been leading you. You shall remember, and shall admire the way, and adore the skill and the fidelity of your guide. —But, as we before proposed, we pass on to consider these words as descriptive,

II. *Of God's inspection, arrangement, and management of things during this twilight-state:* " It shall be one day, which shall be known unto the Lord, not day nor night." This may be intended to set forth—the *infinite knowledge*—the *powerful agency*—and the *astonishing goodness* of God.

1. The Lord sets one thing over against another, so as to connect, balance, and harmonize the whole by his *infinite knowledge.* As the natural day is made up of several hours and of many moments, each of which are productive perhaps of solemn or great events to this or that individual, yet all these are crouded into the same day: So it is respecting the view that God has of the persons and interests of his people. He sees how every event is to be arranged and ordered for their good. His Spirit is in all the wheels of Providence, not those excepted which, for a season, appear to them most alarming and dreadful. There may be many apparent changes and counter-changes in the plan of God's Providence respecting both the church and individuals, but they are all under the

management of one who has wifdom to conduct and perfect fo complicated a defign.— The facred Moralift encourages us, "in the day of profperity to be joyful, but in the day of adverfity to confider: *God alfo,* fays he, *hath fet the one over againft the other, to the end that man fhould find nothing after him.*" * That is, thefe different changes may be as ufeful in the effects which are produced by them, and tend as much to difplay the wifdom of God in their being appointed, as the change of the feafons of the year are conducive to fructify the earth, and calculated for the benefit of its inhabitants. When we come to take a view of the whole performance, there will be found no error in the execution, nor any want of affection to his children who have been more particularly exercifed: It will then appear to them as *one day* which the Lord has been filling up with the evidences of his *infinite knowledge.*

2. As he fets one thing over againft another with the moft confummate fkill and the greateft exactnefs, fo he notices the procefs of the whole work, and difcovers the moft *powerful agency.* Though it requires feveral years, yea feveral thoufands of years, to conduct and finifh any defign, yet before him it is *but as one day.* He works, and takes care that nothing hinder the accomplifhment of what he has in view: Witnefs his predictions to *Abraham* concerning the fojourning of his posterity

* Ecclef. vii. 14.

posterity in *Egypt*, which took up four hundred and thirty years.—To *Jeremiah* respecting the *Babylonish* captivity, and *Israel's* return from it, which required seventy years to accomplish—and, above all, the redemption of sinners by *Jesus Christ*, which required four thousand years to introduce and complete. In all these trials of the faith and patience of his children, he sat by the furnace as a refiner and purifier of silver, to take away their dross, and to make them what it was his pleasure they should be, even holy, and without blame before him in love. Dark, difficult, and inexplicable as many things may appear to the wisest and best of men from the commencement to the close of time, the whole is but as one day which is known unto the Lord.

3. The Lord secures the success of the whole, so as to accomplish that end which shall be the fullest demonstration of *astonishing goodness*. At present we may not be able to see how this trial or that particular occurrence can produce any real good: But we have the gracious assurance of him who cannot be disappointed, that " all things shall work together for good to them who love him." *Joseph* saw in the event that his God meant all that he had passed through for good, and that the good intended was fully accomplished. To us it may appear as though it were *neither day nor night*; but all things lie
naked

naked and open to the eye of our God, and he views the whole as *one day*. He has resolved to sanctify and save his family, and though this work, in their apprehension, may advance very slowly; nay at some seasons they can scarce distinguish whether or not it does advance; yet before the God of our salvation it is but as the *work of a day*, and he will complete it. " The Lord will perfect that which concerneth them, his mercy endureth for ever—he will not forsake the work of his own hands." * It yet remains that we consider the words as descriptive,

III. *Of that happy and glorious end, with which the present state of things shall be concluded:* " It shall come to pass that at eventime it shall be light." This may probably refer to the evening of the world, when error and ignorance shall be removed—the *Jews*, with the fulness of the *Gentiles*, shall be brought in, the earth be filled with the knowledge of the glory of *Jehovah*, and the kingdoms of this world shall become the kingdoms of our God and his Christ. At *evening*—when least expected—and perhaps when hope is ready to expire—*at even-time it shall be light*.

But leaving this—the Psalmist informs us, that " light is sown for the righteous, and joy for the upright in heart." A season is coming when the righteous shall see things as they really are, not detached from, but connected

* Psalm cxxxviii. 8.

connected with each other; not encompassed with clouds, or by the glimmering of twilight, but in the perfect light of heaven. In the evening of the present day it shall be light.

1. *The perfections of God will be more fully unvailed—more gloriously exhibited—and will be viewed to greater advantage than ever they yet have been.* All the knowledge that we have of God at present is conveyed to us by words and signs: We have now a glance of this perfection, by and by of that; but then God will be *seen*—will be *known*—will be enjoyed in all the harmony and splendor of his perfections. " In his light shall they see light;* and shall teach no more every man his neighbour to know the Lord, for all shall know him from the least to the greatest." † Their sun shall no more go down, neither shall their moon withdraw itself, for the Lord shall be their everlasting light, and their God their glory." ‡ Then shall they see him as he is, and know even as they are known.

2. In the evening it shall be light, for then *all the great productions of our God shall be brought to view.* The *works themselves, their reason,* and *their end* shall then be fully made manifest. All the dealings of God with the world, the church, and every individual believer, will be collected together. The whole history of the church's trials and support in

* Psalm xxxvi. 9.—† Jer. xxxi 34.—‡ Isaiah lx. 20.

so many parts of the world, and for so many ages, shall be seen at a single glance: The reason will then be known why one part of the earth, rather than another, was visited with the Gospel. And so just, so wise, so glorious will the whole conduct of God appear in every thing that he has directed, inspected, and performed, that all the church will unite in this exultation: *Great and marvellous are thy works, Lord God Almighty, just and true are all thy ways, thou King of Saints.* And that which shall then be made manifest, concerning the whole church of God, shall be as clear respecting every individual of that company. Then will be seen the expediency of every trial—the mercy that was in every affliction—and the propriety of their being kept so long striving against sin, or walking in this *twilight* state.

3. At even-time it shall be light, for then *the provision that he has been making for the eternal support and entertainment of his people shall be set forth.*——Eye hath not seen, nor can tongue sufficiently describe, what treasures of goodness their God has laid up for them that love and fear him; but the season is coming when all the comforts held out to the faith and hopes of God's people in the Bible, and exhibited to them for so many ages, shall be realized and brought forth for their enjoyment in the heavenly world.——When all the ransomed of the Lord are convened

vened together, as *Joshua* once addressed *Israel*, so will a greater Saviour address his followers, saying, "Ye know in all your hearts, and in all your souls, that not one thing hath failed of all the good things which the Lord your God spake concerning you; all are come to pass unto you, and not one thing hath failed thereof." * Then in God's light shall they see light, receive the end of faith in a full and everlasting salvation, and shall be for ever with the Lord.

The reflection which arises from this subject, and which claims the attention of every unrenewed sinner, is this: In the present twilight state such may pass unnoticed and undetected. Enmity against God may prevail in your hearts, and acts of sin may be secreted. You may presume that no one seeth in secret, and that all shall be well at last. You may trifle with sin, dishonour God, and go on to reject the claims and the counsels of *Jesus Christ*; but the time will come when it will be light without a change, what has been done in darkness shall be exposed as in open day. Your true state will be discovered: Sins long forgotten will be brought to your remembrance——all your mistakes will be corrected, and you will appear to yourselves, and to the whole assembled world, what you now really are in the sight of God.

* Joshua xxiii. 14.

But while this subject proclaims lamentation and woe to the impenitent sinner, it holds forth the greatest encouragement to believers. You, my fellow-travellers, may meet with many a discouragement, and pass under many a shade in the present twilight-state. As you travel through this wilderness, doubts, fears, and trials may greatly discourage, but at even-time it shall be light. All the way in which the Lord has been leading you for so many years, shall appear to have been well chosen.——It shall be seen how goodness and mercy have perpetually followed you therein; and, your course being finished upon earth, you shall have an abundant entrance into his everlasting kingdom, there to unite your testimony with the glorious company already before the throne, in declaring, that HE HATH DONE ALL THINGS WELL. God grant us this honour for *Jesus'* sake. *Amen.*

SERMON

SERMON XX.

Spiritual Gain from Temporal Losses:
Or, the Death of the Widow's Son.

---

1 KINGS xvii. 18.

Art thou come unto me to call my sin unto remembrance, and to slay my son?

A Very strange question must the Prophet have thought this, especially as coming from a person who was under so many obligations to him, both upon her own and her son's account; but upon this occasion she spake unadvisedly with her lips; and when we have glanced upon the solemn Providence which gave rise to this passionate inquiry, we shall both sincerely pity her case, and sympathize with her under that peculiar trial with which she was exercised.

In the beginning of the chapter we find *Elijah*, an inhabitant of *Gilead*, appearing with the greatest solemnity before king *Ahab*, and in the name of the Lord predicting that neither dew nor rain should fall upon that country

try for three years and a half, but according to his word. *

No sooner is the solemn message delivered than he is secretly admonished to retire.—— *Ahab*, though remarkable for his wickedness, is not permitted to lay hand upon him; probably his mind was so powerfully impressed with the alarming message, that he discovered not the least disposition at that season to apprehend the Prophet. A place both of safety and of supply is marked out for *Elijah*: For his supply the brook shall continue to flow, and ravens, the messengers of divine Providence, shall statedly bring him support. *The word of the Lord came to him, saying, Arise, get thee hence, and turn thee eastward, and hide thyself by the brook Cherith, that is before Jordan. And it shall be, that thou shalt drink of the brook, and I have commanded the ravens to feed thee there. So he went and did according unto the word of the Lord: for he went and dwelt by the brook Cherith, that is before Jordan. And the ravens brought him bread and flesh in the morning, and bread and flesh in the evening: and he drank of the brook* ‡

Such was his abode, and such his supply for a considerable season. From the 7th verse of the chapter some have supposed that it was a full year. During this season many, whose eyes had never penetrated this secret recess of the Prophet, would be benefited on his account. Wherever the brook flowed, all who drank

* Verse 1. ‡ Verse 2——6.

of

of it were blessed for *Elijah's* sake. In like manner the wicked receive and enjoy many advantages which are bestowed upon them for the sake of others. The streams of the divine bounty perhaps flow to them and their habitations by virtue of the prayers and piety of persons whom they never knew.——At length, either as the natural effect of the continual drought, for the punishment of others who had not improved this special forbearance of the Almighty towards themselves—or in order to send a blessing to a distant part, the brook becomes dry, and the Prophet is commanded to go to *Zarephath*, or *Sarepta*, a place inhabited by idolaters. Obedient to the heavenly mandate he removes. As he approaches the place, the first object which presents itself to his view is a poor woman gathering sticks. *Elijah*, though an *Israelite*—a faithful servant of the Lord—yea an eminent Prophet, is under the necessity of begging to supply his wants: But he asked in faith—he asked not with the humble importunity of a beggar, but with the authority of one who had his commission from God. The Lord had told him, that he had commanded a widow of that place to sustain him. *

The demand the Prophet made upon this poor woman introduces a very moving scene; and serves at once for a key to open the widow's heart and habitation, the state of her family, and of the whole supply which she had

* Verse 7.

had for herself and her son: *So he arose, and went to Zarephath: And when he came to the gate of the city, behold, the widow woman was there gathering of sticks: and he called to her, and said, Fetch me, I pray thee, a little water in a vessel, that I may drink. And as she was going to fetch it, he called to her, and said, Bring me, I pray thee, a morsel of bread in thine hand. And she said, As the Lord thy God liveth, I have not a cake, but an handful of meal in a barrel, and a little oil in a cruse: And, behold, I am gathering two sticks, that I may go in, and dress it for me and for my son, that we may eat, and die* * Every word she uttered we may suppose would pierce the Prophet's feeling heart. Had he viewed things with an eye of sense, his faith had now staggered, and his language would have been to this effect: " And have I travelled so far under the power of deception? And is *this* the woman who, I was informed, had a command from God to sustain me? And is an handful of meal and a little oil her whole stock of provisions?—Better to have died by the brook *Cherith*, where there was no one to pity or to mock me, than under the eye of so many enemies to the God of *Israel.*"—But he staggered not at the command or the promise of God. He shrunk not at this alarming aspect of his Providence—being strong in faith, he glorified his God. In the name of that God, whom it is probable this woman neither knew nor served,

* Verse 10——12.

served, he spake encouragement and comfort to her: *And Elijah said unto her, Fear not; go, and do as thou hast said: but make me thereof a little cake first, and bring it unto me, and after make for thee and for thy son. For thus saith the Lord God of Israel, the barrel of meal shall not waste, neither shall the cruse of oil fail, until the day that the Lord sendeth rain upon the earth. And she went, and did according to the saying of Elijah: and she, and he, and her house did eat many days.**——There can be no doubt but so good a man, and so zealous a servant of the Lord as *Elijah* was, would endeavour to feed this woman's mind with the knowledge of divine truth, while she, as the instrument in the hand of Providence, fed him with bread. Though the woman was poor, her habitation mean, and the provision plain, their conversation would be profitable, their communion sweet, and their days would be crowned with goodness.—At length an event, little expected, takes place. Black famine had been excluded by a special Providence from this favoured habitation, while perhaps it had been felt in some, if not in every house in *Zarephath*.—— But death hath more ways of access to our habitations than one. *Elijah* was grown old; this widow was in the middle age of life; the bloom of youth probably glowed only upon the cheeks of one of the inhabitants of this tent, and death marks him for

* Verse 13——15.

his

his prey. The difeafe with which he is afflicted makes rapid progrefs—probably during the feafon in which the Prophet walked out into the fields to meditate and to pray, the young man fickens—and dies.

Heretofore the *Prophet's* return to the widow's habitation had been kindly welcomed with a fmile, or with fuch a falutation as this, *Bleſſed be thou of the Lord:* But now he finds her in tears, and his ears are accofted with a very different language: *And ſhe ſaid unto* Elijah, *What have I to do with thee, O thou man of God? Art thou come unto me to call my ſin to remembrance, and to ſlay my ſon?*

What we propofe from this paffage is to make a few general remarks, which we fhall mention, and then enlarge upon.—From thefe words it appears, that there is a great propenfity in the human heart, either to take no notice of thofe inftances in which we fin againft God, or foon to forget the convictions we have had.—That God is pleafed to make ufe of various ways and methods to convince men of their fins, particularly thofe whom he regards with fpecial favour—That by fuch methods the veil is often withdrawn, to let them fee that fuch things were really difpleafing in his fight, which they once thought little of, if not favourably concerning—That there is danger of giving way to a fretful, murmuring frame of fpirit, in feafons of of great trial —That seasons, in which sin is brought to remembrance, are very painful seasons—But that to God's people all their trials shall eventually terminate in their real profit.

Our first remark is,

1. *That there is a great propensity in the human heart, either to take no notice of those instances in which we sin against God, or soon to forget the convictions we have had* Few men pay that attention to the general tenor of their conduct which they ought. Some good men have resolved to stop every thought as it first entered the mind, and investigate its origin, and whither it tended, before they suffered it to pass; but partly through the hurry of business, natural indolence, ignorance, partiality to ourselves, and a variety of things which might be mentioned, those who know the most of themselves will see that, however reasonable, such a method must be exceeding difficult. *Solomon*, who knew as much of the heart as most men, informs us, that there is not a just man who doth good and sinneth not*: And the Apostle *James* confirms the sentiment by that confession he made in his own name, and in the name of all the apostles and first followers of *Jesus Christ*. *In many things we offend all* †. There are so many sins of ignorance, of omission, sinful thoughts and sinful desires, that we find *David* saw reason to humble himself on their account before God. "Who, "says

* Eccles. vii. 28.—† James iii. 2.

"says he," can understand his errors? Cleanse thou me from secret faults†" *Solomon*, with all his extent of understanding; *David*, with all his watchful circumspection, could neither detect nor number them. They defile the soul—from them we must be cleansed.—God alone can cleanse—and it is the duty of all, and will be the practice of all good men, to apply to him for cleansing. So extensive and spiritual is the law of God, that it is impossible for any one to be acquainted with all his defects. Through the error of our judgments, ignorance of the rule of duty, or a selfish partiality in our own favour, how prone are we to account those things innocent in their nature, or that action laudable, which the law of God pronounces sinful, exceeding sinful. There are treasures of deceit and wickedness in the human heart, which are visible alone to God. Hence pride cloaths itself with the garb of humility; covetousness passes amongst men for prudent care; superstition assumes the names of piety and zeal; and the deceitfulness of sin, in ten thousand forms, imposes upon the hearts of men so as to ward off present convictions, or ruin them for ever.

Even where persons have had some convictions that they have been acting a foolish and unreasonable part, how soon do such convictions wear off and are forgotten. Men see their faults at seasons; but, like persons beholding

* Psalm xix. 12.

beholding their faces in a glafs, they go away and forget what manner of men they are. Like the Roman governor, they difmifs their reprovers and their convictions together. Were all thofe convictions and impreffions, which have been made upon the minds of men while attending under the miniftry of the gofpel, as well fixed there, as they are in the book of God's remembrance, what manner of perfons would they be in all holy converfation and godlinefs! But many of our convictions prove like the fhadows of the clouds, and our impreffions are like the early dew which paffeth away. The conduct of a number of perfons proves the truth of this remark, " That there is a great propenfity in the human heart, either to take no notice of thefe inftances in which we fin againft God, or foon to forget the convictions we have had." Whatever the fin, or fins, of this woman had been, fhe feems either to have taken no notice of, or to have forgotten them till this mournful event took p ace. Then fhe cried out, "Art thou come to call my fin to remembrance?'—We notice,

2. *That God is pleafed to make ufe of various ways and methods to convince men of their fins, particularly thofe whom he regards with fpecial favour.* Thefe means are very various in their nature and appearance.

Sometimes he effects this by the *ordinary miniftry of his fervants*, or by fome particular hint,

hint, or remark, which is dropped by them in the courſe of their miniſtry. Though by them the bow be drawn at a venture, the Lord is pleaſed to direct the arrow to the proper, the intended mark. It proves a word with power and in ſeaſon : Without any deſign in the miniſter, to the convinced party it appears as though ſomething perſonal had been intended. It comes to his conſcience, not only as the word of a man, like himſelf, but as the word of God, which, as in an inſtant, ſhews him all that ever he did. Had not *Elijah* been ſent to this widow, probably ſhe would never have ſeen the ſinfulneſs of her former conduct, as ſhe often ſaw it, under his faithful inſtructions and reproofs : And, perhaps, ſhe had never ſeen it ſo peculiarly aggravating as ſhe did upon this occaſion.— And has the miniſtry of the ſervants of God been made thus uſeful to *your* ſouls ? Has this been inſtrumental to introduce the light of divine truth into your hearts, and thrown the light of conviction over the whole of your paſt conduct ? Have ye been convinced of the ſinfulneſs of ſin, your need of a better righteouſneſs than your own, and has the truth and power of the Goſpel been confirmed in you ? If this be the caſe, though miniſters ſhould remain unacquainted with the ſucceſs of their labours while they live, yet you have reaſon to bleſs God that you heard their voice,

voice, and the day will come when they shall also rejoice with you.

Personal trials and afflictions are also employed at times as means to convince men of sins which otherwise they had never seen, which they had forgotten or persevered in. The Psalmist tells us that it was good for him that he had been afflicted, for before he was afflicted he went astray; afterwards he learned the word, and was led in the path of duty: And no doubt many will have eternal reason with him to bless God for those trials and afflictions which have been over-ruled for the profit of their souls: Not that this is the necessary fruit of affliction; for the more some persons are afflicted the more they transgress. But when grace accompanies the affliction, then is it rendered effectual to convince of sin, or to promote obedience. The intention and the effect of afflictions, when under the influence of a divine blessing, is set forth in a very full and striking manner by Elihu: "If they be bound in fetters and be holden in cords of affliction, then he sheweth them their work and their transgressions, that they have exceeded: He openeth also their ear to discipline, and commandeth that they return from iniquity. If they obey and serve him, they shall spend their days in prosperity and their years in pleasures; But if they obey not, they shall perish by the sword, and they shall die without knowledge."*—But to apply this remark

* Job xxxvi. 8——12.

remark to the subject before us.——Though there be reason to conclude, that this widow was a good woman—and that *Elijah's* ministry had been much blessed to the profit of her soul, it is probable this affliction was intended to accomplish some end, perhaps to detect some evil which the Prophet's penetration and faithfulness had never been able to discover or to remove: Not only God's word, but his rod has a voice. He afflicts not willingly, or grieves the children of men; what he does is for their profit—either it is to humble them, to take away sin, or to make them partakers of his holiness.

At other seasons the Lord brings sin to remembrance *by the death of very near relations*, or intimate friends. In his view, who seeth all things as they are, there appears a necessity to remove those out of the way who stand between us and the means of conviction.—— The Lord tears away those " dear delights we fondly call our own;" those who have had such union with our hearts that the removal of them cannot but wound and pain us greatly: Such wounds perhaps are necessary in order to effect the cure of the soul.—— The death of *David's* children, though in most cases just—with respect to themselves, might be intended as punishments for the father's sin· Each one that fell was probably a fresh means to bring his sin to remembrance. Thus " various are the methods which God employs

employs to convince men of their sins, and to bring them to remembrance."—We remark,

3. That by such methods the veil is often withdrawn to let men see that those things were really displeasing in God's sight which they once thought little of, if not favourably concerning. "Art thou come to call my sin to remembrance?" She might have repeatedly heard the Prophet make intercession against *Israel*, saying, "Lord, they have broken down thine altars;" and some have supposed that she apprehended that he had now been pleading against her for the idolatry of her past life; and that in answer to this prayer, the Lord had slain her son.——But I rather apprehend her distress arose from other quarters.

Perhaps this afflicted mother saw that she had been too anxious about her son. Her very life had been bound up in the life of the lad. She had formed great hopes and high expectations respecting him, when grown up to maturity, and she declined in years. As *Lamech* said of *Noah*, so she of her son, *This same shall comfort me.* Ah, how often do we sink our creature-comforts into their graves, by placing those hopes and expectations on them, which we should fix on God only.—Her husband was dead.—She had no one to comfort her—none to minister to her in her old age save this lad—and now behold *he* is dead. Now had she a fuller opportunity than ever

ever to see the folly of all creature-dependencies. This woman had renounced the idols of her country, and the Prophet no doubt thought her to be a real convert to the worship of the true God: But that God, who abhors an idol, espied one in her heart, and he laid it dead in her arms. Ye parents beware lest, like the ape in the fable, by over-affection ye crush your comforts to death.

Or probably she now saw that, on account of the strength of her affection, she had not reproved him in some cases with that fidelity, or instructed him with that diligence she ought to have discovered: All such instances were now brought to her recollection, with all their aggravations. We take it for granted that she indulged the most favourable hopes of the state of her son, concluding his soul was now fixed in a state of everlasting happiness: Yet she gave way to the most unfavourable ideas of her conduct to him, and apprehended this to be one reason why the Lord had taken him from her. Probably something similar to this was the language of her heart upon this occasion: " I have been too indulgent—too inattentive to the seasons of instruction. The Lord saw all this, and in mercy to my child has been pleased to remove him from a parent, who would have ruined him, had he been spared. Had my affections sat more loose upon my child, or had I been more attentive to his best interest, it is probable he might

might have been spared: But my sin—yes, my sin has slain my son."—Ye parents, take the warning, for such reflections over your murdered comforts must prove painful beyond description.—But painful as such reflections may be, they are far less distressing than those which some parents feel, who, after seeing the effects of their faults and follies confirmed in their children, when grown mature in years and in iniquity, have to follow them to their graves. *Eli* reproved not his children, or did it in too gentle a manner.—They sinned, and the Lord flew them. His ears tingled at the tidings, his heart bled, and his gray hairs were brought with sorrow to his grave. What, O what suppose ye must that parent feel who is called to follow to the silent grave his children who are twice dead! Such, perhaps, in some instances, was *David's* case; but more affecting still, if such parents have reason to conclude that their own conduct was the occasion of their children's ruin.—— Be concerned then to train up your children in the way they should go: Grace ye cannot bestow on them, but instruction and reproof ye ought not to withhold. On the one hand, beware that ye provoke them not to wrath; on the other, that ye indulge them not to their everlasting ruin. —Thus having shewn that, by the hand of affliction, the veil is often withdrawn, in order to let men see that those things are very displeasing to God, of which they thought otherwise, We remark further,

4. *That there is danger of giving way to a fretful, murmuring frame of spirit in seasons of great trials.* *Jonah*, when he only sustained the loss of a shadow afforded by a plant, thought that he did well to be angry; and *Elijah* must have considered this not only as very unusual, but very odd language in which the widow addressed him; *What have I to do with thee, O man of God? Art thou come to call my sin to remembrance, and to slay my son?*—What had she to do with him?— Foolish woman—What would she have done without him? Had this Prophet never come to her house perhaps she had still been a poor idolater—Had he never come, probably she had seen her son dead long before this; and what was more affecting than all, she herself had not only died of the famine, but had died in her sin; yet now she says, *What have I to do with thee?* What? Did she need no more instruction from this heavenly messenger? Could the man who had administered comfort to her mind so frequently, under her trials, no longer comfort her, or did she refuse to be comforted? She spake, as if by one act she intended to exclude the Prophet from her house, and the God of the Prophet from her heart; *Art thou come to slay my son?* No, at first he came to feed him with bread, and to instruct him in the knowledge of the true

true God; and even now *Elijah* was come to rescue her son from death, and to fit him both for earth and heaven:—For all this *Elijah* was come.

From this we see how apt men are to attribute their losses and trials to any cause but the right one. Had this thing been omitted, or had that been done, things would have been otherwise than they are: Thus they foolishly argue; as if the Lord had no direction in the case, and nothing to do in the disposal of the event: Whereas a sparrow, yea not an hair from the head falls without his knowledge. Instruments are as nothing independent of the great agent, who employs them to answer or accomplish what he sees to be right. Beware then of supposing that the Lord deals hardly, much less unjustly, with you, in any of the trials you are exercised with. He can do no wrong. Be still, therefore, and own that he is God. Whatever he gives to you, or takes from you, still you have reason to bless his holy name.— We remark once more,

5. *That seasons in which sin is brought to remembrance are very painful seasons.* They open the wounds that have been healed up too soon, and probe them to the bottom. This poor woman must have had a very sorrowful season with her son dead in her bosom, and her sins arranged before her eyes, or rather like so many arrows shot into her heart.

So much she felt, that she hardly knew what she said to the Prophet, and this made some apology for the asperity of her language.—Conviction had seized upon her, and presented a cup mixed with wormwood and gall: Her soul had her sin in remembrance, and was humbled in her.—Our last remark from these words is,

6. *That to God's people all their trials eventually terminate in their real profit.* This woman would, if possible, take more pleasure in the company of her son, after his restoration, than ever she had done before. She had learned some lessons from this event which would prove both for his and her instruction and profit in future: Even this occurrence, painful as it was for a season, was to be numbered among the things which wrought for her good, and for the glory of God. She would receive her son, we may suppose, as *Jochebad* did her *Moses* from the hand of the *Egyptian* Princess, that she might enjoy him as given to her from God, and that she might bring him up for God. Her mind would be more confirmed in the knowledge and worship of the true God; and she would seize and improve this great event in order to convince others of the power of the God of *Israel*, and of the help which might be expected from him.

From this subject we learn, that all our outward comforts in this life are in the hand

and at the difpofal of the Almighty: Like fair flowers, they rife under his hand; open to regale us for a fhort feafon; call our attention to him, who endowed them with every quality which affords us delight: They fade at his pleafure, and are removed at his command. O to be inftructed in the divine art of enjoying God in them; improving them, while they are continued, to his glory; to hold them dependent on his pleafure, and to refign them at his call. The ftreams of our comfort may be cut off; but if our fouls are in a ftate of friendfhip with God, the fountain ftill abides.

From what has been advanced in this difcourfe we venture to infer, that if the remembrance of fin is capable of producing fo much mifery to the mind, even in fo fhort a time,—how infupportable muft it be to have it brought full to view in the future world, without any thing to abate its force, with every thing to add to its poignancy: No comforter at hand—No hope in God—No refuge to fly to—Recollection in the fulleft exercife of its powers—Confcience open to the fulleft conviction—and that mifery begun which fhall have no period.

Finally, if the reftoration of an earthly comfort, though to be enjoyed but for an uncertain feafon, and finally to be removed from or left behind us, if this be productive of fuch felicity, what will it be to meet all

our

our brethren in Christ, the whole family of the faithful before the throne of glory; all of them freed from sin, corruption, and death; all perfect in holiness: Then all who have died in the Lord, and whose bodies we have been called to consign to the grave in the faith of a glorious resurrection, shall come forth to die no more — to live — to be enjoyed — their converse and company enjoyed compleatly, and for ever. Happy, desirable season! may we wait for it with expectation. They who now sleep in Jesus will God bring with him, to be the subjects and the associates of our joy. Even so, *Amen.*

SERMON

SERMON XXI.

Chrift's Charge againſt his profeſſing People.

PSALM lxix. 8.

I am become a ſtranger unto my brethren, and an alien unto my mother's children.

SUCH was the ſituation of *David*, and thus might he juſtly complain in the time of his diſtreſs. After ſtepping forward as the champion of the hoſts of *Iſrael* in the day of their calamity—After ſlaying the object of their fear, and ſaving the whole nation from ſlavery and from ruin; I ſay, after all this, when he was perſecuted by the king of *Iſrael*, as an enemy to his prince and his God; purſued as an outlaw by the very army that owed its preſent exiſtence to his valour; and probably abandoned by the brethren of his father's houſe; with what propriety ought be taken up this complaint, " I am become a ſtranger unto my brethren, and an alien unto my mother's children." Such conduct diſcovered the baſeſt ingratitude on the part of *Iſrael*, and to a generous and feeling mind,

like

like *David's*, it must have proved peculiarly distressing.

But *David*, in this and in many other parts of the book of Psalms, is, we apprehend, to be considered, not simply as an afflicted and persecuted person, but as a prophet foretelling, and as a type representing a far greater sufferer and Saviour. Even *Jesus Christ*, who was not only the *Son of David*, but that true *David*, of whom the once-suffering, the after-exalted *David* was but the type and shadow. Though the Psalmist *David* was truly zealous for the honour of God and his house, and greatly persecuted and insulted, yet several parts of this Psalm are far more applicable to him, to whom they are expressly applied in the New Testament, than they ever were to *David* the son of *Jesse*. You all know to whom the following passages are applied by those who were under the guidance of an unerring Spirit: " The zeal of thine house hath eaten me up, and the reproaches of them that reproached thee are fallen upon me." * And again: " They gave me gall for my meat, and in my thirst they gave me vinegar to drink " † Indeed the whole is peculiarly applicable to *Jesus Christ*.

The manifold sorrows and heavy sufferings of the Son of God, when he appeared as the representative and surety of his church, are described in the beginning of the Psalm: *Save me, O God, for the waters are come in*

* Verse 9.—Ver. 21.

unto

unto my foul. I sink in deep mire where there is no standing: I am come into deep waters where the floods overflow me. * Tribulations are frequently in the sacred writings compared to waters: Here they are represented as waters deep and tempestuated: He sunk into the mire and clay—the waters rushed in upon him—yea the floods passed over him. From this hour of distress, and from these overwhelming afflictions he desired to be delivered; but as that could not be granted, he prays to be supported, and carried through them with honour and success.

While in the days of his flesh, we are told that he wrestled with strong cryings and tears; and though we are informed of only a few sentences that he uttered, while he was in the garden and on the cross, yet he is here represented, while waiting for his God, as crying till he was weary, his throat parched, and his eyes began to fail: *I am weary of my crying, my throat is dried: mine eyes fail while I wait for my God.* †

Though he was without spot, blemish, or any such thing, perfectly innocent, and universally holy: Though he shewed the benevolence of his disposition through the whole of his life, ever going about doing good to all who came in his way; to all who would listen to his instructions, or participate of his favours—yet even *Jesus Christ* had enemies.

The

* Verse 1, 2.—† Ver. 3.

The enemies of this *Jesus* were numerous, and very inveterate: Though every body had cause to love him, yet he was hated, opposed, persecuted even to death: Though the only innocent person in the whole world, he suffered for sin, and made satisfaction for those wrongs which others had done: Nay more, for the crimes of some of those who were his implacable enemies. *They that hate me without a cause are more than the hairs of mine head: they that would destroy me, being mine enemies wrongfully, are mighty: then I restored that which I took not away.* * He both satisfied and honoured the law of God in the place of sinners.

The evangelic *Isaiah* tells us, that " the Lord laid upon him, viz. *Jesus Christ*, the iniquity of us all." He stood chargeable with the sins of men, and satisfaction was required at his hands. He who knew no sin was made sin for us, that we might be made the righteousness of God in him: And as the believer in *Jesus* may now claim interest in his righteousness as his own, seeing it was wrought out for him, and he now stands related to him as his head; so the Lord *Christ* here speaks of the follies and sins of his people, as if they were his own, *O God, thou knowest my foolishness; and my sins are not hid from thee;* † not that he ever indulged a foolish thought, or did a sinful action through the whole course of his life.

* Verse 4.——† Ver. 5.

He

He is further reprefented as pleading that his difciples might not be ftaggered on account of his fufferings, when they faw his requeft rejected, or his foul deprived of confolation while he hung upon his crofs: He prays that they might be convinced of the true reafon of his fufferings: That it was to fecure and eftablifh the glory of God and the falvation of men, that he then appeared loaded with guilt, forfaken, and overwhelmed with difgrace and forrow: *Let not them that wait on thee, O Lord God of hofts, be afhamed for my fake: let not thofe that feek thee be confounded for my fake, O God of Ifrael: Becaufe for thy fake I have borne reproach; fhame hath covered my face.* *

Then follows the complaint and charge againft the profeffing people of God, on account of their carriage towards this true friend of finners, *I am become a ftranger unto my brethren, and an alien unto my mother's children.*

In this difcourfe we propofe,

I. To take a general view of thofe endearing appellations which *Jefus Chrift* is here reprefented as making ufe of, when fpeaking of the profeffing people of God. He calls them *his brethren* and *his mother's children.*

II. We fhall attend to the charge fixed upon them, as it refers to the ancient church, *I am become a ftranger to them.*

III. We

* Ver. 6, 7.

III. We shall consider how far the same charge may be justly preferred against us in the present day.

And may a divine blessing accompany what we have to advance under these several branches.

I. *The endearing appellations which Jesus Christ here uses, when speaking of the professing people of God,* are these two, " my brethren" and ." my mother's children." Strong expressions of that near relation in which he stands to them, and of that ardent affection which he bears towards them. Like *Joseph*, his brethren were angry with him, although he tenderly loved them, readily ministred to their necessities, and in the event saved them when in great distress: Yet they fought, and in effect they accomplished his death, though that was the appointed means of preserving their own lives and securing their salvation. The *brethren* here spoken of, are to be considered as the members of the visible church. That church is the *mother,* and her members are the children: And when such are stiled the *brethren* of *Jesus Christ,* it is expressive both of the love he has for them, and the favour he has shewn them.

1. When *Christ* calls the members of the visible church *his brethren,* it is *expressive of that favour which he bare to human nature in general, and to all his believing family in particular.*

lar. Though he were rich, yet for their ſakes he became poor, that they through his poverty might be made rich.* From everlaſting ages his delights had been with the ſons of men †; and in the fulneſs of time, though he exiſted in the form of God, and thought it not robbery to be equal with God, yet made he himſelf of no reputation, and took upon him the form of a ſervant, and was made in the likeneſs of men; and being found in faſhion as a man, he humbled himſelf, and became obedient unto death, even the death of the croſs. ‡ Such was the love, the condeſcenſion, and compaſſion of the Son of God towards ſinners of the human race. He took not on him the nature of angels, but the ſeed of *Abraham* §, that he might be united to men in the neareſt relation: He put himſelf into a ſituation whereby he could ſuccour them, and have a ſuitable offering to preſent for the expiation of ſin, and the ſatisfaction of divine juſtice. To this end the Word was made fleſh and dwelt amongſt us.‖ God was manifeſt in the fleſh **; and as in *Adam* all his poſterity died, ſo in *Chriſt* all his ſeed are made alive. What an aſtoniſhing ſtoop of Majeſty! What an unparalleled expreſſion of love was this! Becauſe the children were partakers of fleſh and blood, he alſo took part of the ſame. ‖‖ He who, from everlaſting ages, exiſted in *the form of God,* who

---

* 2 Cor. viii. 9.—† Prov. viii. 31.—‡ Phil. ii. 6, &c.—§ Heb. ii. 16. ‖ John i. 14.—** 1 Tim. iii. 16.—‖‖ Heb. ii. 14.

who was *equal* with the Father, as partaking of the same Divine Nature, even while in a certain sense he was so distinct from him that he could humble himself to assume human nature, and in that nature to humble himself still further.——He whom the Father hath now exalted and honoured before and above the whole creation, expressed the greatness of his affection in assuming man's nature that he might die for our sins.

2. When *Jesus Christ* expresses himself under these tender and endearing epithets, calling his professing people his *brethren* and *his mother's children*, it is descriptive also of *the proofs of this his affection which he gave while here upon earth, and still continues to give both on earth and in heaven* *Jacob's* sons saw not the affection of their brother *Joseph* so plainly, while he abode with them in the same family, as they did afterwards. His humiliation, however, was not voluntary, but imposed upon him; but the great Redeemer humbled himself: In his life, but especially by his death, he has commended his love to the notice of men. As the friend of human nature he taught the ignorant; expostulated with transgressors; succoured the afflicted; restored the dead to their weeping and disconsolate friends; and, above all, pronounced pardon to sinful men. All who applied to this Saviour found in him the fidelity of a friend, and the sympathy and affection of a brother.

And

And even now, in confirmation of this his fraternal affection, he sends the Gospel from place to place to inform men what a complete and compassionate Saviour he is. In this Gospel, especially in the Ordinance of the Supper, he represents himself as *Jesus* our Brother, ready to sympathize with us under all our trials, to supply all our necessities, and to make us the friends of God in this world, and prepare us for the enjoyment of him in heaven.——And while his affection is thus displayed upon earth as a brother, he pleads the cause of all the children in the presence of his Father above. He bears the interest of every individual upon his heart, and manages it with success before the throne. There he pleads; *Let not them that wait on thee, O Lord God of hosts, be ashamed for my sake: let not those that seek thee be confounded for my sake, O God of Israel.* * Even now he appears in heaven in the very nature that he assumed upon earth, to shew the union that still subsists between him and all his believing family. *He that sanctifieth, and they who are sanctified, are all of one*; that is, of one nature; *for which cause, he is not ashamed to call them brethren.* † He acknowledges them as his brethren before the throne, and in the presence of all the heavenly hosts.——But we proceed now;

II. To

---

* Verse 6.——† Heb. ii. 11.

II. To attend to *the charge which* Jesus Christ brings against these his brethren, *as it relates to the church of old.* " I am become a stranger to my brethren, and an alien unto my mother's children." This was true of the *Jews* at large, and upon a particular occasion of his own disciples.

1. *It was true of the Jews in general.* Though their own countryman, born amongst them, of the tribe of *Judah* and of the family of *David,* yet they did not receive him with that respect, attention, and cordiality which were due to him. On the contrary, they slighted, contemned, yea persecuted him even to death. Instead of bidding him welcome as the expected Deliverer, long foretold by their Prophets—instead of rejoicing in him as *the mercy* promised to their fathers, we are informed that when " he came to his own, his own received him not.". They treated him with the greatest indignity, and spoke of him with as much derision and contempt, as if they thought that the very mentioning of his name would defile their lips, or be offensive to the ears of others: " We know," say they, " that God spake by *Moses*; as for *this fellow,* we know not from whence he is*." Nay, they appear desirous to represent him as no part of the holy seed, but a wretch under the power of the devil. " Say we not well, that thou art a *Samaritan,* and haft

* John ix. 29.

hast a devil:† And the same historian has told us further, that even his own brethren did not believe in him ‡.

But how came the *Jews* to act in so strange, so unaccountable a manner to *Jesus Christ?* What had he done to merit such treatment from them?—By his power they saw the lame walk, and persons born blind, with whom they had been conversant, have their eyes opened, and the dead restored to friends and to the active scenes of life. They heard persons who had been dumb proclaim him as their deliverer; others testifying how water had been turned into wine; a few loaves of bread multiplied for the supply of thousands; how the waves had subsided at his word, and the winds were still at his command. All elements, all creatures, all diseases, yea the very devils obeyed him; in short, every thing but the obdurate hearts of men. Born at *Bethlehem* the appointed place, at the appointed season also, when the sceptre was departing from *Judah*; and of that very tribe and family which had long before been named.—With all these evidences to confirm their minds, and to corroborate his claims, how came it to pass that he was treated as a stranger by his brethren, and as an alien by his mother's children? The plain reason was, that he opposed their pride in being the descendants of *Abraham*, and their carnal attachment to the honours and glory of the

Vol. II.   E e e   present

† John viii. 48.——‡ John vii. 5.

present evil world: He refuted the opinion they had formed of the law of God, setting it forth in a very different point of view, and objected to their conduct in the service of God, shewing that he required spiritual worship, mercy rather than sacrifice, and preferred the obedience of the heart to the fat of lambs. He purged the house of his father, driving out the buyers and sellers who had assembled therein for the convenience of traffic. On these accounts he was treated as a stranger by his brethren: *For,* says he, in the words which follow the text, *the zeal of thine house hath eaten me up;* and the reproaches of them that reproached thee, are fallen upon me*.

2. Even *his own disciples, while he was in the extremity of his distress, acted as though they knew him not.* They all forsook him and fled, and left him to stand alone at *Pilate's* bar and in *Herod's* presence. *Peter,* instead of acknowledging him, declared that he knew nothing about him, when the question was put to him; nay, pretended to be almost a stranger to his very name.—" I know not the man."—" Woman, I know not what thou sayest."—" Then he began to curse and to swear, saying, I know not the man." Enough *Peter.* The *Jews* knew very well that the disciples of *Jesus Christ* would not curse and swear.—Such language would never betray him to be a christian. After this, we apprehend, not one person would ask him whether

* Ver. 9.

whether or not he belonged to *Jesus*. No, his blustering and bouncing oaths would remove every suspicion from their minds upon this subject.—Let every prophane person take this hint: If you can curse and swear, with what some may call a good grace, a disciple of *Beelzebub* you may be, but it is certain you do not belong to *Jesus Christ*. The man who, in his common conversation, can trifle with, or insult God's name in almost every sentence, proves that he retains no reverence for him in his heart. He blasphemes that very name which angels bless, and trifles with that power before whom devils tremble. But to return from this digression,

Jesus Christ was forsaken by his own family and followers. With propriety might he adopt the language of the Psalmist, and say, *I was a reproach among all mine enemies, but especially among my neighbours, and a fear to mine acquaintance: They that did see me without, fled from me**. The sight of him without the camp, rejected and crucified, caused them to flee. Such was their conduct after all the gracious instructions, manifestations, and promises which he had afforded to them. But their conduct was the effect of fear, of surprize, of the depth of his disgrace, and of the force of temptation. But they repented of their cowardice, returned to their allegiance, and were pardoned and accepted.

* Psalm xxxi. 11.

Having shewn how this was applicable to the church of old, we proceed,

III. *To consider how far the same charge may be justly preferred against us in the present day.* Is not this the language of *Jesus Christ* still? "I am become a stranger to my brethren?" And is not there too much ground for such complaint with respect to several of us?

1. As to many, though born within the pale of the visible church, descended from parents eminent in their day for exemplary piety, privileged with a religious education, and permitted to see the truth of the religion recommended to you, exemplified in the conversation and conduct of your godly parents; though surrounded with advantages and obligations, how many of you have been acting as strangers to *Jesus Christ?* You have not sought his acquaintance, perhaps, on the contrary, you have rather endeavoured to avoid it; though the proposals of this Saviour are so liberal, you have trifled with them, because his requirements are so pure. It may be you have regularly kept your place in the sanctuary, but have you not slighted him in private, by neglecting his word, or restraining prayer? In the world, probably, like *Peter*, you have been afraid that any should think that you belonged to *Jesus Christ*; you have endeavoured, therefore, to convince them of the contrary, if not by a prophane, yet by a vain and

and trifling converſation. Him you have not honoured; no, you have ſlighted and injured him. Though every good you have poſſeſſed in this life, has, in a ſort, been vouchſafed to you upon his account; for were it not for him, every ſtream of divine goodneſs would probably ceaſe to flow; yet this kind, compaſſionate, and gracious Saviour you have not honoured. He never yet received one prayer of faith from your hearts to preſent to his father. He never had the opportunity yet to announce, in the preſence of your relatives now in glory, that the correſpondence was opened between him and you upon earth. No, year after year has paſſed away, and you have all this time continued ſtrangers to *Jeſus Chriſt*. His name you hear and know ſomething of, but you continue ſtrangers to his grace, truth, power, and ſalvation. Seek him now while he may be found, leſt you ſhould remain ſtrangers to him for ever.

2. Others there are, who, though they know him, do not chuſe to own him openly. In ſecret, they treat him as a friend and brother—they conſult him in their difficulties—they correſpond with him, though at a diſtance, they have communion with him: But either through a falſe and unreaſonable dread of him, or the fear of others, they do not acknowledge him openly. Upon ſome of his appointments they attend; but they keep going in and out as ſtrangers do at an inn,

not

not as children who belong to the house. Probably, while the brethren and friends of *Jesus* acknowledge him before God, angels, devils, and men in the way that he hath appointed, these persons will look on, while others of them go out with the men of the world, as if they belonged not to *Christ's* family, although he has expresly commanded them to break bread in remembrance of him. How would professors of this class be startled, were the persons they retire with to address them in the language of *Absalom* to *Hushai*. *Absalom* said to *Hushai*, *Is this thy kindness to thy friend? Why wentest thou not with thy friend**? To confess *Christ* before men is our duty, our privilege, our honour; to deny or not to confess him is our sin. Whosoever is ashamed of him and of his word, of such will he be ashamed in that day, when he appears surrounded with honour and glory. And if *Jesus Christ* has owned you for his brethren, your duty is to associate with his family, and to remember and confess him in the way that he hath appointed. But,

3. Even with respect to us, who have openly and repeatedly acknowledged our relation to this Saviour, is there not too much ground for him to take up this complaint? *I am become a stranger to my brethren.*

Are our thoughts fixed upon him, and our affections going out after him as they were formerly? Is he the pleasing, profitable, habitual

---

* 2 Sam. xvi. 17.

bitual subject of our meditations that he once was? Are you conversing about this Saviour and recommending him to others, as those who know his name and desire to diffuse the favour of it? Is it your desire and determination, through grace, to know nothing amongst men, save *Jesus Christ*, and him crucified? Are ye stirring up your hearts to lay hold upon his strength, grace, and promises, and to attend to and honour his precepts? Are your visits to a throne of grace as frequent as they were formerly; and do you keep up that familiarity there, the benefit of which you have so often found? Do you maintain that steady regard to the means of grace, and that constant attendance upon them which you once observed? Or have you been treating the Saviour with indifference and putting a slight upon him—giving to the world that strength, that time, that ardour of the mind, all which were due to your elder brother? Has *Jesus Christ* no cause to take up this complaint against any of us? "I am become a stranger to my brethren? How often am I deprived of their company in my house; and even while they are there, how frequently do I detect their hearts wandering from me, and left to rove, without a restraint from them?"—If there be cause for such a complaint, and our hearts tell us there is, then let us look up to him for the power of quickening grace to correct our folly. And is there reason for such a complaint against us?—Lord, enable us to listen to it, and regard it. Condescend not only to speak to our ears but to our hearts, and say, Am I not become almost a stranger to you my brethren?

O to hear, and to profit by reproof upon earth, otherwise *Jesus Christ* will carry this complaint against us into the heavenly court, and to the Father of the whole family. He will lodge this complaint against us; "Father, after all that I have done and suffered for my friends upon earth—after all the favours, privileges, and indulgences granted to them—after telling them that it is their duty and interest to remember me—after appointing every mean necessary to promote and increase their correspondence with me; nay, after letting them have the experimental proof of mine abundant condescention and super-abounding grace: After all this, I am become a stranger to my brethren. Father, avenge my cause, in order to awaken these my thoughtless slumbering disciples out of their insensibility."—Should this be the case, *disease* will be commissioned to afflict our bodies—or *death* to slay our near relatives—or *disasters* to strip us of our worldly property, in measure, if not entirely—or what, perhaps, may prove more distressing than any or all of these—*Darkness*, an horror of darkness to seize upon and possess our souls for the remaining

maining days of our pilgrimage upon earth. As the effect of such a conduct towards this compassionate friend of sinners, our future days may be uncomfortable, and our course in this life be concluded in darkness. And has he said, " Them that honour me, I will honour ?" O that we may be enabled so to conduct ourselves towards our elder brother, that he may intercede for us, and not plead against us. May we severally rejoice in the thought, experience the comfort, and possess all the advantage of having an advocate with the father, even *Jesus Christ* the righteous— May we love him more—honour him more— follow him with greater ardour—love all his brethren on earth for his sake—and finally be received by him into his father's palace. Amen.

SERMON XXII.

Acceptable Worship: Or, God approached through a Mediator.

EPHES. ii. 18.

Through him we both have an access by one Spirit unto the Father.

HAD we at this season to appear before our superiors, especially in the courts of princes, where forms and ceremonies are fixed, and strictly required to be attended to, a regard to our own ease and success would powerfully excite us to obtain all possible information upon these articles, that so, upon our appearance, we might be able to conduct ourselves with propriety and advantage: But it is not the ceremonies of the courts of princes that ye would learn, or that I would teach: Our province is to inform you how ye may draw near to God with approbation and acceptance. *Jehovah*, the God of order, has been pleased to signify his pleasure respecting this interesting concern; and it is our desire to shew you the law of the house, that so ye may be enabled to regulate all your addresses

and

and applications agreeable to the pattern that he hath given: May we severally attend to it with that simplicity, that subjection of mind, and that conformity of conduct, which is becoming those who desire continually to receive the law from his mouth.——Certain it is that human invention has nothing to do in the worship of God. The precept and the pattern are to be sought alone from the scriptures, as the only unerring and infallible formula both of faith and worship. To the law, therefore, and the testimony we look for all necessary instruction and direction in this important business, and thither we turn with this confidence, that if a man *desire to do the will of God*, he shall know of the doctrine that proceeds from him, and of the method in which he can be approached by the humble suppliant.

The words now read are chosen with a view to obviate the doubts of some—to explain our own sentiments—and to vindicate our practice in that part of the worship of God to which these words may be considered as having some reference, viz. Prayer. There is, however, one principle which we wish to premise, and which we doubt not will be honoured with the sanction of every one who reveres the Bible as a revelation from God: It is this——There can be no contradictions in that book which proceeds from him who is of one mind and none can turn him, and which is the exprefs revelation of his will to his creatures. True, every part may not appear equally clear at the firft view; every fentence may not afford the fame degree of light into the fame fubject: But where one may feem to fail us, another fteps forward with its fuperior evidence, and when the whole comes to be collected and compared, the fubject appears clear and confiftent; our doubts are filenced, and our difficulties removed. Detached portions of fcripture may feem to countenance almoft any error; but reftore them to their connection, view them in harmony with the reft, and they tend not only to convince you what is truth, but alfo to confirm the mind both in the belief and practice of it.

With a defire to excite the warmeft fentiments of gratitude in the hearts of the *Ephefian* church towards the great Author of their mercies, in the chapter before us, the Apoftle endeavours to lead back their minds to reflect upon that ftate of fpiritual death, in which the Gofpel found them: They were dead in trefpaffes and fins—under the power of Satan, and walking in that courfe of difobedience, which led to everlafting deftruction.—From this confideration he both infers and proves that their falvation muft be wholly of grace. This grace both feparated them for the Lord, and operated in them fo as to form them for himfelf, that they might fhew forth his praife.

The

The subject thus far advanced, naturally led both him and them to the consideration of that happy, that honourable state into which they were now brought, as united to the church of God, and partakers of its invaluable privileges. The veil was rent, the sacred inclosure laid open, and they reconciled unto God by the death of *Jesus Christ*; yea more, they had access to God, as a kind, a gracious, a reconciled Father. *Ver.* 11——18. " Remember that ye being in time past *Gentiles* in the flesh—that at that time ye were without *Christ*, being aliens from the commonwealth of *Israel*, and strangers from the covenants of promise, having no hope, and without God in the world; but now in *Christ Jesus*, ye who sometimes were far off are made nigh by the blood of *Christ*; for he is our peace, who hath made both one, and hath broken down the middle wall of partition between us; having abolished in his flesh the enmity, even the law of commandments, contained in ordinances, for to make in himself of twain one new man, so making peace; and that he might reconcile both unto God in one body by the cross, having slain the enmity thereby; and came and preached peace to you which were afar off, and to them that were nigh: For through him we both have an access by one Spirit unto the Father."

What I propose from these words is,

I. Briefly

I. Briefly to explain the privilege here referred to, *access to God*.
II. Point out the grand mean whereby this privilege was first procured, is still preserved, and will ever be rendered effectual, it is *through Christ*.
III. The suitable and sufficient aid provided for enjoyment of this privilege, it is *by one Spirit:* And,
IV. The ultimate object of our hope and happiness to whom we are permitted to present our humble addresses and supplications, *to the Father*.

But before we enter more particularly into this plan, we beg leave just to remark, that these words, in our apprehension, evidently hold forth the doctrine of the ever-blessed Trinity. The true God is here revealed under a variety of characters or offices, the Father, the Son, and the Holy Spirit, and the fellowship which every believer has with each of them in their respective manifestations, particularly in the duty of prayer, is here clearly evinced: It is through *Jesus Christ* as the Mediator, and by the aid, assistance, and operation of the Holy Spirit, that we have access to the Father—who, as seated upon the throne of grace, claims all the honours, and dispenses all the covenant-blessings of the Deity. It is, properly speaking, the Divine Nature we worship, whatever name be used,

character

character assumed, or office represented. The Son, considered as to his Divine Nature, is in the Father, and the Father in the Son, so as to be properly one; and what we remark of the Son is equally applicable to the Holy Spirit; so that though there be three who bear record in heaven, yet these three are one, that is one glorious Essence, one God.— But let us now proceed to the method already laid down.

I. We propose *briefly to touch upon the glorious privilege here referred to*, viz Access to God. Now the very idea of access supposes in it *previous distance* and *present liberty of approach*.

Previous distance is evidently intimated in the idea. As *Gentiles*, these *Ephesians* had been without God and without hope. They had been held off at an awful distance, excluded from all the privileges of grace and the covenants of promise. But though once far off, they were now made nigh by the blood of *Christ*. Blessed, invaluable privilege! To be translated from under the power of darkness, and introduced into the blessed liberty of God's children. To be admitted through the rent veil of the Redeemer's flesh, into the presence of God as a reconciled friend and father. Remember, brethren, the situation in which your forefathers once were in this nation; yea, reflect upon your own condition, previous to converting grace: Ye were then,

then, without God in the world, or *Chrift* in the heart. O never forget your former diftance while in a ftate of fin and unregeneracy; and let all the honour of the change be afcribed to him to whom the whole honour is due.

Ye were once afar off, now there is *liberty to approach*. There is accefs to God, and acceptance before him through *Jefus Chrift*. The word here tranflated *accefs*, fignifies to be introduced as by the hand into court, and prefented by fome intimate friend, or appointed officer, into the royal prefence: So *Jefus Chrift* is reprefented as introducing all his friends into the prefence of his father. Through him ye are permitted to approach the throne of grace, and by prayer and fupplication to make known your requeft. At all times, in all your trials and difficulties, ye are encouraged to come boldly before his throne, that ye may obtain mercy, and find grace to help you in every time of need. With holy boldnefs ye may open your mouths to tell him all your concerns and troubles. Rejoice, my fellow-finners, in the thought, that there is accefs to God. Every obftacle which once lay in the way is entirely and for ever removed; and the encouragement is, that afk what ye will, while the blefling is contained in the promife, and the plea founded upon the merit and advocacy of *Jefus*, it fhall be done unto you. Aftonifhing privilege,

vilege, that poor worms of the earth, rebels against their God, and sinners against their own souls, can have access to God with hope and confidence, there to plead his promises, and to take shelter under the shadow of his power.——Proceed we,

II. To lay before you the *grand mean, whereby this privilege was first procured, is still preserved, and will ever be found effectual.* It is through Christ.

1. This great privilege of access to God was procured for us by the death of *Jesus Christ*. In *Christ Jesus* ye, who sometimes were far off, are made nigh by the blood of *Christ* *, ver. 13. We have admittance into the holiest of all by the blood of *Jesus*. This is that new and living way whereby we have access to God. Without the shedding of blood there was no remission; without remission, no peace; and without peace, no prospects that could excite our hope, or draw forth our desires. Brethren, whenever ye approach a throne of grace, never forget at what an amazing expence, and by what an extraordinary exertion that way was laid open for you. Justice, with its extensive demands; holiness, with its no less extensive requirements, and wrath, with its inconceivable and accumulated curses, stood in the way. These were not to be removed by your cries for pity, or resolutions to be more obedient for the future. These had still entirely and

eternally

eternally blocked up the way, had not the blessed *Jesus* graciously, seasonably, and powerfully interposed himself; and he has removed sin by bearing the punishment due to it, satisfied justice, honoured the claims of holiness, and sprinkled the way to the throne of grace with his own blood, that, in every step you take in your approach to it, ye may both see and feel to whom ye stand indebted for this high, this honourable privilege. And as his blood first procured this access, so,

2. He still preserves this way of access open for us. Hence he represents himself as the *door* by which we have access, and as the *way* in which we are to walk; and further, we are expressly told that no man cometh to the Father but by him. It is in his name and in his right that we enjoy this invaluable privilege. There is no access to God but *by* and *through* a Mediator. He, as the great high priest of our profession, hath entered within the veil; and the connection, the indissoluble connection that subsists betwixt him and his people, still keeps the way open. Because he lives, they shall live also. Dying, he opened the way, and, living, he preserves it open for the encouragement of all his friends and family. How would our sins, our ingratitude, our incredulity, our innumerable departures from the living God, how would these, long ere this, have closed up the way, had not the blessed Redeemer constantly

constantly exerted himself to keep it open! It is through him who was dead, but is alive again, that we have access, with confidence, into the grace wherein we stand, and rejoice in hope of the glory of God. Let this consideration influence your conduct whenever ye find your minds oppressed with fears or distress through your own conduct: It is not in your own name, or on your own account, but through him, that ye have this access to, God.

3. This gracious privilege of access to God, as to our Father, is rendered effectual and acceptable by *Jesus Christ*. He ever lives to make intercession for us, to perfume the petitions of his people with the incense of his own merit, and to perfect the imperfections which attend their supplications by the addition of his infinite wisdom and divine authority. Our very petitions would be sufficient to prove our ruin, had we not an advocate with the Father to prevent the effects of our folly, and to procure what we saw not the necessity of asking. He, gracious intercessor, throws the whole of his interest into the scale, which would otherwise be found infinitely too light. Acquainted with all your wants, and with all your weaknesses, he overlooks not the least concern of the lowest believer. It is not your arguments, however forcible in their own nature, that prevail—not your zeal, however fervent—not

your frames, however lively, that give efficacy to your prayers—or however dull, that prevent their being heard. It is the merit and intercession of *Jesus* which renders the work prevalent. His " FATHER I WILL" carries such efficacy along with it, as renders even sighs significant, and gives to the most broken petitions of the heart all the force of heavenly oratory. His presence above renders your access to God both effectual and acceptable; for sinners are now accepted in the beloved to the praise of the glory of his grace. We now go on to consider,

III. *The suitable and sufficient aid provided for our enjoyment of this blessed privilege*, it is by one spirit that we approach the Father.

Three things become necessary for the success and improvement of this important privilege, *Knowledge, Grace*, and *Liberty*.

1. *Knowledge*. It is the office of the blessed Spirit, by the instrumentality of the word, so to shine *upon* the heart, as to discover our guilt, misery, wants, and wretchedness; and so to shine *into* us, or to vouchsafe such discoveries of the will, the grace, and the power of God, as well as of the glory, the suitableness, and sufficiency of the Lord *Jesus Christ*, as shall assist us to pray. How should creatures, so ignorant as we are, know what to pray for, or how to perform the duty, did not the Spirit graciously and powerfully enlighten the mind with respect to the will and character

racter of God, and also help our infirmities. It is this Spirit which leads into all truth, takes of the things of *Christ*, and shews them to the mind, and enables the soul to derive all its arguments from the word of eternal truth. He enlightens the mind to see the truth, enables us to embrace it, and then to plead it before God in such language as this; " Establish the word to thy servant, upon which thou hast caused me to hope." And O what light hath shone upon some doctrine! What comfort through some promise, when ye have been solemnly engaged with God in the duty of prayer. Ye both saw your wants, and how his honour stood engaged amply to supply them.

2. *Grace* also is in this duty drawn forth into exercise. *Faith* goes forth to meet the approaching blessing; *hope* enters into future and distant prospects; *love* kindles the fire beneath the sacrifice; *patience* bows to the will of heaven; and *expectation* pants for the blessings of a gracious Father. The Spirit of grace and of supplications is shed on you abundantly, that so your converse with God may be suitably conducted, and your communion with him increased. Thus the true believer approaches God with grace in his heart; and without this, especially without faith, it is impossible to please him. " The Spirit himself maketh intercession for us with groanings that cannot be uttered." He puts

a cry into the heart even for the salvation of God, and enables the soul to ask in faith nothing doubting. Be it your chief concern, that the several graces be in proper exercise in all your approaches to God. Indeed without *that*, it is no approach to him, but a standing still, that you may mock him to his face.

3. *Liberty* is another blessing which is received from the Spirit, in order to assist us in our access to God. He enlarges the heart with suitable conceptions of what God is through *Jesus Christ*, opens the mouth to plead with him, and enables the soul, at seasons, to approach with freedom of speech, and to tell the Lord all its wants. He brings the argument to the mind, enables the soul to enter into it, and fills the plea with all the invincible importunity of faith. Like *Jacob*, the soul becomes *resolute*—it wrestles for the blessing—it cannot be *put off*—it will not recede—and finally, it *obtains*; "for where the Spirit of the Lord is, there is liberty." Such draw near with boldness to a throne of grace, that they may obtain mercy, and find grace to help them in time of need.

This Spirit is the only true source of uniformity in the worship of God. The gifts that he bestows may be various, and each of his gifts may be vouchsafed in different degrees upon different persons; but this Spirit is the author of all these refreshing discoveries,

veries, all those necessary graces, and all that happy liberty which are so necessary to the comfortable access which every believer finds to his God. And pity it is that any thing should ever intrude into our worship, that should tend to impede that exercise of the mind, that lively exertion of the several graces, or that holy liberty which this Spirit is the author of. However, so far as the access is real and approved, it is by this *one Spirit* that all the family of God, in every age and place, and of every denomination, have access to him as a gracious, compassionate, and reconciled Father in *Christ Jesus*. This brings us to the *fourth* and last thing we proposed, viz.

IV. *The ultimate object of our hope and happiness, to whom we are privileged to present our humble addresses and supplications, it is to the Father.* But seeing the Son and Spirit, though distinct in their office-characters, are represented in the scripture as equally possessed of every possible perfection, and equally participants of Deity, why are they not to be equally addressed with the Father? Certainly they may; nor are we left destitute of evidence from scripture, that, in certain cases, and upon particular occasions, they may.* Thus *Stephen*, in his dying moments, commended his departing spirit to *Jesus Christ*, saying, Lord *Jesus*, receive my spirit.

* 2 Cor. xiii. 14.

spirit *. And thus *Paul*, when grievously afflicted with the thorn in the flesh, besought the Lord, that is the Lord *Christ*, as the sequel proves, to take it away from him; but the only answer he could obtain was this, "My grace is sufficient for thee, for my strength is made perfect in weakness†:" But, properly speaking, it was not the office-character of *Jesus Christ* that was the object of faith to the one, or of desire in the other; but it was the Deity which gave efficacy to the office, and manifested itself through it. Strictly speaking, it is Deity alone which is the proper object of religious worship. "Thou shalt worship the Lord thy God, and him only shalt thou serve;" and, therefore, while as on the one hand we are careful strenuously to maintain their distinct personality, the strictest care is necessary on the other, both upon our own and on account of others, that in every act of religious worship we shew that we address ourselves to, and adore but one God. "To us there is but one God, the Father of whom are all things, and we in him, and one Lord *Jesus Christ*. by whom are all things, and we by him ‡," Thus we apprehend the Father sustains the whole honour of the Deity in the grand œconomy of our salvation: But the Son and Spirit considered as to their divine nature, are in the Father, and He in them. So that though either of these divine persons

may

* Acts vii. 59.——† 2 Cor. xii. 8, 9.——‡ 1 Cor. viii. 6.

may be diſtinctly addreſſed, yet by the ſcripture we are taught more commonly to addreſs ourſelves to the Father: But be it the Father, the Son, or the Holy Spirit that is addreſſed by us, our worſhip properly terminates in, and has reſpect to not the Father, as a Father; not the Son, as a Son; not the Holy Ghoſt, as the Holy Ghoſt, but as God over all, bleſſed for ever. The whole Godhead is addreſſed by us. Senſible I am, that every ſimilitude or repreſentation taken from natural things, however it tends in ſome things to illuſtrate the ſubject, muſt impair the repreſentation almoſt as much in others; yet ſuch a method ſometimes greatly aſſiſts the weakneſs of the human mind to conceive of divine ſubjects. I will attempt to explain my idea by ſuch a method: Under the *Jewiſh* polity you will remember there were certain cities of refuge appointed for the ſafety and ſecurity of the man-ſlayer, who, without intention, had taken away the life of a brother *Iſraelite*. Let us ſuppoſe that there might be *three* ways which led to one of theſe cities—*two* of them had been uſed occaſionally and in particular caſes, the *other* was the more frequented and proper road. Now the ſafety of the perſon lay neither in this way nor in that. The city was the object that he had in view, nor did he judge himſelf ſecure till he had obtained entrance within the walls: So, if our worſhip ſhould terminate in any office-character,

racter, without centering in Deity, we come short of the mark that we ought to aim at; for it is through *Christ* that by one Spirit we have access to the Father.

But we rest not the matter upon any private opinion; as, under the law, in the mouth of two or three witnesses every word was to be established, we shall now bring forward the testimony upon this head, of perhaps three as great luminaries as ever graced the christian church in later ages.

The *first* witness we introduce is Dr. *Gill*. His words are these: " Prayer is a part of
" divine and religious worship, which is
" made to the Father, and indeed is generally
" made to him; the access and address are
" most frequently unto him; not but that
" they may be equally made to the other two
" persons; but the reason why they are
" usually made to him is, because he bears
" no office, whereas the others do; and an
" office which is concerned in the business of
" prayer. *Christ* is the Mediator through
" whom the access is, and the Spirit is the
" Spirit of supplication by whose aid and as-
" sistance prayer is made *."

The next witness we would bring forward is the pious Dr. *Watts*. " It is a very na-
" tural inquiry," says he, " whether we may
" distinctly address ourselves in prayer to the
" Son or Spirit of God to bestow divine in-
" fluences upon us, to which I answer, that
                                                " the

---
* Gill's Body of Divinity, vol. III. p. 3.

"the scripture which is indited by the Spirit
"himself, generally instructs us to make God
"the Father the more direct object of our
"addresses in prayer, and to intreat the Fa-
"ther to bestow his Spirit on us; because it
"is He sustains the supreme dignity and ma-
"jesty of Godhead, as the Lord and Sove-
"reign of all, as the prime agent in our sal-
"vation, and prime object of our worship.
"It is the Father of light that is the giver
"of every good and perfect gift*. It is the
"Father that gives his Holy Spirit to them
"that ask him †. It is the God and Father
"of our Lord *Jesus Christ* to whom St. *Paul*
"bowed his knees, that he would strengthen
"his saints, by his Spirit in the inner man ‡.
"And he prays, that the God of our Lord
"*Jesus Christ*, the Father of glory, would
"give them the Spirit of wisdom and reve-
"lation §. It is evident, by the general
"current of scripture, both in its counsels
"and in its examples, that we are chiefly to
"seek the aids of the blessed Spirit from
"God the Father, through the mediation
"of his Son *Jesus Christ*; and, doubtless,
"this always has been, and this will be the
"most usual practice of Christians, who make
"the word of God the rule and guide of
"their worship∥."

* James i. 17.—† Luke xi. 13.—‡ Eph. iii. 16.——§ Eph. i. 17.——
∥ Watts's Sermons, vol. II. p. 475.

Dr. *Owen*, whose praise is in all the churches, shall bring up the rear with his testimony: "This," says he, "is the general order of Gospel-worship, the great rubric of our service: Here in general lies its decency, that it respects the mediation of the Son, through whom we have access, and the supplies and assistance of the Spirit, and a regard unto God as a Father. He that fails in any one of these, he breaks all order in Gospel-worship. If either we come not to it by *Jesus Christ*, or perform it not in the strength of the Holy Ghost, or in it go not to God as a Father, we transgress all the rules of this worship. This is the great canon which, if it be neglected, there is no decency in whatever is done in this way." *

To the same purpose, and in the same discourse †, "The immediate object of worship is God. We have access to God. It is the Father who is here peculiarly intended; God as God: He who is the beginning and end of all; whose nature is attended with infinite perfection: He, from whom as sovereignty over all doth proceed, is the formal object of all divine and religious worship. Hence divine worship respects, as its object, each person in the blessed Trinity equally; not as this or that person,

---

* Complete Collection of Sermons by *J. Owen*, D. D. Folio, p. 3.
† Page 4.

"son, but as this or that person is God; that is, the formal reason of all divine worship: But yet, as the second person is considered as vested with his office of mediation, and the Holy Ghost, as the comforter and sanctifier of his saints; so God the Father is in a peculiar manner the object of our faith, and love, and worship. So *Peter* tells us, *That through Christ we believe in God that raised him up from the dead, and gave him glory.** *Christ* being considered as Mediator, God that raised him from the dead, that is the Father, is regarded as the ultimate object of our worship; though worshipping him who is the Father as God, the other persons are in the same nature worshipped."

In another place he expresseth himself thus: "We worship the Lord *Christ* who is God and man; he is so in one person; and his person who is God and Man is the object of that worship: For the *formal reason* and object of it is the Divine Nature in that person. Give me leave to say, God himself could not command the Lord *Christ* to be worshipped with divine religious adoration, were he not *God by nature*, for the thing itself implieth a contradiction. Religious worship is nothing but an assignation of that honour which is due to divine excel-

* 1 Peter i. 21.

"excellencies; namely, to trust, believe, fear,
"obey, love, and submit to infinite holiness,
"goodness, righteousness, power in the first
"cause, last end, and Sovereign Lord of all.
"Now to assign glory proper to divine ex-
"cellencies, and which receiveth its nature
"from its object, where divine excellencies
"are not, is openly contradictory. Besides,
"God hath said, *I am the Lord, that is my
"name, and my glory will I not give unto an-
"other.* He that hath not the *Name of God;*
"that is, his Nature, shall not, nor can have
"his glory, which is to be the object of the
"worship." *

Such is the testimony upon this head which has been borne by these three eminent champions for evangelic truth—and in the steps of such eminently great and good men, I wish humbly to tread so long as I am honoured to minister in the christian sanctuary—and united in worship and society with such *Men* I hope to spend a blessed eternity.

To conclude: A throne of grace is erected. It is now accessible.—Thither direct all your petitions and requests.—It is your Father that fills it, and we have an advocate with him, *Jesus Christ* the righteous, and he is the propitiation for our sins, and not for ours only, but for the sins of the whole world. Come boldly

* *Owen on Hebrews,* vol. II. p. 38.

boldly to this throne.—Aſk what ye will.—Caſt all your care upon God.—It is his *honour* to hear prayer—it is your *duty* to preſent it; and he that aſks ſhall have, he that ſeeks ſhall find. May God teach you to pray—enable you to prevail——and glorify himſelf by the anſwer. Even ſo. *Amen.*

THE END.

www.ingramcontent.com/pod-product-compliance
Lightning Source LLC
Chambersburg PA
CBHW022141300426
44115CB00006B/295